Kinect Hacks

Jared St. Jean

Beijing · Cambridge · Farnham · Köln · Sebastopol · Tokyo

Kinect Hacks

by Jared St. Jean

Published by O'Reilly Media, Inc., 1005 Gravenstein Highway North, Sebastopol, CA 95472.

O'Reilly books may be purchased for educational, business, or sales promotional use. Online editions are also available for most titles (*http://my.safaribooksonline.com*). For more information, contact our corporate/institutional sales department: 800-998-9938 or *corporate@oreilly.com*.

Editor: Shawn Wallace
Production Editor: Melanie Yarbrough
Copyeditor: Rachel Monaghan

Proofreader: Linley Dolby
Indexer: Judy McConville
Cover Designer: Karen Montgomery
Interior Designer: David Futato
Illustrator: Rebecca Demarest

November 2012:   First Edition

Revision History for the First Edition:

2012-11-02   First release

See *http://oreilly.com/catalog/errata.csp?isbn=9781449315207* for release details.

ISBN: 978-1-449-31520-7

[LSI]

Table of Contents

Preface

The way we interact with machines is always changing. As technology evolves, new ways of interacting with computers become available to us, one innovative breakthrough after the next. If we go back 10 years, RIM was just starting to implement phone capabilities into their line of Blackberry mobile devices. Now we have touch screens capable of delivering a full computing experience in the palm of our hands. Voice recognition software is finally becoming mainstream with the introduction of Siri on the iPhone 4S. We are rapidly entering an age in which being tethered to an accessory or peripheral, such as a mouse or keyboard, will be considered an archaic way of getting things done.

Touch screen interfaces are all the rage right now, but the next true evolution in human/computer interaction won't require you to physically touch a thing. You've seen it before in a number of sci-fi films: some guy in a futuristic get up is waving his hands around, barking orders at a computer that seamlessly tracks his movement and executes every command with flawless accuracy. The proper name for this type of computer interaction is called a *Natural User Interface* (NUI), which describes the ability to issue commands to a device using nothing more than your own natural body movements, gestures, and voice. You'll no longer need to clean those germ-infested keyboards and touch screens or pick up new batteries for your wireless mouse or gaming controller. The possibilities are truly endless, and we're already starting to see deployments of NUI interactivity all over the world. Soon you'll see NUIs in store windows, bus stations, malls, as well as many other places that could benefit from adding natural human interaction to the process of selling and providing information.

One great piece of tech that has ushered in this new wave of creative development is the Microsoft Kinect. The Kinect has introduced itself to the masses at the best possible time. In its short existence, it has proven to be a great option for those looking to spice up the way we work with computers. For starters, the Kinect is a fraction of the cost of most professional 3D depth sensing cameras. A wide assortment of programs allow you to use Kinect 3D depth data with Windows, Linux, and Mac machines. Whether you're an innovative professional interested in bleeding edge tech, or a part time hobbyist with a great new idea, the Kinect is easy to set up, it's cheap, and it's loaded with potential to change the way we interact with machines.

My intention from the start was to write a book that everyone could take something from. Whether you're completely new to the scene or have been tinkering around with the Kinect since its debut, there's something in here for everyone. Some of the hacks range from basic installation of tool sets or programs to detailed code write-ups relating to a wide range of available IDEs such as Processing and openFrameworks.

There are gesture-based solutions that work with a quite a few diverse applications in this book. For music related application, there is information on how to set up Ableton Live with Kinectar. If mocap is your thing, there are tips and tricks for using Blender or Animata with NI mate. HTML5 and JavaScript integration is included using Zigfu's ZDK along with full-on 3D object and scene recreation written in C++ using PCL and OpenCV. If visual effects are your thing, be sure to check out all the diverse Kinect hacks using open source IDEs such as Processing and openFrameworks.

Whether you're looking for some fun projects to work on in your spare time or finding the perfect jump off spot to get started on your next big project, I believe you'll be able to find something in here that will appeal to you. Whatever is your proverbial cup of tea, there's definitely something in here for everyone to enjoy working on.

The Story

Writing this book was one of the best experiences of my life, hands down. I had a pretty good idea of what was out there and how to set things up, but what I learned going through the amount of diverse hacks that would eventually compose the content of this book truly made me aware of the great work people are doing with the Kinect. I got to know many of the talented people involved in the scene from around the world and learned an incredible amount in the process.

I started off by writing the guides necessary to get you started on your preferred OS. The great thing about the Kinect scene is that it was born out of the open source community. This ensured that drivers would be released across all platforms. From there, various libraries were released allowing people to start playing around with Kinect data in other open source IDEs such as Processing, openFrameworks, and Cinder. Getting the Kinect up and running and installing the proper libraries for your IDE of choice is the first step. After that, the real fun begins.

After completing the first two chapters, things really started to get interesting. A wide assortment of new tools became available to play around with. For example, working with Chris Vik's amazing Kinectar app, which allows you to be your very own hands-free composer and musician, and Stephan Howell's Kinect2Scratch, which uses the Scratch IDE, was an unbelievable experience. I had a blast settings things up and then playing around with the end results. I can honestly tell you that I loved working on this book from beginning to end.

Acknowledgments

A big huge juicy thank you to everyone at O'Reilly Media for taking a chance on this lowly blogger. I never thought in my wildest dreams that putting a bit of work into a niche scene like Kinect hacking would result in something like this. In my opinion, they took a huge chance with me and I hope I was able to deliver a great product to add to their impeccable track record in the world of technical writing.

Even though O'Reilly Media made this thing you're holding in your hands a reality, I would have never had the opportunity if it wasn't for Greg Mackenzie and the Dashhacks network. His passion for hacking and modding electronics eventually produced the best network of hacking sites on the Internet. The journey seemed short in hindsight, but what I got out of it has changed my life forever. Mad props for letting me do my own thing, GregCube.

Last but certainly not least, the amazing folks who took time out of their lives to develop such incredible projects using Kinect's 3D depth sensing capabilities. You are an inspiration and also responsible for making us think beyond the keyboard and mouse, ushering in a new age of interacting with machines. In no particular order, here is my "I'm not worthy!" list of incredible contributors to both this book and the scene in general. Without the efforts of each and all of you—I can't complete this sentence because I don't even want to think about it!

Thanks to Daniel Shiffman, Joshua Blake, Kyle McDonald, Nicolas Burrus, Shawn Wallace, Brian Jepson, Ryan Challinor, Chris Vik, Julius Tuomisto, Peter Nash, RJ Durran, Ning Ma, Kris Temmerman, Mike Newell, Andrew Berg, Felix Endres, Stephen Howell, Jordi Llobet Torrens, Anna Fusté Lleixà, Jeremy Archer, Taylor Veltrop, Takashi Nishibayashi, Daniel Ho, Javier Graciá Carpio, Theodore Blackman, Amir Hirsch, and Stefan Stegmueller.

Conventions Used in This Book

The following typographical conventions are used in this book:

Italic

Indicates new terms, URLs, email addresses, filenames, and file extensions.

Constant width

> Used for program listings, as well as within paragraphs to refer to program elements such as variable or function names, databases, data types, environment variables, statements, and keywords.

Constant width bold

> Shows commands or other text that should be typed literally by the user.

Constant width italic

> Shows text that should be replaced with user-supplied values or by values determined by context.

These lines signify a tip, suggestion, warning, caution, or general note.

Using Code Examples

This book is here to help you get your job done. In general, you may use the code in this book in your programs and documentation. You do not need to contact us for permission unless you're reproducing a significant portion of the code. For example, writing a program that uses several chunks of code from this book does not require permission. Selling or distributing a CD-ROM of examples from O'Reilly books does require permission. Answering a question by citing this book and quoting example code does not require permission. Incorporating a significant amount of example code from this book into your product's documentation does require permission.

We appreciate, but do not require, attribution. An attribution usually includes the title, author, publisher, and ISBN. For example: "*Kinect Hacks* by Jared St. Jean (O'Reilly). Copyright 2013 Jared St. Jean, 978-1-449-31520-7."

If you feel your use of code examples falls outside fair use or the permission given above, feel free to contact us at *permissions@oreilly.com*.

Safari® Books Online

Safari Books Online is an on-demand digital library that lets you easily search over 7,500 technology and creative reference books and videos to find the answers you need quickly.

With a subscription, you can read any page and watch any video from our library online. Read books on your cell phone and mobile devices. Access new titles before they are available for print, and get exclusive access to manuscripts in development and post feedback for the authors. Copy and paste code samples, organize your favorites, download chapters, bookmark key sections, create notes, print out pages, and benefit from tons of other time-saving features.

O'Reilly Media has uploaded this book to the Safari Books Online service. To have full digital access to this book and others on similar topics from O'Reilly and other publishers, sign up for free at *http://my.safaribooksonline.com*.

How to Contact Us

Please address comments and questions concerning this book to the publisher:

O'Reilly Media, Inc.
1005 Gravenstein Highway North
Sebastopol, CA 95472
800-998-9938 (in the United States or Canada)
707-829-0515 (international or local)
707-829-0104 (fax)

We have a web page for this book, where we list errata, examples, and any additional information. You can access this page at:

http://oreil.ly/kinect_hacks

To comment or ask technical questions about this book, send email to:

bookquestions@oreilly.com

For more information about our books, courses, conferences, and news, see our website at *http://www.oreilly.com*.

Find us on Facebook: *http://facebook.com/oreilly*

Follow us on Twitter: *http://twitter.com/oreillymedia*

Watch us on YouTube: *http://www.youtube.com/oreillymedia*

Contributors

Anna Fusté Lleixà (*hi@annafuste.com*) is a Multimedia Engineering student at La Salle Barcelona (Ramon Llull University), an Audiovisual Communication Graduate (Pompeu Fabra University), and an Intern at la Salle HCI Department. Find out more at *http://www.annafuste.com*.

Peter Nash is a creative technologist based in London. He thrives on variety, including taking on hardcore academic challenges (he achieved "top of the year" for researching Nanotechnology in College) and experimenting with interactive installations, programming mobile apps and web, and working with big high street retailers to keep *with it*. He is currently pioneering a start-up dedicated to making the lives of smartphone app developers and designers easier. Peter contributed Hack #17.

Reach him via LinkedIn (*http://www.linkedin.com/pub/peter-nash/1a/25b/8b3*), Twitter (*https://twitter.com/pedronash*), or his personal website (*http://pedro-nash.com/*).

RJ Duran is a Computational Artist & Engineer exploring the inherent properties and aesthetics of biological and emergent pattern formation through Media Arts & Technology. His fascination with natural systems, engineering, traditional art forms such as music and architecture, and philosophy inform and guide his artistic pursuits. His mission as a creator is to understand the "deep complexity" embedded within systems in order to develop engaging, interactive and experiential audio, visual, and physical tools and experiences for education, exploration, and enlightenment.

He holds a BS in Electrical Engineering from Colorado State University, a certificate in Audio Engineering from The Conservatory of Recording Arts & Sciences, and a certificate in Digital Culture & Creative Technology from Boulder Digital Works. He is currently a Graduate Student Researcher in the Media Arts & Technology program at the University of California Santa Barbara. RJ contributed Hack #18. He can be reached at his website (*http://rjduran.net*) or via email at *rjduranjr@gmail.com*.

Born in China, **Ning Ma** now lives in Germany and has received his Master's Degree in Computational Engineering in Faculty Civil and Environmental Engineering from Ruhr-Bochum University. He is currently a PhD candidate.

Apart from his studies, he is very interested in digital graphics. He is self-taught to work with design tools, playing around with images and animations. His recent experiments with Kinect extends the field of his hobby. He loves actually interacting with graphics by programming is fun and exciting. Ning contributed Hack #19 and Hack #20.

Mike Newell works for Goodby Silverstein & Partners (*http://goodbysilver-stein.com/*). Mike contributed Hack #21.

He can be reached via his personal website (*http://iwearshorts.com/blog/*), via email at *mike@iwearshorts.com*, on Twitter at @newshorts, or on Google+ (*https://plus.google.com/116936126718533638419/posts/p/pub*).

Stephen Howell is a Computing Lecturer in the Computing Dept. at the Institute of Technology Tallaght, Dublin. He lectures on Kinect software development in modules called Interactive Media Design & Interactive Media Development. Visit his website at *http://scratch.saorog.com*. Stephen contributed Hack #47, Hack #48, and Hack #49.

Stephen can be contacted by email at *stephen.r.howell@gmail.com*.

Jordi Llobet (*jordi.llobet@me.com*) is a Multimedia Engineering student at La Salle Barcelona (Ramon Llull University). He's also a team member at the Interactive Prototype Design Group (La Salle HCI Department). Find out more at *http://www.jordi lobet.es*. Jordi contributed Hack #50.

Jeremy Archer (*https://github.com/fatlotus*) is a student at the University of Chicago. He works on various open-source projects, primarily for scientific computing, at Chicago's Computation Institute (*http://ci.uchicago.edu/*). He is also co-founder of Carbonless Community, a green energy software company based in Chicago. Jeremy contributed Hack #51.

Taylor Veltrop grew up near Chicago surrounded by Lego, Meccano, and computers. His first humanoid robot was made from wood (mostly by his father) at the age of 6. He studied Japanese and computer science at the engineering school in the University of Colorado and eventually found himself in Japan chasing robot dreams. There he came across Kinect-based teleoperation while exploring solutions for robot hand-eye coordination and navigation. Taylor currently resides in Paris working with Aldebaran Robotics. Taylor contributed Hack #52 and Hack #53.

Taylor can be reached via email at *taylor@veltrop.com*, at his personal website (*http://taylor.veltrop.com*), or on YouTube (*http://www.youtube.com/user/taylorveltrop*).

Stefan Stegmueller is a professional Software Architect/Developer from Switzerland (Master of Science in Computer Science). Candescent.ch is his private development project. I runs candescent.ch to publish programs which he writes mainly for himself but could be useful for others too.

One of his current fields of interest is natural user interaction. Stefan believes that after the Command Line Interface (CLI) and the Graphical User Interface (GUI) the Natural User Interface (NUI) is the next big thing in human-machine interaction. Stephan contributed Hack #54.

Stefan can be reached via email at *info@candescent.ch*, at his website (*http://www.candescent.ch*), blog (*http://blog.candescent.ch*), and on Twitter at @CandescentCH.

Winect is a final year project by **Daniel Ho** in National University of Singapore, School of Computing. Since graduation, he had continued this project during his free time at *http://ixorastudios.com/software/winect/*. Daniel contributed Hack #56.

Kris Temmerman contributed Hack #22: Create a Hairy Effect.

Andrew Berg contributed Hack #23: Create Hand Tracking Trails Using Cinder.

Chris Vik contributed Hack #25: Install Kinectar; Hack #26: Map Parameters in Ableton Live With Kinectar; Hack #27: Set Up a Drum Kit with Kinectar; and Hack #28: Create a Dubstep Wobble Bassline with Kinectar.

Javier Graciá Carpio contributed Hack #36: Use Processing to Create a 3D Scanner with Mesh Viewer.

Felix Endres contributed Hack #38: Set Up PCL and OpenCV; Hack #39: Display a Colored Point Cloud; Hack #40: Use Features to Track Camera Image Motion; Hack #41: Fuse Point Clouds into a Consistent 3D Model; Hack #42: Add Convenience Functionality to 3D Model; and Hack #43: Next Steps; SLAM, OctoMaps, Surface Reconstruction.

Takashi Nishibayashi contributed Hack #55: Use Kinect Justure for Mac.

1

Getting Up and Running

The Kinect was designed and marketed as an accessory to the Xbox 360 with the intention of breathing new life into Microsoft's gaming division without the company having to release a brand new console. The multimillion dollar idea was to offer a new and exciting way for Xbox 360 owners to play video games. Microsoft's marketing department hit the nail on the head with the catchy tag line "You are the controller"; in other words, the Kinect offers a natural user interface free of any cables, chargers, or controllers. When you move your hand, the game or dashboard interface responds accordingly. The Kinect was launched on November 4th in North America at a retail price of $150 and allowed users to simply plug the device into their Xbox 360 and start playing right away.

What Microsoft may not have anticipated was that its affordable gaming accessory was capable of many great things once placed in the hands of creative developers around the world. A mere six days after its launch, the Kinect was hacked and people started experimenting with it, shortly thereafter discovering what they could do with this affordable depth-sensing camera.

To truly get an idea of the amazing things you can do with the Kinect, you need to understand what it actually is and what it can do.

How the Kinect Works

The Kinect is a pretty impressive piece of tech. Sporting an RGB camera, multiarray microphones, and a depth sensor capable of full-body 3D motion capture along with facial and voice recognition capabilities, this video game accessory packs a serious punch. The Kinect uses both hardware and software simultaneously to capture and interpret depth data on the fly. The software, developed by a company called Prime-Sense, is able to recognize humans based on their skeletal structure (Figure 1-1). People have the distinct advantage of, well, standing on two legs and having arms. This is how the Kinect is able to determine that a human being is present. It can then focus on capturing data from the movements of that recognized "player." Unless you have apes frequently interrupting your game time by busting into your living room, this is a pretty rock-solid means of isolating and tracking a human skeleton in the room and disregarding everything else.

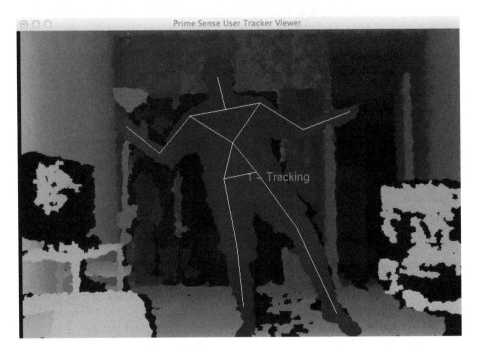

Figure 1-1.
PrimeSense skeletal tracking viewer

At its core, the Microsoft Kinect's true innovation and technical prowess lie within its depth-sensing technology. An infrared (IR) cluster of light (also referred to as a *point cloud*) is produced and spread out across a room, carrying with it encoded information in the form of varying light patterns—picture hundreds of little laser-point–size dots covering the room. The IR beams that are being emitted are undetectable to the naked eye, but when viewed in the dark through night vision goggles, they are on brilliant display (Figure 1-2).

Point cloud data is accurate only at a distance of approximately 1.2 to 3.5 m (3.9 to 11 ft) but within this range, data is collected and sent back, relaying information such as the distance of any detected objects based on any deformations in the IR light patterns. Two onboard complementary metal-oxide semiconductor (CMOS) cameras are used in individual capacities to further analyze any data that's been collected from the IR light patterns. The RGB camera collects 30 frames per second of actual real-time events at a 640x480 resolution, while the other handles the 3D depth imaging.

An onboard processor then renders the collected data in the form of 3D images so everything is wrapped up in a nice little package—and all of this for a measly $150. If only it did things other than rate my pathetic dance moves or let me pet jungle cats. If only....

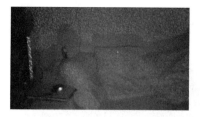

Figure 1-2.
IR light pattern using night vision

How the Kinect Was Hacked

I think it's a pretty safe bet to say that the Kinect would have been hacked at some point or another. Its potential was just too great to have people sit around idly waiting for Microsoft to release its own software development kit (SDK) for the device. For all we know, it may never have even released its SDK were it not for the efforts of the OpenKinect community. Actually, I'm getting a little bit ahead of myself. Let's back it up to the fledgling days of the Kinect's launch and talk about a little bounty put forth by the good folks over at Adafruit.

The bounty, called the X prize, was to be awarded to the first person able to produce open source drivers for the Kinect. The drivers could be functional on any operating system and had to be accompanied by an application that demonstrated their functionality by displaying a split window of the depth data and the RGB camera. Microsoft caught wind of this little competition, and its initial response was that of any company undergoing a major hardware launch. Since the Xbox 360 was hacked quite some time ago, this knee-jerk response was issued from a Microsoft PR rep:

> Microsoft does not condone the modification of its products... With Kinect, Microsoft built in numerous hardware and software safeguards designed to reduce the chances of product tampering. Microsoft will continue to make advances in these types of safeguards and work closely with law enforcement and product safety groups to keep Kinect tamper-resistant.

Most would cower in fear thinking of what Microsoft, with its deep pockets, could do to keep this sort of thing from catching the world's attention, but what actually happened was the complete opposite. Microsoft's response enticed Adafruit to increase the bounty of its X prize, not shy away. Fast-forward six days, and a winner was announced! Héctor Martin took the prize and dubbed his open source Kinect drivers "libfreenect." With this, a new generation of open source Kinect development was under way, and excited developers interested in working with Kinect wasted no time getting involved. The OpenKinect project was born, and a community of programmers and developers began building futuristic applications using the Kinect's depth-sensing capabilities.

On December 9, 2010, PrimeSense embraced the work being put forth by the open source community with the release of OpenNI and NITE. Things were really starting to get cooking at this point. With the backing of the developers responsible for the Kinect hardware, a wave of hacks began gaining a lot of attention all around the world. Wrappers started pouring in at this point, enabling people to toy around with their favorite programming language or framework in order to start experimenting with their own Kinect-related projects.

If ever there were a case for presenting the term "hacker" in a positive light, the efforts of the OpenKinect community would be it.

Choose a Framework and Driver

This section is all about getting your Kinect set up on your computer so you can get started on that next game changer. We'll be covering the installation process with a few different methods to get up and running. Step-by-step walkthroughs are available for Windows 7, Mac OS X, and Ubuntu that cover installing the libfreenect drivers, OpenNI, NITE, and SensorKinect, along with the Kinect SDK. For the sake of consistency, the guides formulated in this section have been successfully tested on a Mac running OS X 10.7, Windows 7, and Ubuntu 11.10.

Although having a wide variety of options can be a great thing, at times, the potential of getting mixed up in things can always rear its nasty little head. So we'll focus on two main options. As I mentioned earlier, libfreenect was the first set of open source-compatible Kinect drivers made available to the public. It is maintained by the Open Kinect community of developers and can be downloaded at *https://github.com/Open Kinect/libfreenect*.

PrimeSense, the developers behind the Kinect's depth-sensing technology, released OpenNI, a derivative of the open source LGPL PrimeSense code. You'll need to also install the avin2 SensorKinect module, built specifically for the Kinect based on code from the PrimeSense sensor driver, if you want to use OpenNI.

So what we're left with is two completely viable options available for us to use when working with Kinect depth data. The question now is, which one is right for you?

Well, for starters, if you plan on releasing your program in some commercial form, OpenNI and libfreenect are both fine to use, so you can scratch that off of your list. If you're interested in motor control, however, go with libfreenect; OpenNI with

SensorKinect does not support it. For higher-level NUI support, OpenNI has its NITE middleware integration available. libfreenect has a much more complicated installation process, so if you're unfamiliar with compilers and are more comfortable dealing with binary installers, OpenNI/NITE involves a much less complicated installation process. Whichever route you decide to take, you'll be in good hands. Both organizations have a huge, supportive community with great online forums.

There are usually two different methods of installing the open source drivers required to capture data from the Kinect sensor. You can compile the latest builds from scratch, or just install the binaries if available. We'll cover both methods in case one or the other just doesn't quite work out the way it was supposed to. It's always good to have a plan B, right?

HACK 01 Install OpenNI, SensorKinect, and NITE for Windows 7

For the sake of simplicity, we'll start things off the nice and easy way. Since PrimeSense was kind enough to release its own binary installers, we'll begin with this route.

The title of this hack is a bit deceiving. You can apply these guidelines to a Windows XP or Vista machine, if that's all you have. As I mentioned before, however, I used a Windows 7 machine for all of these guides.

Download the OpenNI package installer from *http://www.openni.org/Downloads/ OpenNIModules.aspx*.

Select OpenNI Packages from the first drop-down menu. From the next drop-down, select Stable, and then choose PrimeSense Package Stable Build for Windows-Development Edition.

Be sure to download the appropriate 32- or 64-bit versions depending on your system. If you don't know what you're running, go to Control Panel → System and Security → System, and see System Type.

Launch the executable file to begin installing OpenNI and NITE.

Download the Kinect sensor drivers from *https://github.com/avin2/SensorKinect*.

Once you've downloaded the package, extract the contents and install the driver mod by executing the binary located in the *Bin* folder. Be sure to choose the right 64- or 32-bit installer.

To see if everything was installed correctly, plug the Kinect into a USB port and make sure it is plugged into a power source as well. Go to your Start Menu → All Programs → OpenNI → NiViewer. After a few seconds, a window should open showing you a simple depth view from the Kinect sensor (Figure 1-3).

Figure 1-3.
A NiSimpleViewer demo

To see if the NITE samples are working, you'll need to copy all of the sample XML files from the *PrimeSense/NITE/Data* folder to the *PrimeSense/Sensor/Data* folder. Once they've been copied over, go to Start → All Programs → PrimeSense → NITE 64 bit (for those who installed the 64-bit version) → Samples → Sample-Box64 (Figure 1-4).

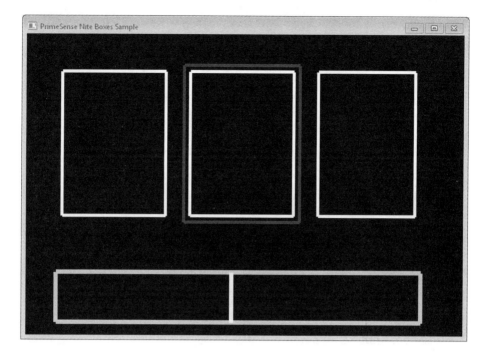

Figure 1-4.
PrimeSense NITE SampleBox

HACK 02 Install OpenNI, NITE, and SensorKinect for OS X

Before we get started, you'll need the following applications installed and configured:

- Xcode
- CMake
- MacPorts
- Git

You'll need to install a few library dependencies as well. Using MacPorts, install *libtool* and *libusb-devel + universal*. Open up your Terminal application (Applications → Utilities → Terminal) and run the following command:

```
sudo port install libtool
```

Restart your Mac. Open up your Terminal again and install libusb-devel + universal as follows:

```
sudo port install libusb-devel +universal
```

Restart your computer once again. Create a directory in which you'll store all of our installers. We'll create a *Kinect* folder in the *Home* directory.

```
cd ~/
mkdir Kinect
cd Kinect
```

Download the latest version of OpenNI from its GitHub repository.

```
sudo git clone https://github.com/OpenNI/OpenNI.git
```

Change the working directory to *OpenNI/Platform/Linux-x86/CreateRedist* and run RedistMaker.

```
sudo ./RedistMaker
```

Once the build has finished, back out of that directory and make your current working directory *Bin/Release*.

```
cd ../Bin/Release
```

Run one of the examples to make sure everything is working properly.

```
sudo ./Sample-NiUserTracker
```

Next, we'll need to install the avin2 SensorKinect driver mod to retrieve data captured by the Kinect. Navigate back to the *Kinect* directory and use Git to download the latest version of SensorKinect.

```
cd ~/Kinect
sudo git clone https://github.com/avin2/SensorKinect.git
```

Change your working directory to *~/Kinect/SensorKinect/Bin* and extract the contents of *SensorKinect-Bin-MacOSX-v*...*tar.bz2*.

Navigate into the newly extracted directory and run the installer script.

```
sudo ./install.sh
```

Last but not least, we'll want to install NITE. Download the latest unstable build of NITE from *http://www.openni.org* and place it in your *Kinect* directory. (Go to *http://open ni.org/Downloads/OpenNIModules.aspx* and select OpenNI Compliant Middleware Binaries → Unstable Release → PrimeSense NITE Mac OSX.)

I will refer to the NITE root directory as *NITE* to keep things consistent. If you'd like to rename it, by all means do so.

```
mv nite-bin-macosx-v*.*.*.* NITE
```

Extract the contents of the file, change the working directory to the *NITE* folder, and run the install script.

```
sudo ./install.sh
```

You will then be prompted to enter the PrimeSense license key, which is 0KOIk2JeIBYClPWVnMoRKn5cdY4=.

We're almost done! If you want to run some of the examples, you'll need to move the sample XML files from the *SensorKinect/Data* directory over to *NITE/Data*. You can do this in the Finder or in a Terminal.

Cruise on over to the *Samples* directory and try one out for size! (See Figure 1-5.)

```
cd ~/Kinect/NITE/Samples/Bin/Release
sudo ./Sample-PointViewer
```

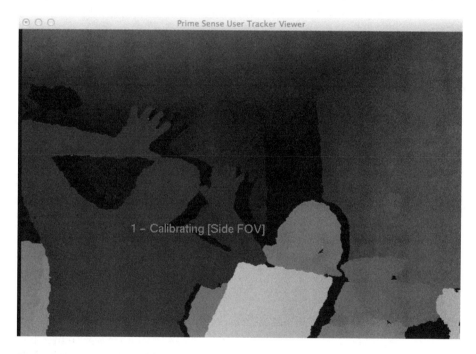

Figure 1-5.
PrimeSense NiUserTracker sample

`HACK 03` Install OpenNI, NITE, and SensorKinect for Ubuntu

Getting your Kinect working with Ubuntu is pretty straightforward. It will definitely help if you're comfortable working on a command line. We'll be using *apt* to download everything except the NITE middleware package, so things should go smoothly.

First, as always, we'll need to ensure that all of the required libraries and other dependencies are installed before we'll be able to download the required SDK, drivers, and middleware from the usual spots.

We'll install OpenNI first.

The order in which we install each component is important, so try not to veer off course and install NITE or SensorKinect before OpenNI!

There are a few libraries that we need to install, so we'll tackle those before moving on. I've listed the requirement names along with the official sites that host the downloads. Instead of installing them all manually, apt commands you to install everything in one swift motion.

Open up your Terminal application and enter the following commands, allowing time for each install to finish successfully before moving on to the next one.

```
sudo apt-get install git-core cmake g++ python \
freeglut3-dev pkg-config build-essential \
libxmu-dev libxi-dev libusb-1.0-0-dev \
doxygen graphviz
```

Don't be surprised if this takes a lifetime to complete, especially if you're using a fresh Ubuntu installation.

You'll also need to install the Java Development Kit. I used a separate session of apt since I needed to build a repository.

```
sudo add-apt-repository "deb http://archive.canonical.com/ lucid partner"
sudo apt-get update
sudo apt-get install sun-java6-jdk
```

Hopefully everything installs properly without your having to cruise the backwaters of the Internet in search of dependencies for those dependencies. Always remember, in times of trouble, Copy, Google, and Paste are your best friends in the whole wide Web. Moving on, create a *Kinect* directory wherever you'd like. I chose the *Home* directory.

```
mkdir ~/Kinect
cd ~/Kinect
```

Download OpenNI using Git and make sure you're dealing with the unstable version.

```
sudo git clone https://github.com/OpenNI/OpenNI.git
sudo git checkout unstable
```

To check out some of the samples, you'll need to build them first.

```
cd OpenNI/Platform/Linux-x86/Build
sudo ./RedistMaker
```

If you're unable to run the previous command, you may need to change the file permissions. Type chmod 777 * *while in the* Build *directory.*

After compiling everything, we can now move on to installing the SensorKinect driver.

```
cd ~/Kinect
sudo git clone https://github.com/avin2/SensorKinect
```

Change the working directory to *CreateRedist* to compile and create a redist package.

```
cd SensorKinect/Platform/Linux-x86/CreateRedist
```

Run the script RedistMaker.

```
sudo ./RedistMaker
```

Navigate to the newly created *Redist* directory located inside of *Build* and run the installation script.

```
cd ../Build/Redist
sudo ./install.sh
```

Change the working directory to *Build* and run **make** and then **make install**.

```
cd ~/Kinect/SensorKinect/Platform/Linux-x86/Build
sudo make && sudo make install
```

That's it for SensorKinect. The final step is to install the PrimeSense NITE Middleware package. First download the version of PrimeSense NITE from *http://www.open ni.org/Downloads/OpenNIModules.aspx*. In the first drop-down, select OpenNI Compliant Middleware Binaries. Then select the unstable version. Download the package that corresponds to your Ubuntu installation (32- or 64-bit).

I created a new directory called NITE *in which I placed the contents of the extracted* NITE *package. This is just to keep things consistent, as version numbers may be different at the time this book is released.*

If you want to try out some of the sample programs, you'll need to edit the XML files located in the *Data* directory to include the PrimeSense license key, as shown in Figure 1-6. To do this, you'll need to change the third line of the XML sample files from:

```
<License vendor="PrimeSense" key=""/>
```

to:

```
<License vendor="PrimeSense"
key="0KOIk2JeIBYClPWVnMoRKn5cdY4="/>
```

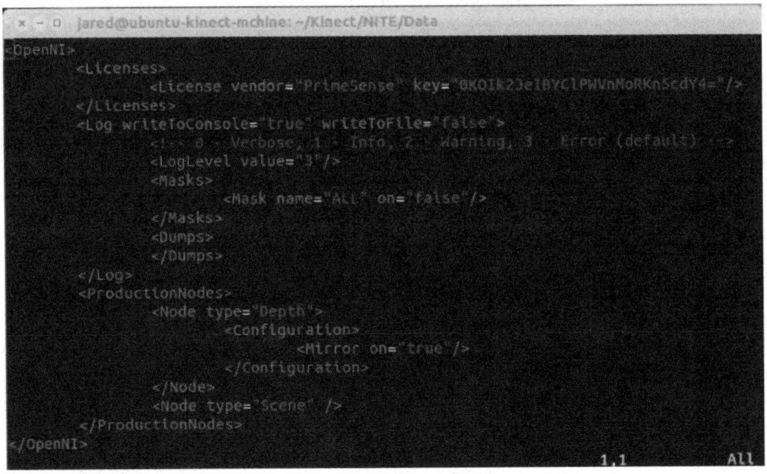

Figure 1-6.
NITE XML sample key

Change the working directory to *NITE* and run the installation script.

```
cd ~/Kinect/NITE
./sudo install.sh
```

Right away, you'll be prompted to enter the PrimeSense license key. Enter the following key to complete the installation process.

```
0KOIk2JeIBYClPWVnMoRKn5cdY4=
```

Newer versions do not require a license key.

```
At this point, you should be ready to see if the samples are working. Con
nect your Kinect to a USB port and ensure that the power adapter is also
plugged in.
```

Change the working directory to *NITE Sample* and execute one of the accompanying demos (Figure 1-7).

```
cd ~/Kinect/NITE/Samples/Bin/Release
sudo ./Sample-PointViewer
```

KINECT HACKS

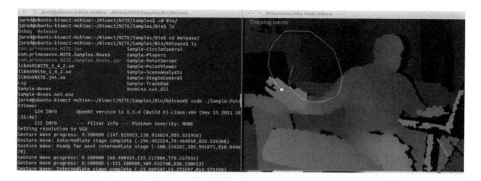

Figure 1-7.
NITE sample point viewer running on Ubuntu

If you are continuously running into the "InitFromXML failed: Failed to set USB Interface! Error," shown in Figure 1-8, try the following (it solved my problem right away):

```
sudo rmmod gspca_kinect
```

```
jared@ubuntu-kinect-mchine:~/Kinect/OpenNI/Platform/Linux$ cd Bin/
jared@ubuntu-kinect-mchine:~/Kinect/OpenNI/Platform/Linux/Bin$ ls
x86-Release
jared@ubuntu-kinect-mchine:~/Kinect/OpenNI/Platform/Linux/Bin$ cd x86-Release/
jared@ubuntu-kinect-mchine:~/Kinect/OpenNI/Platform/Linux/Bin/x86-Release$ ls
libnimCodecs.so                org.OpenNI.Samples.UserTracker
libnimMockNodes.so             org.OpenNI.Samples.UserTracker.jar
libnimRecorder.so              Sample-NiAudioSample
libOpenNI.jni.so               Sample-NiBackRecorder
libOpenNI.so                   Sample-NiConvertXToONI
libSample-NiSampleModule.so    Sample-NiCRead
niLicense                      Sample-NiRecordSynthetic
niReg                          Sample-NiSimpleCreate
NiViewer                       Sample-NiSimpleRead
OpenNI.net.dll                 Sample-NiSimpleViewer
org.OpenNI.jar                 Sample-NiUserTracker
org.OpenNI.Samples.SimpleRead  SimpleRead.net.exe
org.OpenNI.Samples.SimpleRead.jar  SimpleViewer.net.exe
org.OpenNI.Samples.SimpleViewer  UserTracker.net.exe
org.OpenNI:Samples.SimpleViewer.jar
jared@ubuntu-kinect-mchine:~/Kinect/OpenNI/Platform/Linux/Bin/x86-Release$ sudo
./NiViewer
Open failed: Failed to set USB interface!
Press any key to continue . . .
```

Figure 1-8.
OpenNI USB interface error

HACK 04 Install libfreenect for Mac OS X

For this guide, we will be using MacPorts to download and configure the libraries along with other components. We'll perform the majority of the work using the Terminal application located in your *Utilities* directory: *Applications/Utilities/Terminal*. You will need to install Git to process the latest repository builds from GitHub and install the libtool and libusb-devel libraries. You'll need to issue the following commands to download and install the prerequisites and dependencies for compiling libfreenect:

```
sudo port install git-core
sudo port install
sudo port install libusb-devel
```

*The **sudo** command requires the admin-level password for Mac, which grants you temporary root-level access.*

You will also need to download and install CMake to compile libreenect. You can find the latest version at *http://www.cmake.org/cmake/resources/software.html*. Create a directory from which you would like to work. It can be named anything and placed anywhere. For the sake of simplicity, we will create the directory *OpenKinect* located in your *Home* directory.

```
cd ~/
mkdir OpenKinect
cd OpenKinect
```

Download the latest libfreenect repository using the **git clone** command in your current working directory:

```
sudo git clone https://github.com/OpenKinect/libfreenect.git
```

Navigate to the *libfreenect* directory:

```
cd ~/OpenKinect/libfreenect
```

Create a new *build* directory, navigate into it, and compile the source code:

```
mkdir build
cd build
ccmake ..
```

When prompted, press the C key to begin compiling.

If the **ccmake** command fails, you will need to manually change the *LIBUSB_1_IN-CLUDE_DIR* path to *usr/local/include/libusb-1.0*.

Press C to restart the build.

Press the G key to generate and then type the following once everything has been completed:

```
ccmake ..
```

Once this process has completed and the cursor prompt has returned, run the following commands:

```
sudo make && sudo make install
```

The installation should be complete at this point. Navigate to the *libfreenect/build/bin* directory and run the glview demo to see if things are working properly.

```
cd ~/libfreenect/build/bin
sudo ./glview
```

HACK 05 Install libfreenect for Ubuntu

As with the Windows installation method described in Hack #01, there is a binary package available for Ubuntu installations of OpenKinect that allows us to easily install the drivers. You can find precompiled RPM and Deb packages by visiting *http://bit.ly/TlFy5x*.

These packages are rather old, so if you run into any installation problems, skip to the next section, which covers compiling libfreenect from source.

If you're using a fresh install of Ubuntu, you'll more than likely have to install quite a few dependencies on your machine to get started. A quick way to get things moving is to manually install everything at once by issuing the following command:

```
sudo apt-get install git-core cmake freeglut3-dev \
pkg-config build-essential libxmu-dev libxi-dev libusb-1.0-0-dev
```

After the library dependencies have all been successfully installed, we can now move on to compiling libfreenect from source. For the sake of this tutorial, I created a *Kinect* folder in my *Home* directory. This is where we'll place the extracted contents of libfreenect.

```
mkdir ~/Kinect
cd ~/Kinect
```

Download libfreenect using Git and then create and move into a *build* directory.

```
git clone https://github.com/OpenKinect/libfreenect.git
cd libfreenect
mkdir build
cd build
sudo cmake ..
```

Once CMake is done compiling, you can now run **make** and then **make install**.

```
sudo make
sudo make install
```

Then there's one last command before we can run some of the sample demos.

```
sudo ldconfig /usr/local/lib64/
```

Navigate to *bin* inside the *build* directory and run the glview demo. Make sure your Kinect sensor is connected via USB and that the power adapter is plugged in as well.

```
cd /libfreenect/build/bin
sudo ./glview
```

If glview opens properly, you should now be looking at the famous dual view of the RGB and depth camera output that the Kinect is currently capturing. See Figure 1-9.

Figure 1-9.
libfreenect glview sample for Ubuntu

HACK 06 Install libfreenect for Windows 7

Get ready for quite the ride if you're interested in compiling and building libfreenect on a Windows machine. It is by far the most involved process, requiring a lot of tinkering around with library dependencies to properly compile and build libfreenect.

Before we get started, we'll need to download and install CMake and Visual Studio 2010 from the following places:

Visual C++ 2010 Express
http://www.microsoft.com/visualstudio/eng/downloads

CMake Windows Binary Installer
http://cmake.org/cmake/resources/software.html

Farther down the road, you'll need to manually assign the path for certain library files and includes to finish compiling libfreenect in CMake. I've added them all to a nice little ZIP file, which you can download at *http://developkinect.com/resource/library/libfreenect-windows-dependencies*.

If, for whatever reason, you need to download the files individually, here are their names and download locations:

libus-win32

   http://sourceforge.net/apps/trac/libusb-win32/wiki

pthreads-win32

   http://sourceware.org/pthreads-win32/

Glut

   http://www.xmission.com/~nate/glut.html

Following are the steps required to install the drivers for the Kinect sensor.

Download and extract the libfreenect drivers from GitHub: *https://github.com/Open Kinect/libfreenect/zipball/master*.

   For the sake of consistency, create an OpenKinect *folder on your desktop where all these downloads will be placed.*

Extract the contents of the ZIP file into the *OpenKinect* folder.

   I'll refer to this new folder simply as libfreenect, *although it may be labeled differently on your computer.*

At this point, we'll install the drivers for the Kinect sensor. Plug the Kinect sensor into a USB port on your computer and make sure the AC adapter is plugged in as well. You will be presented with an "install drivers" pop-up notification. Cancel it.

Navigate to your Device Manager: Start → Control Panel → System and Security → System → Device Manager.

You will see a device called Xbox NUI Motor with a yellow exclamation mark indicating that the device is unknown and drivers need to be installed. Select (highlight) the device and click the Update Driver Software icon. When prompted for where to search for updated drivers, select Browse My Computer for the driver software.

Select the *inf* directory located within the *libfreenect* source folder (*libfreenect/platform/windows/inf*). Once you click Next, you'll encounter a warning stating that the driver is not certified. Disregard this and continue with the installation.

Once the driver is installed, you should notice that the green LED on the Kinect sensor will now be lit up. Repeat the previous step for the two other unknown devices, Xbox NUI Camera and Xbox NUI Audio.

The necessary drivers should now be successfully installed for your Kinect sensor. Now that that's over with, you will need to download and install (if you haven't already, of course) CMake and Visual Studio 2010.

Before we start compiling libfreenect, create a *build* folder in the *libfreenect* directory. This is where we'll point the output of the CMake compiled binaries.

Open the CMake GUI and set the "Where is the source code" path to */libfreenect*.

Set the "Where to build the binaries" browse build path to */libfreenect/build*. Click Configure. It will fail (as shown in Figure 1-10), but don't worry about it. We still need to set a few includes and library paths, among other things.

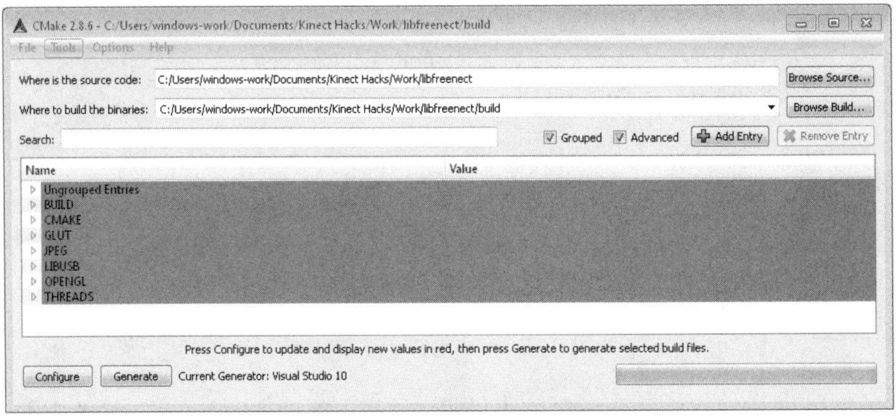

Figure 1-10.
CMake compile failure

First up, take the following actions in the expanded configuration list (Figure 1-11):

1. Uncheck BUILD_FAKENECT.
2. Uncheck BUILD_CPP.
3. Check BUILD_AS3_SERVER.

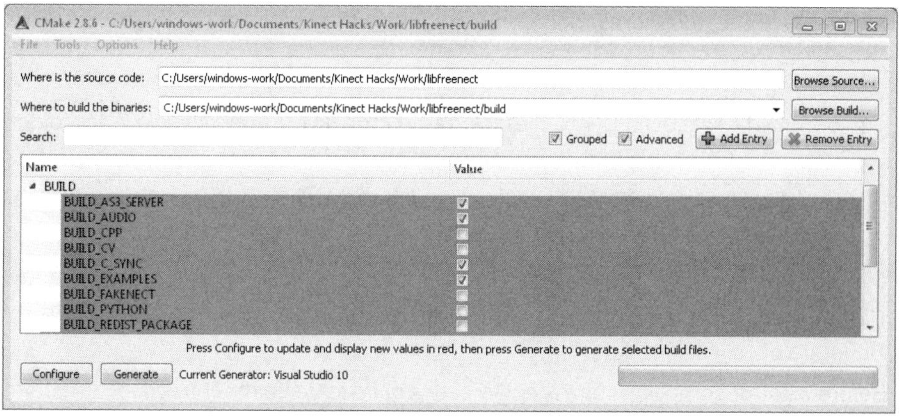

Figure 1-11.
CMake libfreenect build checkboxes

You will now need to point certain build paths to the *freenect_win_deps* folder you downloaded earlier. If you haven't done so already, download it from *http://develop kinect.com/resource/library/libfreenect-windows-dependencies* and extract the contents of the ZIP file. Remember its location. Now do the following:

1. Set LIBUSB_1_INCLUDE to the *freenect_win_deps/include* folder of the uncompressed *freenect_win_deps*.

2. Set LIBUSB_1_LIBRARY to point to the *libusb.lib* file inside the uncompressed *freenect_win_deps* folder located at *freenect_win_deps/lib/msvc/libusb.lib*.

3. Set THREADS_PTHREADS_INCLUDE_DIR to the *freenect_win_deps/include* folder within *freenect_win_deps*.

4. Set THREADS_PTHREADS_WIN32_LIBRARY to point to the *pthreadVC2.lib* file inside the uncompressed *freenect_win_deps* located at *freenect_win_deps/lib/ pthreadVC2.lib*.

5. Set JPEG_INCLUDE_DIR to *freenect_win_deps/include*, located within the uncompressed *freenect_win_deps* folder.

6. Set JPEG_LIBRARY to point to the *libjpeg.lib* file inside the uncompressed *freenect_win_deps* located at *freenect_win_deps/lib/libjpeg.lib*.

Click Configure again. It should successfully complete the process this time, but we still need to add the Glut references.

At the top of the configuration list, you should now see four notices in red that need to be fixed.

1. Set GLUT_INCLUDE_DIR to the *include* directory in the *freenect_win_deps* folder, (*freenect_win_deps/include*).

2. Set GLUT_glut_LIBRARY to point to the *glut32.lib* file inside the *freenect_win_deps* folder as well (*freenect_win_deps/lib/glut32.lib*).

Click Configure, and it should successfully complete this time (Figure 1-12). Click Generate once it's complete.

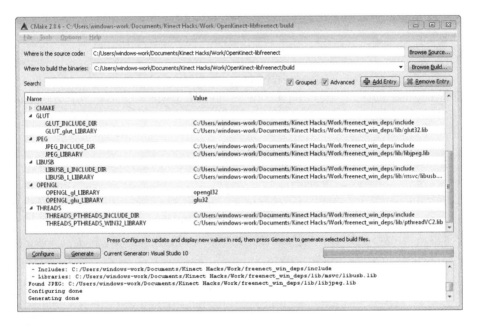

Figure 1-12.
CMake successful build paths

You can now open the *libfreenect.sln* file from the *build* folder in which the output was placed (*/libfreenect/build/*).

Open *libfreenect.sln* in Visual Studio and build the project.

You will receive a few errors when building the solution, but it should compile correctly regardless. The binaries of the build will be placed in the *build/bin/Debug* folder.

The final step is to place a few *.dll* files in the appropriate folders as follows, and then we can run some of the samples provided:

1. Copy *freenect.dll* and *freenect_sync.dll* from *build\lib\Debug* to *build\bin\Debug*.
2. Copy *pthreadVC2.dll* from *freenect_win_deps\lib* to *build\bin\Debug*.
3. Copy *libjpeg-8.dll* from *freenect_win_deps\lib* to *build\bin\Debug*.
4. Copy *glut32.dll* from *freenect_win_deps\lib* to *build\bin\Debug*.
5. Copy *libusb0.dll* from *platform\windows\inf\xbox nui camera\amd64* to *build\bin\Debug*.

If you're compiling for a 32-bit version of Windows, copy *libusb0_x86.dll* from *libfreenect\platform\windows\inf\xbox nui camera\x86* to *libfreenect\build\bin\Debug*.

That's it. The libfreenet package should be fully installed. You can now try running a few of the samples, such as tiltdemo and glview (Figure 1-13).

Figure 1-13.
glpclview libfreenect demo running on Windows 7

HACK 07 Install the Kinect for Windows SDK

Microsoft released its own SDK on June 16, 2011, roughly seven months after it launched the Kinect for Xbox 360. After the incredible reception of all of the custom hacks built by the community of open source developers, what choice did Microsoft have, really? Sit back and watch these creative hobbyists and enthusiasts change the world with its Xbox peripheral? With the release of its own SDK, Microsoft opened up the channels for voice recognition and other audio capabilities, features that are currently unavailable with the libfreenect drivers.

The Kinect SDK has a ton of great features but a few limitations as well. For instance, at the time of this writing, the Kinect SDK toolkit is available only for Windows 7, so if you haven't upgraded from Vista or are still rocking XP, you're out of luck. Development using the Kinect SDK is for noncommercial use only. You'll need DirectX 9.0 runtime installed, and you'll be required to develop your projects in C++, C#, or Visual Basic using Visual Studio 2010. There's also no built-in support for recording or playing back to disk, and it tracks only the full body—there's no upper-body or hands-only mode.

On the upside, it's easy to install, does not require the "Freeze! Hands in the air!" calibration pose (the Psi pose), has audio capabilities, and supports motor tilt as well.

The beauty of the Microsoft Kinect SDK is that it's pretty much plug and play. You will, however, need to meet a few system requirements to get up and running:

- Standalone Kinect sensor with power adaptor (sold separately from Xbox 3601/n bundled Kinect)
- Computer with a dual-core, 2.66 GHz or faster processor
- Windows 7–compatible graphics card that supports DirectX 9.0 capabilities
- 2 GB RAM (4 GB RAM recommended)
- Windows 7 (x86 or x64)
- Visual Studio 2010 Express (or other 2010 edition)
- Microsoft .NET Framework 4.0 (comes with Visual Studio 2010)

If all systems are go, you're pretty much in the clear. Simply download the Kinect SDK (32- or 64-bit) from *http://www.microsoft.com/en-us/kinectforwindows/develop/overview.aspx* and run the installer.

To see if everything is working properly, go to your Start menu, locate the newly installed Microsoft Kinect SDK application, and check out the Skeletal Viewer and Shape Game (Figure 1-14).

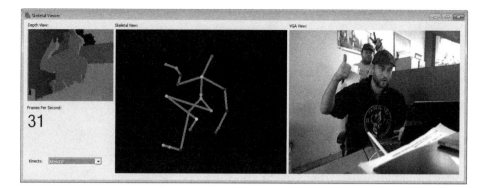

Figure 1-14.
Kinect SDK Skeletal Viewer sample

If you try to run the Skeletal Viewer demo and receive the "NuiInstaller Failed" error message, try removing any devices that are currently occupying USB ports on your computer. You may also need to close applications that use your webcam, such as MSN Messenger, AIM, or Skype. This also applies to the Shape Game sample if the Kinect isn't tracking any users. For more, visit Microsoft's support forums at http://social.msdn.microsoft.com/Forums/en-US/category/kinectsdk.

2

Programming Options

Congratulations! After getting set up with your preferred development environment, you have experienced your first interaction with the Kinect sensor on your computer. As fun as it is to play around with all those samples, there's much more in store once we start looking into the programming side of Kinect hacking.

This chapter will introduce you to a wide assortment of programming languages and tools you can use to build that next killer app. Not only does the Kinect have its own official SDK for you to try out, but there's also a good chance you'll be able to take advantage of your preferred programming language so you can jump right into Kinect hacking. One aspect of programming for the Kinect that's very appealing to most developers is that they're not constrained to a few options in order to create something truly amazing. A large assortment of frameworks, wrappers, application programming interfaces (APIs), and integrated development environments (IDEs) is available for some of the most popular and widely used programming languages, allowing developers to implement a natural user interface for their next project.

The Kinect is a brilliant piece of tech to work with as well. The Kinect is dirt cheap in comparison to other depth-sensing cameras on the market. You can use it to render 3D motion capture techniques in real time, add visual effects to tracked users, provide localization data, or create a new and inventive way to approach traditional video gaming. The list goes on and on. With the right tools by your side, you can open up your world to an entirely new way of interacting with digital media. This chapter will cover the programming languages, tools, and IDEs that are available for you to develop with as well as the add-ons and other applications that are compatible with the Kinect. Short and easy guides accompany each programming option to ensure that you get set up properly and can start developing applications using the Kinect. Let's take a look at what you can use to get started today.

HACK 08 Get to Know openFrameworks

openFrameworks is a very popular tool used by programmers for a wide assortment of Kinect-related projects, ranging from visual effects and games to musical application. It's free to download and works with Windows, Mac OS X, and Linux. If you're interested in learning more about openFrameworks, visit the official site at *http:// openframeworks.cc*.

The following hacks will cover the steps required to install openFrameworks on Windows, Mac OS X, and Linux. You'll need different software installed depending on which OS you choose to use as your development workstation, which we will cover before installing openFrameworks.

You can download openFrameworks from the official site at *http://www.openframe works.cc/download*. You can also download the latest builds and grab the source code for all operating systems from GitHub at *https://github.com/openframeworks/open Frameworks*.

Be sure to always check out the README *file if you happen to run into any problems during the installation.*

For an extensive catalog of reported issues along with general help with anything relating to openFrameworks, be sure to visit the forums at http://forum.openfra meworks.cc.

HACK 09 Install openFrameworks for Windows

For the purpose of this installation guide, I used Code::Blocks (Figure 2-1) as my compiler to build and run openFrameworks examples.

1. Download the Code::Blocks installation of openFrameworks from *http:// www.openframeworks.cc/download*.

2. Download and install the Code::Blocks binaries using MinGW from *http:// www.codeblocks.org/downloads/binaries*.

3. Download the Code::Blocks openFrameworks additions from *http://www.open frameworks.cc/content/files/codeblocks_additions.zip*.

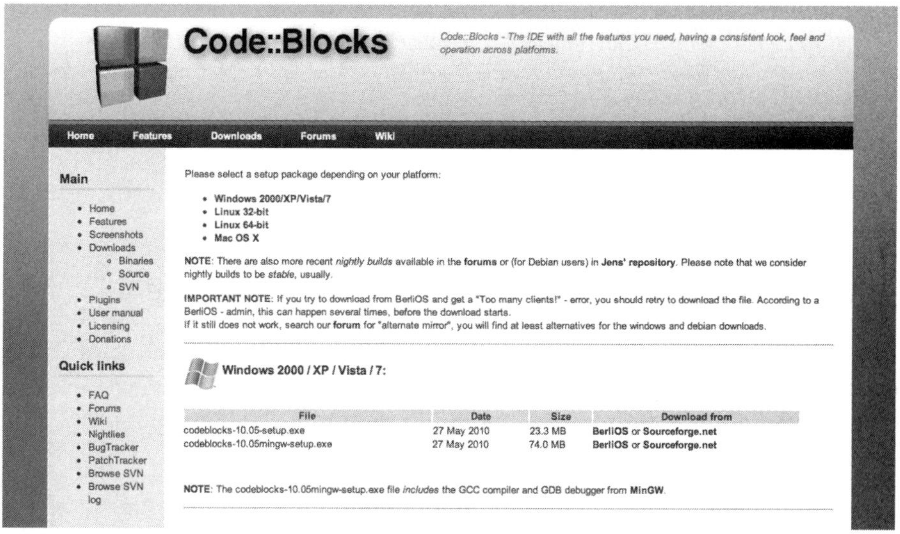

Figure 2-1.
Code::Blocks download page

Inside the *codeblocks_additions.zip* file are two folders. You'll need to place the *add_to_codeblocks_mingw_include* folder into *C:\Program Files\CodeBlocks \MinGW\include* and add *add_to_codeblocks_mingw_lib* to *C:\Program Files\Co- deBlocks\MinGW\lib*.

Once you've completed these steps, try running some of the openFrameworks examples by going to the downloaded openFrameworks folder (originally labeled *of_preRelease_v007_win_cb* for version 007) and launch any of the *.workspace* files in */apps/examples/*.

HACK 10 Install openFrameworks for OS X

To install openFrameworks for your Mac, you'll need to download and install Xcode, Apple's free, GCC-based IDE.

If you haven't installed Xcode yet, you can find everything you need to know about how to get up and running at *http://developer.apple.com/xcode*.

This is probably one of the most straightforward installation processes for openFra- meworks. If Xcode is installed, you can get started right away by downloading the Mac OS X version of openFrameworks from *http://www.openframeworks.cc/download*. Using Finder or Xcode itself, go to the *apps/examples* folder within the *of_preRe- lease_v007_osx* folder. Here, you'll see a wide variety of examples to choose from. Launch or open the *.xcodeproj* file from any of the examples to make sure everything is working OK.

If you are running a Mac with OS X 10.7, you will need to change the Base SDK setting under Build Settings in XCode from "latest Mac OS X (Mac OS X 10.7)" to "Mac OS X 10.6." See Figure 2-2.

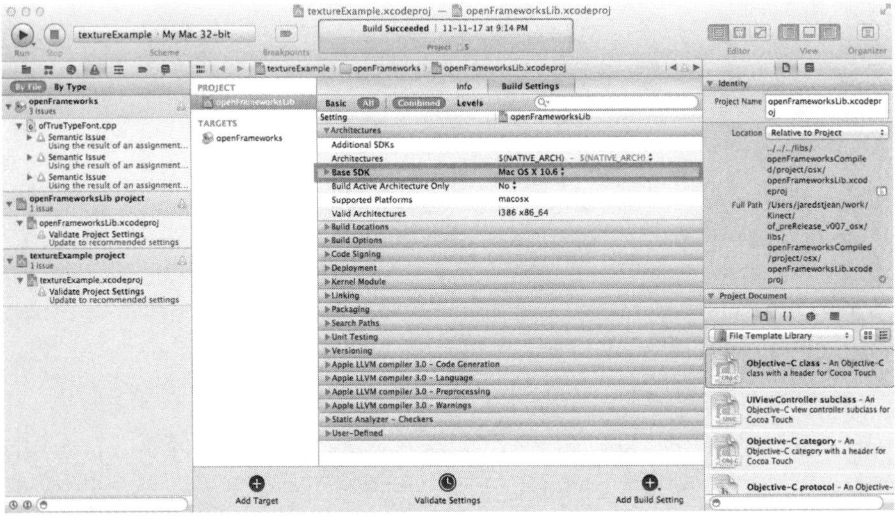

Figure 2-2.
openFrameworks texture example Xcode fix

HACK 11 Install openFrameworks for Ubuntu

openFrameworks recommends the use of Code::Blocks as its preferred IDE, so we'll need to install and configure that before we go any further. You'll need to invoke several commands with root-level privileges, so open up your trusty Terminal application of choice, and let's get started!

Download openFrameworks from *http://www.openframeworks.cc/download*. Inside the *openFrameworks* folder, navigate to the *Ubuntu* directory.

```
cd openFrameworks/scripts/Linux/Ubuntu
```

Install the latest version of Code::Blocks and its dependencies.

```
sudo ./install_codeblocks.sh
sudo ./install_dependencies.sh
```

Install video/audio codecs (optional).

```
sudo ./install_codecs.sh
```

That's it. To see if things are working, you will need to build an openFrameworks example. Navigate to the *app/examples* folder.

```
cd /apps/examples/
```

Enter the *graphicsExample* directory, for example, and run **make**.

```
sudo make
```

Change the working directory to *bin* and launch the example file (Figure 2-3).

```
cd bin
sudo ./graphicsExample
```

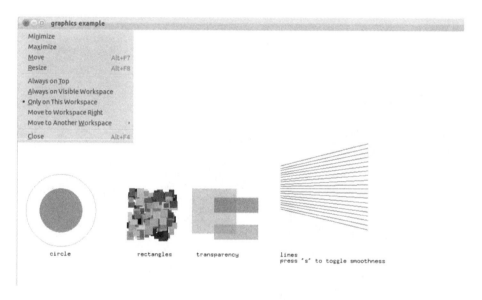

Figure 2-3.
openFrameworks graphics example

HACK 12 Install the ofxKinect Add-on for openFrameworks

To get openFrameworks working with the Kinect, we'll need to install the ofxKinect add-on. ofxKinect is a cross-platform add-on for developing Kinect applications in openFrameworks. It was developed by Kyle MacDonald under the MIT license and can be used with Windows, Mac OS X, and Linux. You can download it from the GitHub repository at *https://github.com/ofTheo/ofxKinect*.

Alternatively, if you choose to use Git to clone the latest repository, be sure to specify the version of openFrameworks. For openFrameworks, you'll need to issue the following command for the latest 007 version:

```
sudo git clone https://github.com/ofTheo/ofxKinect.git 007
```

> The 007 *refers to the version of openFrameworks that you're using. You can find out what version openFrameworks you have by looking at the name of the extracted of* preRelease_v/ *folder.*

I renamed the *007* folder to *ofxKinect* and placed it into the *of_PreRelease_v/ addons/* folder.

If you're using a Mac, build and run the *ofxKinectExample.xcodeproj* file located inside the *ofxKinect/examples* folder with Xcode. See Figure 2-4.

Figure 2-4.
ofxKinect openFrameworks add-on example

On Linux, run **make**, change to the *bin* directory, and then run the example:

```
cd ofxKinect
sudo make
cd bin
sudo ./example
```

On Windows, simply open the *ofxKinectExample_win.workplace* file in the *addons/ ofxKinect/examples* folder. See Figure 2-5.

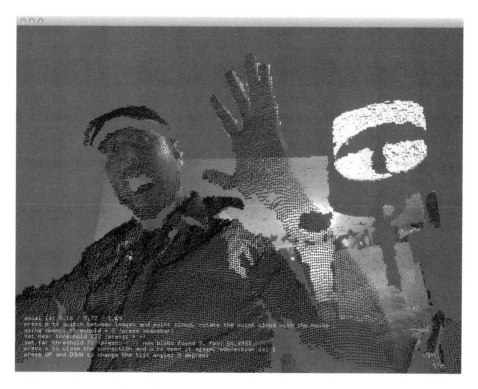

Figure 2-5.
ofxKinect example point cloud

HACK 13 Use Processing

Processing is an open source programming language and IDE that draws several comparisons to openFrameworks, but runs on the Java programming language as opposed to C++. Originally designed as a software sketchbook, Processing has evolved into much more and is widely used by an assortment of programmers interested in learning, prototyping, and production. One of the touted upsides of developing projects using Processing is its intuitive, visual learning style. Compared to other visual programming IDEs, Processing makes it relatively easy for you to get your feet wet, and in a short amount of time, which is perfect for those interested in interactive art, web design, and dynamic visual illustrations.

Since Processing is open source, there are tons of resources and guides available online. The main site, *http://processing.com* (Figure 2-6), has everything you need, including an active and growing community that hangs out in the forums. If you get stumped at any time during development, this is the place to find what you're looking for.

Figure 2-6.
Processing home page

Download and install Processing from *http://processing.org/download*.

By default, Processing creates a sketchbook folder in your Documents *directory called* Processing. *You may, however, need to create a* libraries *directory. If one is not already present in the* Processing *directory, create a new folder called* libraries.

HACK 14 Install SimpleOpenNI and OpenKinect Processing Libraries

You'll need to download a great, easy-to-implement wrapper called SimpleOpenNI to bridge Processing with your Kinect sensor. You can grab SimpleOpenNI for Linux, Windows, and Mac at *http://code.google.com/p/simple-openni/downloads/list*.

For Mac users, all you'll need to do is place the extracted *SimpleOpenNI* directory and all of its contents in the *Processing/libraries* folder. You'll also need to download and run the *OpenNI_NITE_Installer-OSX-x.xx.zip* file to add a few other libraries to run some of the examples. Downloading the simple-to-use installer also ensures that the SimpleOpenNI Processing library will work seamlessly with OpenNI. You can download it at *http://code.google.com/p/simple-openni/downloads/list*.

To see if everything is working OK, launch the Processing application and open up one of the example files located in the *Documents/Processing/SimpleOpenNI/examples/* directory. You do this by using the application's File → Open method or just by double-clicking any file with a *.pde* extension. Once the *.pde* file is loaded into Processing, make sure your Kinect is connected to your computer and a power outlet, then click the Run icon to see it in action.

If you're using Linux, just add the contents in the *~/sketchbook/libraries* directory. That's it. A boatload of examples come with SimpleOpenNI, so feel free to check them out and get started on your latest Processing project using the Microsoft Kinect.

Some Processing sketches referenced later in this book require you to import Daniel Shiffman's OpenKinect library. Follow the same installation instructions as SimpleOpenNI by placing the folder in the *libraries* directory with Processing. The library can be downloaded from *http://www.shiffman.net/p5/kinect/*.

HACK 15 Install Cinder-Kinect for Mac OS X

Cinder (Figure 2-7) is another great open source solution for building amazing graphical, audio, and video applications. It's available to use on Windows and Mac OS X. The learning curve may be a bit steep depending on your familiarity with Processing; Cinder uses C++, so it tends to draw more comparisons to Processing. For more information about Cinder, check out its official site at *http://libcinder.org/*.

Figure 2-7.
Official Cinder site

For the purposes of this installation guide, we'll be using Git to download Cinder for OS X, as shown in Figure 2-8. This is a good idea if you plan on staying up to date with the latest and greatest that Cinder has to offer by easily pulling the master branch down. If using Git isn't your cup of tea, you can always check Cinder's download page to see if a new version is available.

Find yourself a nice cozy directory to store all your Cinder-related files, and run the following commands using a Terminal application:

```
sudo git clone git://github.com/cinder/Cinder.git cinder_master
```

You'll need to download and extract the contents of *boost* to properly build Cinder projects due to a few required headers. You can download a copy of Boost from *http://sourceforge.net/projects/boost/files/boost/1.44.0*.

Extract the contents of the *.zip* file, rename the *boost_1_44_0* folder to simply *boost*, and place it in the *Cinder* root-level directory.

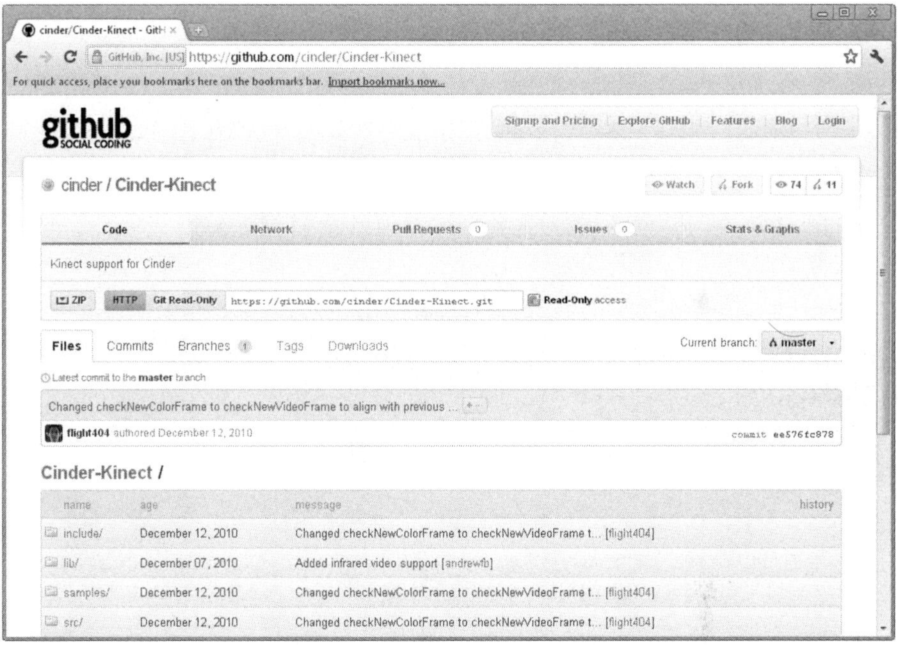

Figure 2-8.
GitHub download

Next up, download the Cinder-Kinect block into the *blocks* directory.

```
cd path/to/cinder/blocks
sudo git clone git://github.com/cinder/Cinder-Kinect.git
```

You'll now be able to try out some of the examples to see if everything is in working order.

3

Visual Effects

If you're looking for the perfect DIY, low-budget special effects solution, look no further than the Kinect. The Kinect shines when it comes to overlaying spectacular digital effects on any user being tracked by the sensor. This truly makes it the perfect solution for those on a tight budget. Using an open source IDE such as Processing, for example, you can apply an extensive library of visual effects supplied by the amazing and abundant community of programmers.

In this chapter, you will learn what options are available to use for your next visually stunning project, along with how to properly install any dependencies required to get up and running. Each hack will be presented in an easy-to-understand manner that will help get you started. By the end of the chapter, you will be able to apply particle effects, colors, and a wide assortment of geometric shapes and patterns that will transform your subject into a real-time, live action, digital masterpiece.

Whether you're interested in adding real-time effects for a live performance or digital enhancements for video-editing post-processing work, the Kinect will provide the means for you to add that perfect touch to any project on a shoestring budget.

HACK 16 Use Quartz Composer with Synapse for Kinect

Quartz Composer is a great visual programming language that comes free with Xcode, Apple's development environment for Mac OS X. This application is available only for Mac and provides a relatively simple means of creating great visual effects. For more on Quartz Composer, check out Apple's online Quartz Composer User Guide at *http://bit.ly/XgdmXm*.

The best way to start building Quartz Composer visual programs with the Kinect is to use Ryan Challinor's Synapse for Kinect application. Synapse is a great tool that was designed to take a lot of the heavy lifting out of getting your Kinect sensor working with applications such as Ableton Live, Quartz Composer, and Max/MSP/Jitter. Synapse for Kinect is designed to pass open sound control (OSC) events to Quartz Composer as well as Ableton Live and Max/MSP.

The program not only works with Quartz Composer, Ableton Live, and Max/MSP, but also *any* application that uses the OSC protocol, so there are plenty of options available when you're using Synapse. I highly recommend this tool if you just want to dive right in and start Kinect hacking.

To show you how easy it is, Ryan has put together some great video examples to get you on your way; they are available on his site, *http://synapsekinect.tumblr.com*. For this hack, I've transcribed one of his step-by-step guides to get you started on your first Kinect integrated Quartz Composer visual program.

Before you begin, make sure you have a copy of Xcode installed on your Mac. You can download it for free at *http://developer.apple.com/xcode/*.

The end result of this hack will be a cool particle halo effect that follows your hand around (see Figure 3-1).

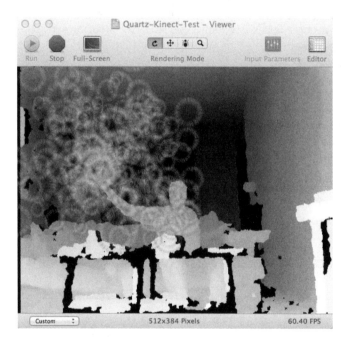

Figure 3-1.
Particle effects following your left hand on the x- and y-axis

Download and extract the contents of Synapse for Mac from *http://bit.ly/TzPFdp* into a directory that you can easily access.

You'll also need to download the *Quartz Composer example project plugins* directory from the same location. Extract the contents of the *QuartzKinect.zip* file, and place the *SynapseKinect.plugin* and *qcOSC.plugin* files in *Username/Library/Graphics/ Quartz Composer Plug-Ins/*.

Make sure your Kinect is connected to your Mac and also plugged into a power outlet. Open the Synapse application from the *Synapse* folder. Perform the Psi calibration pose, as seen in Figure 3-2. Wait until all the joints have been mapped and proceed to the next step.

Psi pose is the proper terminology for the "Freeze! Hands in the air!" calibration pose. This initiates skeletal tracking when you're using OpenNI.

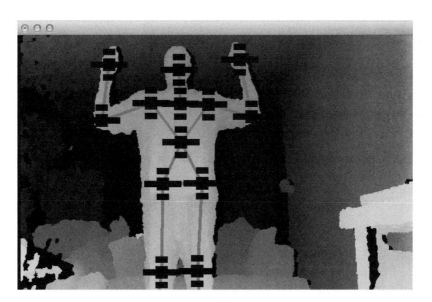

Figure 3-2.
A successful calibration pose with Synapse

Open Quartz Composer. I was able to easily launch the application by searching for Quartz Composer in Spotlight.

In the extracted *QuartzKinect* directory you just downloaded, open the *quartz_pass-through* file and let it run in the background.

Open a new blank project in Quartz Composer by pressing Shift-Command-N or go to File → New Blank.

Click the Patch Library icon in the upper-left corner and add a new sprite. Assign a width of 2 and a height value of 1.5.

Click the Patch Library icon again and add the Synapse plug-in we added earlier by typing in **Synapse**. Connect the Synapse plug-in to the sprite's image. At this point, you should be able to see the Kinect's depth image in the sprite window.

To demonstrate the visual effects we can set up, we'll add some particles that will eventually follow your hand wherever it goes:

1. Click Patch Library.
2. Type **Particle System** and press Enter.
3. Spice up the particles by typing **Halo** and opening the Lenticular Halo library.
4. Attach the Lenticular Halo Image to the particle.

Next up, we'll have to add the qcOSC plug-in using the Patch library. Once it's been added, perform the following steps:

1. Click the Patch Inspector icon in the upper-left corner.
2. Click the drop-down menu and select "settings."
3. Under Network, add **12348** as the port.

If you're still being tracked within the Synapse application, you should see a bunch of new structures added to the qcOSC Macro Patch.

Next we need to add another macro and a few math equations:

1. Click the Patch Library icon and add Structure Index Member.
2. Attach the righthand_pos_screen or lefthand_pos_screen option to the Structure Index Member structure query.

If you need a frame of reference, Figure 3-3 illustrates how everything connects in the end.

---

3. Connect the resulting value of the first math operation to the initial value of the next math operation. Do this again for the last math operation.
4. Set the first math operation value to divide by 640.
5. Set the second math operation value to subtract by 1.5.
6. Set the third math operation value to multiply by 2.
7. Connect the last math operation value to the *x* position of the particle system.

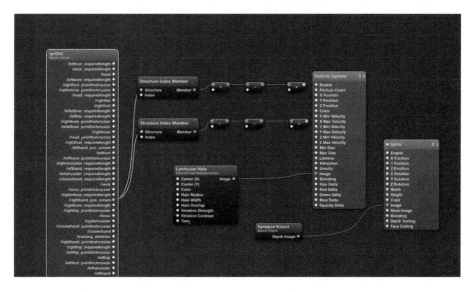

Figure 3-3.
Quartz Composer final layout

At this point, you should be able to see the particle effects follow your hand from left and right on the x-axis. The last step is to get the y-axis working.

Copy and paste the Structure Index Member and the math values to save yourself a bit of time. You could just repeat the whole process, but this method is much easier. Simply drag your cursor around the math values and use the hot key Command+C to copy, and then paste with Command+V.

1. Set the new Structure Index Member value to 1.
2. Change the values of the first math operation to 480, maintaining the current division function.
3. Do not change anything related to the second math operation.
4. Change the value of the last math operation to −2.
5. Connect the last math operation to the *y* position of the particle system.

Hopefully, everything works out OK, and you're now waving a colorful, visual-particle-effect-enhanced hand around in the Quartz Composer Viewer.

For more on Synapse, be sure to visit Ryan Challinor's Synapse page at *http://synap sekinect.tumblr.com*.

HACK 17 Draw in the Air with Processing

This fun little Processing sketch was developed by Peter Nash. Using OpenNI for skeletal tracking, this hack enables you to draw shapes in midair by gesturing. Each shape is generated by the Fisica Processing library by Ricard Marxer, a two-dimensional physics simulator based on JBox2D.

The Processing project contains just one file. This is responsible for identifying users and capturing their hand movements to create and manipulate shapes inside a 2D world. Let's look at the code, beginning with importing the necessary Processing libraries.

```
import SimpleOpenNI.*;
import fisica.*;
import java.awt.*;
```

Declare a **SimpleOpenNI** context; this will be used later to capture hand movements. You can tweak the gesture to start the sketch here, although **RaiseHand** is a good choice, because it is the most robust.

```
SimpleOpenNI context;
String gestureToRecognize = "RaiseHand";
```

Next we need a physics world that provides realistic interaction between the shapes with a gravitational pull. Declare an **FWorld world**, which is a container for all our shapes; an **FPoly temporaryShape**, where we store any shapes being created; and an **FBody lastSelectedBody**, which tracks user selection.

```
FWorld world;         // all drawn shapes exist in this world.
FPoly temporaryShape; // the shape the user is currently drawing.

/** State **/
FBody lastSelectedBody;
```

To implement a good user experience, we need to add a bit of polish—for example, measuring if a user is keeping his hand still and responding accordingly. The following variable declarations will be used to help improve the user experience.

```
long handStillSince;
PVector hand = null;
PVector lastHand = null;
PVector lastFinger;
ArrayList handPositions = new ArrayList();
```

Processing sketches hang off two main methods: setup(), which is called only once, and draw(), which is called every frame. To detect movements from our Kinect library, we implement a few more methods specifically around detecting the loss of hands from view.

The following setup method initializes the onscreen window to draw to, then calls setupWorld() and setupKinect().

```
void setup() {
  size(640,480);
  smooth();

  setupWorld();
  setupKinect();
}
```

setupWorld() is responsible for initializing the 2D world. Try tweaking the gravity settings; the two parameters are the x and y components of the force.

```
void setupWorld() {
  Fisica.init(this);
  world = new FWorld();
  world.setGravity(0, 200);
  world.setEdges();
  world.setEdgesRestitution(0);
}
```

setupKinect() is responsible for initializing the Kinect. This is mostly boilerplate code that puts the Kinect in RGB mode, enables depth field readings, and turns on hand tracking. The Kinect library calls a specific set of movement detection methods, which are implemented as follows:

```
void setupKinect() {
  context = new SimpleOpenNI(this);
  context.setMirror(false);
  if(context.enableDepth() == false)
  {
    println("Can't open the depthMap, maybe the camera is not connected!");
    exit();
    return;
  }

  context.enableGesture();
  context.enableHands();
```

```
    context.enableRGB();
    context.setSmoothingHands(0.1);
    context.addGesture(gestureToRecognize);
}
```

At this point, the library will detect gestures and call a set of predefined methods. These are:

- onRecognizeGesture() when a RaiseHand gesture is detected
- onUpdateHands() when a hand movement is detected
- onDestroyHands() when a hand has been lost from view

These methods are very straightforward and simply change state for our draw() method to process.

```
void onRecognizeGesture(String strGesture, PVector idPosition,
  PVector endPosition) {
    context.removeGesture(gestureToRecognize);
    context.startTrackingHands(endPosition);
}
```

Once a RaiseHand gesture is detected, we ask the library to stop detecting any more gestures so there's only one user being tracked. We then ask the library to start tracking this hand.

```
void onUpdateHands(int handId,PVector pos,float time) {
    PVector tempHand = new PVector();
    context.convertRealWorldToProjective(pos, tempHand);
    hand = new PVector(640-tempHand.x, tempHand.y); // mirror
}
```

Any hand movements are detected with this method, which converts the coordinate to our 640×480 screen output and stores it as a global variable for the draw() method to process.

```
void onDestroyHands(int handId,float time) {
    hand=null;
    context.addGesture(gestureToRecognize);
}
```

When a hand is lost, the preceding method is called. This deletes our hand object and tells the Kinect library to start looking for the RaiseHand gesture again.

Next, the draw() method, which Processing will call every frame, is responsible for updating state and displaying it.

```
void draw() {
  background(0);

  context.update();
  drawRGB();
  world.step();
  world.draw(this);

  // if user is currently drawing a shape, show it.
  if (temporaryShape != null) {
    temporaryShape.draw(this);
  }
  processUserInputs();

  lastHand = hand;
}
```

For each frame, we first reset the output screen, using the standard black background call. Then, we call **update()** to prompt the Kinect library to update its state. The **drawRGB()** method displays the RGB video from the Kinect on the output screen. Next, we update the world's state by calling **step()**. Calling **step()** tells the world that some notion of time has passed and all objects should move a bit.

Next, we draw the world's state (all through library code) and any shapes the user is currently drawing. After we've updated the world states, we process any user hand signals detected by the Kinect library. Finally, the old reference to the user's location is updated.

Now it's time to introduce how to process the hands into state changes.

```
void processUserInputs() {
    Boolean isDrawingShape = false;
    Boolean hasSelectedShape = lastSelectedBody != null;
```

The preceding two convenience variables, **isDrawingShape** and **hasSelectedShape**, determine the user's state. The following states are possible:

- No user interaction.
- User is drawing an object.
- User is selecting an object.
- User is moving an object.

The following **if** statements ensure that user interaction is detected and a shape is not already being drawn (the recorded hand position is empty).

```
if(lastHand != null && hand != null) {
  if (handPositions.isEmpty() ) {
```

In this block, the user's hand has been detected. First we determine if the user is selecting an object by returning any object in the world at the user's hand coordinates, and saving the object as **b**.

```
FBody b = world.getBody(hand.x,hand.y);
if(b != null && !hasSelectedShape && handsBeenStillFor
  (lastHand, hand, 500)) {
```

In this block, the user has selected an object (**b** is an object) for the first time (there is no previously selected object), and his hands have been still for half a second. We add the wait time to improve the user experience.

We update the state by capturing the last finger position and what the user selected; we need these to work out a movement if the user throws the object.

```
println("Selected Object: "+ b);
// IF TOUCHING AN EXISTING OBJECT, RECORD OBJECT
lastSelectedBody = b;
lastFinger = hand;
b.setFill(120, 120, 120);
}
else if(lastSelectedBody != null && lastSelectedBody != b) {
```

In this block, the user moved an object. The **if** statement determines that the user has previously selected an object and has now selected a different object.

We calculate a user's movement in the following lines by applying a force proportional to how fast the user moved his hand.

```
println("Moving  Object");

// IF NEW OBJECT IS DIFFERENT FROM OLD THEN OBJECT HAS BEEN MOVED
float dx = (lastFinger.x-hand.x);
float dy= (lastFinger.y-hand.y);

if(dx != 0 && dy != 0) {
  lastSelectedBody.setVelocity(-20*dx,-20*dy);
}

lastSelectedBody.setFill(120, 30, 90);
lastSelectedBody=null;
} else if (!hasSelectedShape && handsBeenStillFor(lastHand, hand,
2000)){
```

In this block, the user has created an object. The `if` statement determines that the user has not previously selected a shape and his hands have been still for two seconds.

In this case, we set the flag `isDrawingShape`, which we'll interpret later.

```
    println("Creating new Object");
    isDrawingShape=true;
} else if (hasSelectedShape){
```

Finally, if the user has previously selected a shape, change the color as follows.

```
    b.setFill(120, 120, 120);
  }
}
```

If a user is already drawing a shape, the following `if` statement is executed. The following block watches the user's hand, and if the hand has not moved for two seconds, it finishes the shape.

```
if(!handPositions.isEmpty()) {

  if(!handsBeenStillFor(lastHand, hand, 2000)) {
    println("Extending Object");
    isDrawingShape=true;
  } else {
    // ADD OBJECT TO WORLD
    println("Finished new Object");
    world.add(temporaryShape);
    temporaryShape = null;
    handPositions.clear();
  }
}
```

At this point, we've done all the state changes we needed. All that's left is to finish drawing the current shape (see Figure 3-4).

```
if (isDrawingShape) {
  println("Refreshing Object");
  handPositions.add(hand);
  temporaryShape = new FPoly();
  temporaryShape.setStrokeWeight(3);
  temporaryShape.setFill(120, 30, 90);
  temporaryShape.setDensity(10);
  temporaryShape.setRestitution(0);
  for (int i = 0; i < handPositions.size(); i++) {
```

```
        PVector p = (PVector) handPositions.get(i);
        temporaryShape.vertex(p.x,p.y);
    }
}
```

The following code is responsible for displaying the user's hand and changing the color to assist the user (see Figure 3-5).

```
if(isDrawingShape || hasSelectedShape) {
    fill(0,255,0,64);
    stroke(0,255,0);
} else {
    fill(255,0,0,64);
    stroke(255,0,0);
}

ellipse(hand.x, hand.y, 20, 20);
    }
}
```

Figure 3-4.
A completed gesture-based shape drawn in air

The remaining methods are utility methods, which are responsible for specific reusable tasks.

```
void drawRGB() {
  pushMatrix();
  scale(-1.0, 1.0); // draw mirrored
  image(context.rgbImage(),-context.rgbImage().width,0);
  popMatrix();
}

boolean handsBeenStillFor(PVector oldHand, PVector newHand, int timeOut) {
  float dis = oldHand.dist(newHand);
  if(dis > 10.0 || handStillSince == 0) {
    // reset system timer
    handStillSince = System.currentTimeMillis();
    return false;
  }
  else if (System.currentTimeMillis() - handStillSince > timeOut) {
    handStillSince=0;
    return true;
  }
  return false;
}

void keyPressed() {
  if ( key=='c' ) {
    world.clear();
    setupWorld();
  }
}
```

And that's it. Feel free to play around with the original setup or change the code to implement your own adjustments. While you're at it, be sure to check out Peter Nash's blog at *http://pedronash.com*.

Download the complete Sketch at *https://github.com/pablonosh/DIYAngryBirds*

Figure 3-5.
The shape will turn gray when being controlled

Press C to clear the screen and reset the simulation.

HACK 18 Create a Gravitational Particle Effect

This hack was developed by RJ Duran (*http://rjduran.net*) and simulates the behavior of orbiting bodies around a single kinetic attractor. As a user moves from side to side, the gravitational red attractor follows. Movement forward and backward will increase or decrease both the size of the attractor along with its gravitational force on all the particles. You can use a series of key commands to change colors and reset particle behavior.

There are 5,000 particles within the system, each with its own position, velocity, and acceleration. The motion of each particle is dependent on the position of the red attractor, which has its own position and gravity. The underlying functionality is based on Newton's Law of Universal Gravitation, which states that every point mass in the universe attracts every other point mass with a force that is directly proportional to the product of their masses and inversely proportional to the square of the distance between them.

This hack uses the following software:

- Processing 1.5.1 (OS X)
- OpenKinect by Daniel Shiffman (*http://www.shiffman.net/p5/kinect/*)

The key commands are:

S
> Save screenshot

R
> Reset particle behavior

0–4
> Change particle colors (white, blue, red, yellow, green)

Up/down arrows
> Adjust tilt of Kinect sensor (default is 10 degrees)

To start, do the following:

1. Download and extract *Kinect_Particle_System.zip* from *http://bit.ly/XUc98t*.
2. Run *Kinect_Particle_System.pde* and move around in front of the Kinect sensor.
3. Experiment with the code and make something amazing!

The Kinect Particle System example demonstrates the usage of tracking data and depth data gathered from the Microsoft Kinect sensor. The Processing project is divided into several files and classes. The primary sketch is called *Kinect_Particle_System.pde*, and it uses the `KinectTracker`, `Attractor`, and `Mover` classes contained in their accordingly named *.pde* files. The keyboard functionality is separated to simplify the code in our case, but it could be placed in the primary sketch file as well.

We'll begin by looking at the primary Processing sketch, *Kinect_Particle_System.pde*. The first few lines under the header comments are used to import the required libraries to access the Kinect sensor.

```
import org.openkinect.*;
import org.openkinect.processing.*;
```

The library we need is Daniel Shiffman's OpenKinect, which can be downloaded at *http://www.shiffman.net/p5/kinect*. There are a variety of methods for accessing the Kinect sensor data, but this is one of the easiest libraries to get started with in Processing.

The global variables are defined next. The Kinect class is used to access all Kinect device methods. For more information about the available methods, look at Daniel Shiffman's library, mentioned previously. The `KinectTracker` class is used to wrap functionality of the `kinect` object into a simple-to-use interface for accessing the data pulled from the camera. The **x** and **y** variables keep track of the position of our primary attractor. The `numOfParticles` variable defines the total number of **Mover**s that will be active in the system and attracted to the **Attractor**. The `Mover[]` array will contain all our **Mover** objects. Finally, the **Attractor** a is our single **Attractor** object, which is ultimately what the user will control.

```
Kinect kinect;
KinectTracker tracker;

float x;
float y;

int numOfParticles = 100;
Mover[] movers = new Mover[numOfParticles];
Attractor a;
```

Next, as with any Processing sketch, you want to look at the `setup()` and `draw()` methods. In `setup()`, we are taking care of a few things to get the sketch running. We set up the sketch size and drawing style with `size()` and `smooth()`, respectively, and then define the `Kinect()` and `KinectTracker()` objects. After this, we define the **Mover**s with a mass of 1 and random *x* and *y* coordinates within the sketch window. We then define the single **Attractor** object with a mass of 100, gravity of 0.1, and a position at the center of the screen.

```
for (int i = 0; i < movers.length; i++) {
  movers[i] = new Mover(1, random(width), random(height));
}
a = new Attractor(100, 0.1, width/2, height/2);
```

The `draw()` loop is where all the magic happens. Each time the `draw()` loop is called, the background is redrawn, the **Attractor** is drawn, the **Tracker** object tracks, the linearly interpolated position of the tracked object is stored in **v1**, the gravity of the **Attractor** is updated based on the user's proximity to the camera within a given range, and the **Mover**s' positions are updated in the sketch.

```
void draw() {
  background(0);
  a.display();

  tracker.track();
  PVector v1 = tracker.getLerpedPos();

  // update gravity based on distance user is from kinect
  // within range 50 to 900
  float area = tracker.getDepthArea();
```

```
    float aScale = area*0.001;
    a.updateGravity(aScale);

    // map position to fit the width and height of sketch
    x = map(v1.x, 0, 640, 0, width);
    y = map(v1.y, 0, 480, 0, height);

    for (int i = 0; i < movers.length; i++) {
      PVector force = a.attract(movers[i]);
      movers[i].applyForce(force);
      movers[i].update();
      movers[i].display();
    }
    a.updateLocation(new PVector(x, y));
  }
```

We can examine the detail of each method used by the **Attractor** and **Mover**s within each class file. The tracker function **getDepthArea()** is used to calculate the area of exposure. As the user comes closer to the Kinect sensor, the area the camera sees increases. We can then increase or decrease the **Attractor** radius using **a.updateGravity(aScale)**.

Inside the **KinectTracker** class, there are a few things worth noting and even more worth experimenting with. The **minDepth** and **maxDepth** values are used to set the minimum and maximum range for detecting an object (i.e., user). Experiment with these values to get the best results for your setup. A **minDepth** of 50 is about 2–3 feet away from the sensor, and a **maxDepth** of 900 is about 6–7 feet away from the sensor. The **kAngle** value is set to a default tilt of 10 degrees and can be moved up and down via the up and down arrow keys.

```
int kAngle   =  10;   // degrees tilt
int minDepth =  50;
int maxDepth = 900;
```

The final result is shown in Figure 3-6.

Figure 3-6.
Process Kinect gravitational particle effect

For further reference to the library, check out Daniel Shiffman's site at *http://www.shiff man.net/p5/kinect/* and Processing.org.

HACK 19 Make Objects Follow a Tracked User's Hand

This great little hack was pieced together by a relative newcomer to the Kinect hacking game. Thanks to the Hand Tracking chapter from Greg Borenstein's *Making Things See*, Ning Ma has managed to build on the experiences of others to produce a great example of what you can do with Kinect and Processing.

Start off by including the **import** statement for the Toxiclibs and SimpleOpenNI libraries.

```
import toxi.geom.*;
import SimpleOpenNI.*;
SimpleOpenNI kinect;
```

Load the **Agent** array, which is responsible for the objects tracking the target.

```
Agent[] a; // a Agent array, will be multiple agent objects chasing the tar
get
boolean handTrackFlag = false;
PVector handPos = new PVector(); // location of tracked hand
```

Now we can begin setting things up.

```
void setup() {
  size(640, 480, P2D);
  kinect = new SimpleOpenNI( this );

  kinect.setMirror( true );
```

Enable **depthMap** generation.

```
  kinect.enableDepth();
```

Enable **Hands** and **Gesture** generation.

```
  kinect.enableGesture();
  kinect.enableHands();
  kinect.setSmoothingHands(.5);
  kinect.addGesture( "RaiseHand" );// we're interested in the gesture
                                   //"Raise Hand"
  frameRate(30);

  smooth();
  background(0);
  colorMode(HSB, 360, 100, 100); // we use HSB color mode
  a= new Agent[25]; // initializing the agents

  for (int i = 0; i < a.length; i++) {// initializing each agent member
    a[i] = new Agent();
  }
}

void draw() {
  kinect.update();
```

The following lines create the fade-in effect.

```
fill(0, 30);
rect(0, 0, width, height);
```

The following code is responsible for drawing our target, a magenta ellipse with a white dot in the center.

```
fill(300, 100, 100);
ellipse(handPos.x, handPos.y, 25, 25);
fill(360);
ellipse(handPos.x, handPos.y, 10, 10);

if ( handTrackFlag ) { // if hand is being tracked
                       // we start drawing the Agents

    for (int i = 0; i < a.length; i++) {

      a[i].run();
    }
  }
}
```

The following tracks the desired gesture-based events. In this example, we'll be using **RaiseHand**.

```
void onRecognizeGesture( String strGesture, PVector idPosition,
PVector endPosition ) {
  kinect.startTrackingHands( endPosition );
  kinect.removeGesture( "RaiseHand");

}
```

The following code enables hand tracking and is called only once.

```
void onCreateHands( int handId, PVector pos, float time ) {
  handTrackFlag = true;
  kinect.convertRealWorldToProjective( pos, handPos );
}
```

Now track the hand repeatedly.

```
void onUpdateHands( int handId, PVector pos, float time ) {
  kinect.convertRealWorldToProjective( pos, handPos );

}
```

If the hand that was being tracked is lost, call it once again.

```
void onDestroyHands( int handId, float time ) {
  handTrackFlag = false;
  kinect.addGesture( "RaiseHand" );
}
```

This sketch requires the inclusion of another *.pde* file, which is responsible for the objects following the tracked hand. It was developed based on the great Vimeo video tutorial *Tutorial 16 Follow Target* by Jose Sanchez at *https://vimeo.com/19641319*.

Here is the *Agent.pde* code in its entirety (the final product is shown in Figure 3-7).

```
class Agent
{
  Vec3D loc;
  Vec3D vel=new Vec3D(0, 0, 0); // speed
  Vec3D acc= new Vec3D(0, 0, 0); // acceleration
  Agent()
  {
    // when one agent is created, the location is randomly drawn on the
    // canvas
    loc =new Vec3D(random(width), random(height), 0);
  }

  float hv=random(200);// I just want a certain range (0-200) of hue value

  void run() {

    display();
    update(); // update the position of the agent
    followHand(); // follow the moving hand
  }

    void display() {

    noStroke();
    fill(hv, 100, 100);
    rect(loc.x, loc.y, 20, 20);
  }

  void update() {
    vel.addSelf(acc);
    //toxi.geom
    //Class Vec3D addSelf(float a, float b, float c)
    //Adds vector {a,b,c} and overrides coordinates with result.

    vel.limit(5);//maximum velocity
```

```
        loc.addSelf(vel);

        acc= new Vec3D(0, 0, 0);// we have new acc every frame
    }

    void followHand() {
        Vec3D target= new Vec3D(handPos.x, handPos.y, 0);
        Vec3D dif=target.sub(loc);
        float distance = dif.magnitude();
        dif.normalize();// direction
        dif.scaleSelf(15/distance);
        //Scales vector uniformly and overrides coordinates with result.

        acc.addSelf(dif);
    }

}
```

Figure 3-7.
Objects following a gesture-controlled target

Download this sketch at *http://developkinect.com/resource/application/follow-target-processing-sketch*.

Dynamically Change Colors and Background Perspective

Brought to you once again by Ning Ma, the following hack uses Yser C's Flashes Processing sketch, which you can view at *http://www.openprocessing.org/sketch/2373*. The idea behind this hack is rather simple but creates a great effect. The user's outline (once calibrated) dynamically changes color while the background perspective changes based on the position of the calibrated user relative to the Kinect sensor.

Add the **import** statement for the SimpleOpenNI library. If you don't have it yet, download it from *http://code.google.com/p/simple-openni/*.

```
import SimpleOpenNI.*;
import processing.opengl.*;


SimpleOpenNI kinect;
int[] userMap;// storing user pixels
float farbeR;
float farbeG;
float farbeB;
int c=0; // for the hue value color when drawing the userimage
```

The following array creates the flashing rectangle effects from the Flashes *.pde* file.

```
Flash[] flashes; // array for creating rect flashes
float  maxSpeed;
float minSpeed = 0;
```

This code determines the location of the tracked hand.

```
boolean handTrackFlag = false;
PVector posScr = new PVector(); // location of tracked hand

void setup() {
  size(640, 480, P3D);
  kinect = new SimpleOpenNI(this);
  kinect.setMirror( true );
  // enable depthMap generation
  kinect.enableDepth();
```

Here, you can see the depth image of the user.

```
kinect.enableUser(SimpleOpenNI.SKEL_PROFILE_NONE);
```

Enable **Hands** and **Gesture** generation.

```
kinect.enableGesture();
kinect.enableHands();
kinect.setSmoothingHands(.5);
```

Invoke the **RaiseHand** OpenNI gesture.

```
kinect.addGesture( "RaiseHand" );
```

```
maxSpeed = 10;
flashes = new Flash[1000];// initializing each Flash member
for (int i = 0; i<flashes.length; i++) {
  flashes[i] = new Flash(random(-20, 20));
}
```

```
frameRate(30);
}
```

```
void draw() {
  colorMode(HSB, 360, 100, 100);// we use HSB color mode
  background(0);
   kinect.update();
```

Draw the flashing rectangles.

```
// draw the flash rect
for (int i = 0; i<flashes.length; i++) {
  flashes[i].update();
  flashes[i].display();
}
```

```
if ( handTrackFlag ) {
  // if hand is tracked, set camera position with the hand position
  // other values are just experimented
  camera(posScr.x*1.3, posScr.y*1.3, (height/2) / tan(PI*60/ 360.0),
    width/2.0, height/2.0, -60, 0, 1, 0);
}
```

For the purpose of generating a layered effect, add the Flash rectangles again.

```
for (int i = 0; i<flashes.length; i++) {
  flashes[i].update();
  flashes[i].display();
}
```

Draw the user depth image.

```
if (kinect.getNumberOfUsers()>0)
{
```

```
        userMap = kinect.getUsersPixels(SimpleOpenNI.USERS_ALL);
        loadPixels();
        for (int i=0;i<userMap.length;i++)
        {
          if (userMap[i]!=0)
          {
            pixels[i]=color(c*10, 100, 100); // the color of user is changing
          }
        }
        c++;
        if (c > 36) {
          c = 0;
        }


        updatePixels();
    }
}
```

Finish up with the **Hands** and **Gesture** events.

```
// Track the desired gesture, here is "RaiseHand"
void onRecognizeGesture( String strGesture, PVector idPosition,
PVector endPosition ) {
  kinect.startTrackingHands( endPosition );
  kinect.removeGesture( "RaiseHand");
}


// Hands Events
void onCreateHands( int handId, PVector pos, float time ) {
  handTrackFlag = true;
  kinect.convertRealWorldToProjective( pos, posScr );
}

//tracking the hand, called repeatedly
void onUpdateHands( int handId, PVector pos, float time ) {
  kinect.convertRealWorldToProjective( pos, posScr );

}

//called once when we lose the hand
void onDestroyHands( int handId, float time ) {
```

```
    println( "onDestroyHands - handId: " + handId + ", time: " + time );
    handTrackFlag = false;
    kinect.addGesture( "RaiseHand" );
}
```

The final result appears in Figure 3-8.

Figure 3-8.
Colored rectangles with changing background perspective

Download this Processing sketch in its entirety at *http://bit.ly/RubNBU*.

HACK 21 Create a Live 3D Rendered Effect with Processing

This sketch takes point cloud data from the Kinect, marches over the points using a marching cubes algorithm, and renders a polygonal mesh. The end result is a bubble-like representation of your skeletal data being passed from the Kinect to the Processing sketch.

This Processing hack is composed of four sketches:

• *live_render_3d.pde*
• *MCTriangle.java*

- *MarchingCubes.java*
- *MarchingCubesTables.java*

For the purpose of this tutorial, we'll be covering the code represented in the *live_render_3d.pde* and *MarchingCubes.java* files only. Adding all the required Java files makes things a bit messy for what we're trying to do. Thankfully, you can check out the GitHub repo at *https://github.com/newshorts/Live-Render-3D* for the full project and all accompanying Java files.

To get things up and running, you'll need to download and place the following libraries in your *Processing/libraries* directory:

- OpenKinect: *http://www.shiffman.net/p5/kinect*
- Toxiclibs: *http://hg.postspectacular.com/toxiclibs/downloads/*

Remember to restart Processing whenever you add a new library, or it will not be able to import the library into the sketch!

Open a new sketch and begin by typing in the following code:

```
import toxi.geom.Vec3D;
import processing.opengl.*;
//import rui.marchingCubes.*;

// kinect
import org.openkinect.*;
import org.openkinect.processing.*;

//import processing.core.PApplet;

import java.lang.Math;
import java.util.ArrayList;
import toxi.geom.Vec3D;

MarchingCubes mc;
Vec3D rotationAxis;

Boolean bUseFill;

// kinect
Kinect kinect;
float a = 0;
```

The following determines the size of Kinect image.

```
int w = 640;
int h = 480;
int kWidth  = 640;
int kHeight = 480;
```

This refers to the depth mapping and tilt.

```
boolean depth = true;
boolean rgb = false;
boolean ir = false;
float deg = 8; // Start at 15 degrees
PImage depthImg;
int minDepth =  40;
int maxDepth = 860;
```

Set the initial record to **false**.

```
boolean record = false;
int counter = 0;
```

Print a custom file.

```
boolean printFile = false;
ArrayList points;
PrintWriter output;
```

We'll use a lookup table so that we don't have to repeat the math over and over.

```
float[] depthLookUp = new float[2048];

void setup(){
  size(1024, 600, OPENGL);
  Vec3D aabbMin = new Vec3D(-width/2, -height/2, -250);
  Vec3D aabbMax = new Vec3D(width/2, height/2, 250);
  Vec3D numPoints = new Vec3D(50,50,50);
  float isoLevel = 1;
  mc = new MarchingCubes(this, aabbMin, aabbMax, numPoints, isoLevel);

  rotationAxis = new Vec3D();

  bUseFill = false;

  // kinect
```

```
kinect = new Kinect(this);
kinect.start();
kinect.enableDepth(true);
kinect.tilt(deg);
```

We don't need the grayscale image in this example, so this makes it more efficient.

```
kinect.processDepthImage(false);
```

Get depthImg to constrain.

```
depthImg = new PImage(kWidth, kHeight);
```

Access the lookup table for all possible depth values (0–2047).

```
for (int i = 0; i < depthLookUp.length; i++) {
  depthLookUp[i] = rawDepthToMeters(i);
}
points = new ArrayList();
output = createWriter("points.txt");


}

void draw(){
  background(255);
  lights();

  // kinect
  int[] depth = kinect.getRawDepth();
  int skip = 50;
  //Translate(width/750,height/750,-50);

    mc.reset();

    // original for loop
    println("entering loop");
    int nBalls = 0;
    for(int x=0; x<w; x+=skip) {
      for(int y=0; y<h; y+=skip) {
        int offset = x+y*w;
        int rawDepth = depth[offset];

        if(rawDepth >= minDepth && rawDepth <= maxDepth) {
          PVector v = depthToWorld(x,y,rawDepth);
          Vec3D metaBallPos = new Vec3D(v.x * 500, v.y * 300, v.z*300);
          mc.addMetaBall(metaBallPos, 100, 1);
          nBalls++;
```

```
        }

      }
    }
    println("done with loop, " + nBalls + " balls");
    // end original for loop

  mc.createMesh();
  if(bUseFill){
    fill(0,255,0);
    noStroke();
  }
  else {
    noFill();
    stroke(127);
  }

  pushMatrix();
  translate(width/2, height/2, 0);
  rotateX(rotationAxis.x);
  rotateY(rotationAxis.y);
  mc.renderMesh();
  popMatrix();
}

PVector depthToWorld(int x, int y, int depthValue) {

  final double fx_d = 1.0 / 5.9421434211923247e+02;
  final double fy_d = 1.0 / 5.9104053696870778e+02;
  final double cx_d = 3.3930780975300314e+02;
  final double cy_d = 2.4273913761751615e+02;

  PVector result = new PVector();
  double depth =  depthLookUp[depthValue];
  result.x = (float)((x - cx_d) * depth * fx_d);
  result.y = (float)((y - cy_d) * depth * fy_d);
  result.z = (float)(depth);
  return result;
}

float rawDepthToMeters(int depthValue) {
  if (depthValue < 2047) {
    return (float)(1.0 / ((double)(depthValue) * -0.00307 + 3.33094));
  }
```

```
      return 0.0f;
    }

    void keyPressed(){
      if(key == CODED){
        if(keyCode == LEFT) rotationAxis.y += 0.05;
        if(keyCode == RIGHT) rotationAxis.y -= 0.05;
        if(keyCode == UP) rotationAxis.x -= 0.05;
        if(keyCode == DOWN) rotationAxis.x += 0.05;
      }
      else {
        if(key == ' '){
          bUseFill = !bUseFill;
        }
        if(key == 'r' || key == 'R'){
          mc.reset();
          rotationAxis.set(0,0,0);
        }
      }
    }

    void stop() {
      kinect.quit();
      super.stop();
    }
```

The following example represents one of the Java files necessary to complete the effect. For the purpose of this hack, we'll be covering only the *MarchingCubes.java* file.

```
package rui.marchingCubes;

import processing.core.PApplet;

import java.lang.Math;
import java.util.ArrayList;
import toxi.geom.Vec3D;

public class MarchingCubes {

    PApplet p5;

    public float voxelValues[][][];
    protected Vec3D voxels[][][];
    protected Vec3D numPoints, aabbMin, aabbMax;
    protected Vec3D cubeSize;
```

```
protected Vec3D worldSize;
protected float isoLevel;

private Vec3D vertList[];

protected ArrayList<MCTriangle> triangles;

/**
 * constructor:
 * you must define the world bounds, the number of points that
 * will make the grid (in a Vec3D),
 * and the isoLevel.
 * @param _p5
 * @param _aabbMin
 * @param _aabbMax
 * @param _numPoints
 * @param _isoLevel
 */

public MarchingCubes(PApplet _p5, Vec3D _aabbMin, Vec3D _aabbMax,
        Vec3D _numPoints, float _isoLevel){
    p5 = _p5;
    aabbMin = new Vec3D(_aabbMin);
    aabbMax = new Vec3D(_aabbMax);
    worldSize = aabbMax.sub(aabbMin);
    numPoints = new Vec3D(_numPoints);
    cubeSize = new Vec3D(worldSize.x / (numPoints.x-1),
        worldSize.y / (numPoints.y-1), worldSize.z /
        (numPoints.z-1));
    voxelValues = new float[(int)numPoints.x][(int)numPoints.y]
    [(int)numPoints.z];
    voxels = new Vec3D[(int)numPoints.x][(int)numPoints.y]
    [(int)numPoints.z];

    _internalReset();
    isoLevel = _isoLevel;

    vertList = new Vec3D[12];
    triangles = new ArrayList<MCTriangle>();

}
```

The following code is responsible for creating the mesh.

```
public void createMesh(){
    triangles = new ArrayList<MCTriangle>();
    for(int i=0; i<numPoints.x-1; i++){
        for(int j=0; j<numPoints.y-1; j++){
            for(int k=0; k<numPoints.z-1; k++){
                polygonise(i, j, k);
            }
        }
    }
}
```

This returns an **ArrayList** of MCTriangles with all the triangles that make up the mesh.

```
public ArrayList<MCTriangle> getMesh(){
    return triangles;
}
```

The following code copies the mesh triangles into an array and returns.

```
public MCTriangle[] getMeshToArray(){
    MCTriangle _triArray[] = new MCTriangle[triangles.size()];
    triangles.toArray(_triArray);
    return _triArray;
}
```

This is the default rendering for the mesh.

```
public void renderMesh(){
    MCTriangle tri;
    p5.beginShape(PApplet.TRIANGLES);
    for(int i=0; i<triangles.size(); i++){
        tri = triangles.get(i);
        p5.vertex(tri.a.x, tri.a.y, tri.a.z);
        p5.vertex(tri.b.x, tri.b.y, tri.b.z);
        p5.vertex(tri.c.x, tri.c.y, tri.c.z);
    }
    p5.endShape();
}
```

This code renders the ISO grid—very useful for debugging.

```
public void renderGrid(){
    p5.noFill();
    p5.stroke(127);
    p5.beginShape(PApplet.LINES);
    for(int i=0; i<numPoints.x; i++){
        for(int j=0; j<numPoints.y; j++){
```

```
        for(int k=0; k<numPoints.z-1; k++){
            p5.vertex(voxels[i][j][k].x, voxels[i][j][k].y,
                voxels[i][j][k].z);
            p5.vertex(voxels[i][j][k+1].x,
            voxels[i][j][k+1].y, voxels[i][j][k+1].z);
        }
    }
}
for(int i=0; i<numPoints.x; i++){
    for(int j=0; j<numPoints.y-1; j++){
        for(int k=0; k<numPoints.z; k++){
            p5.vertex(voxels[i][j][k].x, voxels[i][j][k].y,
                voxels[i][j][k].z);
            p5.vertex(voxels[i][j+1][k].x,
            voxels[i][j+1][k].y, voxels[i][j+1][k].z);
        }
    }
}

for(int i=0; i<numPoints.x-1; i++){
    for(int j=0; j<numPoints.y; j++){
        for(int k=0; k<numPoints.z; k++){
            p5.vertex(voxels[i][j][k].x, voxels[i][j][k].y,
                voxels[i][j][k].z);
            p5.vertex(voxels[i+1][j][k].x,
            voxels[i+1][j][k].y, voxels[i+1][j][k].z);
        }
    }
}
p5.endShape();
}
```

The following code returns a tridimensional array of the values that each voxel has. You can use this to define the value of each voxel.

```
public float[][][] getValues(){
    return voxelValues;
}
```

Here we return the voxel grid that makes up the ISO space, in a three-dimensional array.

```
public Vec3D[][][] getVoxels(){
    return voxels;
}
```

This sets the ISO value of a voxel:

```
public void setValue(int indexX, int indexY,
int indexZ, float value){
    if(indexX > -1 && indexX < numPoints.x &&
        indexY > -1 && indexY < numPoints.y &&
        indexZ > -1 && indexZ < numPoints.z){
        voxelValues[indexX][indexY][indexZ] = value;
    }
}
```

This block gets the value of the specified voxel:

```
public float getValue(int posX, int posY, int posZ){
    if(posX > -1 && posX < numPoints.x &&
        posY > -1 && posY < numPoints.y &&
        posZ > -1 && posZ < numPoints.z){
        return voxelValues[posX][posY][posZ];
    }
    return 0;
}
```

This returns a specific voxel of the ISO space.

```
public Vec3D getVoxel(int posX, int posY, int posZ){
    if(posX > -1 && posX < numPoints.x &&
        posY > -1 && posY < numPoints.y &&
        posZ > -1 && posZ < numPoints.z){
        return voxels[posX][posY][posZ];
    }
    return new Vec3D(0,0,0);
}
```

These lines check if the specified point is inside a voxel cube and return the voxel, returning a new **Vec3D** if the point is outside the grid.

```
public Vec3D getVoxelAtWorldCoord(Vec3D point){
    for(int i=0; i<voxels.length-1; i++){
        for(int j=0; j<voxels[i].length-1; j++){
            for(int k=0; k<voxels[i][j].length-1; k++){
                if(point.x >= voxels[i][j][k].x &&
                    point.y >= voxels[i][j][k].y &&
                    point.z >= voxels[i][j][k].z &&
                    point.x <= voxels[i+1][j+1][k+1].x &&
                    point.y <= voxels[i+1][j+1][k+1].y &&
                    point.z <= voxels[i+1][j+1][k+1].z){
                    return voxels[i][j][k];
                }
            }
        }
```

```
        }
    }
    return new Vec3D();
}
```

This code block adds a **MetaBall** with the specified radius; the grid points inside the radius will be added to the **metaValue**.

```
public void addMetaBall(Vec3D pos, float radius,
    float metaValue){
    float radiusSQ = radius*radius;
    float distSQ;

    for(int i=0; i<voxels.length; i++){
        for(int j=0; j<voxels[i].length; j++){
            for(int k=0; k<voxels[i][j].length; k++){
                distSQ = voxels[i][j][k].distanceToSquared(pos);
                if(distSQ < radiusSQ){
                    voxelValues[i][j][k] += (1-distSQ / radiusSQ)
                    * metaValue;
                }
            }
        }
    }
}

public void addMetaBox(Vec3D aabbMin, Vec3D aabbMax,
float metaValue){
    for(int i=0; i<voxels.length; i++){
        for(int j=0; j<voxels[i].length; j++){
            for(int k=0; k<voxels[i][j].length; k++){
                if (voxels[i][j][k].x > aabbMin.x &&
                    voxels[i][j][k].y > aabbMin.y &&
                    voxels[i][j][k].z > aabbMin.z &&
                    voxels[i][j][k].x < aabbMax.x &&
                    voxels[i][j][k].y < aabbMax.y &&
                    voxels[i][j][k].z < aabbMax.z){
                    PApplet.println("added");
                    voxelValues[i][j][k] += metaValue;
                }
            }
        }
    }
}
```

Here we return the maximum voxel value:

72

```
public float getMax(){
    float _max = voxelValues[0][0][0];
    for(int i=0; i<voxels.length; i++){
        for(int j=0; j<voxels[i].length; j++){
            for(int k=1; k<voxels[i][j].length; k++){
                if(_max < voxelValues[i][j][k])_max =
                voxelValues[i][j][k];
            }
        }
    }
    return _max;
}
```

This returns the lowest voxel value.

```
public float getMin(){
    float _min = voxelValues[0][0][0];
    for(int i=0; i<voxels.length; i++){
        for(int j=0; j<voxels[i].length; j++){
            for(int k=1; k<voxels[i][j].length; k++){
                if(_min > voxelValues[i][j][k])_min =
                    voxelValues[i][j][k];
            }
        }
    }

    return _min;
}
```

This block multiplies all grid values with **val**.

```
public void scale(float _val){
    for(int i=0; i<voxels.length; i++){
        for(int j=0; j<voxels[i].length; j++){
            for(int k=0; k<voxels[i][j].length; k++){
                voxelValues[i][j][k] *= _val;
            }
        }
    }
}
```

Here, all grid values are set with **val**:

```
public void set(float _val){
    for(int i=0; i<voxels.length; i++){
        for(int j=0; j<voxels[i].length; j++){
            for(int k=0; k<voxels[i][j].length; k++){
```

```
                voxelValues[i][j][k] = _val;
            }
        }
    }
}
```

This sets the grid point with the specified index with the value:

```
public void set(int indexX, int indexY, int indexZ, float val){
    if(indexX >-1 && indexX < numPoints.x &&
       indexY >-1 && indexY < numPoints.y &&
       indexZ >-1 && indexZ < numPoints.z){
       voxelValues[indexX][indexY][indexZ] = val;
    }
}
```

This block normalizes the voxel values.

```
public void normalize(){
    float maxVal = 0;
    for(int i=0; i<numPoints.x; i++){
        for(int j=0; j<numPoints.y; j++){
            for(int k=0; k<numPoints.z; k++){
                if(voxelValues[i][j][k] > maxVal)
                maxVal = voxelValues[i][j][k];
            }
        }
    }
    float invertMaxVal = 1.0f/maxVal;
    for(int i=0; i<numPoints.x; i++){
        for(int j=0; j<numPoints.y; j++){
            for(int k=0; k<numPoints.z; k++){
                voxelValues[i][j][k] *= invertMaxVal;
            }
        }
    }
}
```

Here, we reset the voxel values to zero.

```
public void reset(){
    for(int i=0; i<numPoints.x; i++){
        for(int j=0; j<numPoints.y; j++){
            for(int k=0; k<numPoints.z; k++){
                voxelValues[i][j][k] = 0;
```

```
            }
         }
      }
   }
```

And then we redefine the minimum bounds of the ISO space.

```
public void setAABBMin(Vec3D _aabbMin){
    aabbMin.set(_aabbMin);
    _internalReset();
}
```

This code returns the minimum bound of the ISO space.

```
public Vec3D getAABBMin(){
    return aabbMin;
}
```

This block redefines the maximum bound of the ISO space.

```
public void setAABBMax(Vec3D _aabbMax){
    aabbMax.set(_aabbMax);
    _internalReset();
}
```

Here, the maximum bound of the ISO space is returned.

```
public Vec3D getAABBMax(){
    return aabbMax;
}
```

These lines return the number of triangles that make up the mesh.

```
public int getNumTriangles(){
    return triangles.size();
}
```

And these return the ISO level.

```
public float getIsoLevel(){
    return isoLevel;
}
```

These lines set the ISO level.

```
public void setIsoLevel(float _isoLevel){
    isoLevel = _isoLevel;
}
```

This snippet returns the number of vertices that make up the ISO space in a **Vec3D**: the x value represents the number of elements along the x-axis; the **y** value represents the number of elements along the y-axis; and the **z** value represents the number of elements along the z-axis.

```
public Vec3D getNumVoxels(){
    return numPoints;
}
```

Here we redefine the number of voxels that make up the grid.

```
public void setNumVoxels(Vec3D _numPoints){
    numPoints.set(_numPoints.x, _numPoints.y, _numPoints.z);
    voxels = new Vec3D[(int)numPoints.x][(int)numPoints.y]
        [(int)numPoints.z];
    voxelValues = new float[(int)numPoints.x][(int)numPoints.y]
        [(int)numPoints.z];
    _internalReset();
}
```

This chunk returns the size of a single cube of the ISO space.

```
public Vec3D getCubeSize(){
    return cubeSize;
}
```

And this one returns the total size of the ISO space.

```
public Vec3D getWorldSize(){
    return worldSize;
}
```

```
//Internals
protected void _internalReset(){
    for(int i=0; i<numPoints.x; i++){
        for(int j=0; j<numPoints.y; j++){
            for(int k=0; k<numPoints.z; k++){
                voxels[i][j][k] = new Vec3D(cubeSize.x * i,
                    cubeSize.y * j, cubeSize.z * k);
                voxels[i][j][k].x += aabbMin.x;
                voxels[i][j][k].y += aabbMin.y;
                voxels[i][j][k].z += aabbMin.z;
                voxelValues[i][j][k] = 0;

            }
        }
    }
}
```

```
    }

    protected void polygonise(int i, int j, int k){
        int cubeIndex = 0;
        if (voxelValues[i][j][k] < isoLevel) cubeIndex |= 1;
        if (voxelValues[i+1][j][k] < isoLevel) cubeIndex |= 2;
        if (voxelValues[i+1][j+1][k] < isoLevel) cubeIndex |= 4;
        if (voxelValues[i][j+1][k] < isoLevel) cubeIndex |= 8;
        if (voxelValues[i][j][k+1] < isoLevel) cubeIndex |= 16;
        if (voxelValues[i+1][j][k+1] < isoLevel) cubeIndex |= 32;
        if (voxelValues[i+1][j+1][k+1] < isoLevel) cubeIndex |= 64;
        if (voxelValues[i][j+1][k+1] < isoLevel) cubeIndex |= 128;
        /* Cube is entirely in/out of the surface */
        if (MarchingCubesTables.edgeTable[cubeIndex] == 0){
            return;
        }
```

Find the vertices where the surface intersects the cube.

```
        if ((MarchingCubesTables.edgeTable[cubeIndex] & 1) > 0){
            vertList[0] = vertexInterp(isoLevel, voxels[i][j][k],
                voxels[i+1][j][k], voxelValues[i][j][k],
                voxelValues[i+1][j][k]);
        }
        if ((MarchingCubesTables.edgeTable[cubeIndex] & 2) > 0){
            vertList[1] = vertexInterp(isoLevel, voxels[i+1][j][k],
                voxels[i+1][j+1][k], voxelValues[i+1][j][k],
                voxelValues[i+1][j+1][k]);
        }
        if ((MarchingCubesTables.edgeTable[cubeIndex] & 4) > 0){
            vertList[2] = vertexInterp(isoLevel, voxels[i+1][j+1][k],
                voxels[i][j+1][k], voxelValues[i+1][j+1][k],
                voxelValues[i][j+1][k]);
        }
        if ((MarchingCubesTables.edgeTable[cubeIndex] & 8 ) > 0){
            vertList[3] = vertexInterp(isoLevel, voxels[i][j+1][k],
                voxels[i][j][k], voxelValues[i][j+1][k],
                voxelValues[i][j][k]);
        }
        if ((MarchingCubesTables.edgeTable[cubeIndex] & 16) > 0){
            vertList[4] = vertexInterp(isoLevel, voxels[i][j][k+1],
                voxels[i+1][j][k+1], voxelValues[i][j][k+1],
                voxelValues[i+1][j][k+1]);
        }
        if ((MarchingCubesTables.edgeTable[cubeIndex] & 32) > 0){
```

```
            vertList[5] = vertexInterp(isoLevel, voxels[i+1][j][k+1],
                voxels[i+1][j+1][k+1], voxelValues[i+1][j][k+1],
                voxelValues[i+1][j+1][k+1]);
        }
        if ((MarchingCubesTables.edgeTable[cubeIndex] & 64) > 0){
            vertList[6] = vertexInterp(isoLevel, voxels[i+1][j+1][k+1],
                voxels[i][j+1][k+1], voxelValues[i+1][j+1][k+1],
                voxelValues[i][j+1][k+1]);
        }
        if ((MarchingCubesTables.edgeTable[cubeIndex] & 128) > 0){
            vertList[7] = vertexInterp(isoLevel, voxels[i][j+1][k+1],
                voxels[i][j][k+1], voxelValues[i][j+1][k+1],
                voxelValues[i][j][k+1]);
        }
        if ((MarchingCubesTables.edgeTable[cubeIndex] & 256) > 0){
            vertList[8] = vertexInterp(isoLevel, voxels[i][j][k],
                voxels[i][j][k+1], voxelValues[i][j][k],
                voxelValues[i][j][k+1]);
        }
        if ((MarchingCubesTables.edgeTable[cubeIndex] & 512) > 0){
            vertList[9] = vertexInterp(isoLevel, voxels[i+1][j][k],
                voxels[i+1][j][k+1], voxelValues[i+1][j][k],
                voxelValues[i+1][j][k+1]);
        }
        if ((MarchingCubesTables.edgeTable[cubeIndex] & 1024) > 0){
            vertList[10] = vertexInterp(isoLevel, voxels[i+1][j+1][k],
                voxels[i+1][j+1][k+1], voxelValues[i+1][j+1][k],
                voxelValues[i+1][j+1][k+1]);
        }
        if ((MarchingCubesTables.edgeTable[cubeIndex] & 2048) > 0){
            vertList[11] = vertexInterp(isoLevel, voxels[i][j+1][k],
                voxels[i][j+1][k+1], voxelValues[i][j+1][k],
                voxelValues[i][j+1][k+1]);
        }

    Vec3D vecA;
    Vec3D vecB;
    Vec3D normalVec = new Vec3D();
    for(i=0; MarchingCubesTables.triTable
        [cubeIndex][i] != -1; i+=3){

        vecA = vertList[MarchingCubesTables.triTable[cubeIndex]
        [i+1]].sub(vertList[MarchingCubesTables.triTable[cubeIndex]
        [i]]);
```

```java
            vecB = vertList[MarchingCubesTables.triTable[cubeIndex]
            [i+2]].sub(vertList[MarchingCubesTables.triTable[cubeIndex]
            [i+1]]);
            normalVec = vecA.cross(vecB);

            Vec3D triA = new Vec3D(vertList[MarchingCubesTables.triTable
            [cubeIndex]
            [i]].x,
                vertList[MarchingCubesTables.triTable[cubeIndex][i]].y,
                vertList[MarchingCubesTables.triTable[cubeIndex][i]].z);
            Vec3D triB = new Vec3D(vertList[MarchingCubesTables.triTable
            [cubeIndex][i+1]].x,
                vertList[MarchingCubesTables.triTable[cubeIndex][i+1]].y,
                vertList[MarchingCubesTables.triTable[cubeIndex][i+1]].z);
            Vec3D triC = new Vec3D(vertList[MarchingCubesTables.triTable
            [cubeIndex][i+2]].x,
                vertList[MarchingCubesTables.triTable[cubeIndex][i+2]].y,
                vertList[MarchingCubesTables.triTable[cubeIndex][i+2]].z);
            triangles.add(new MCTriangle(triA, triB, triC, normalVec));
        }
    }

    protected Vec3D vertexInterp(float _isoLevel, Vec3D vertice,
        Vec3D vertice2, float valP1, float valP2){
        float mu;
        Vec3D p = new Vec3D();

        if (Math.abs(isoLevel-valP1) < 0.00001)
            return(vertice);
        if (Math.abs(isoLevel-valP2) < 0.00001)
            return(vertice2);
        if (Math.abs(valP1-valP2) < 0.00001)
            return(vertice);
        mu = (isoLevel - valP1) / (valP2 - valP1);
        p.x = vertice.x + mu * (vertice2.x - vertice.x);
        p.y = vertice.y + mu * (vertice2.y - vertice.y);
        p.z = vertice.z + mu * (vertice2.z - vertice.z);

        return p;
    }

}
```

That's it! You can see the result in Figure 3-9. As I mentioned at the beginning of this hack, you can download the remaining files you need to get up and running from the GitHub repo at *https://github.com/newshorts/Live-Render-3D/*. Alternatively, you can download them from Mike Newell's blog at *https://s3.amazonaws.com/iwearshorts-random/bubbleBoy2.1.zip*.

Once everything is running properly, try pressing the space bar to turn the mesh output green.

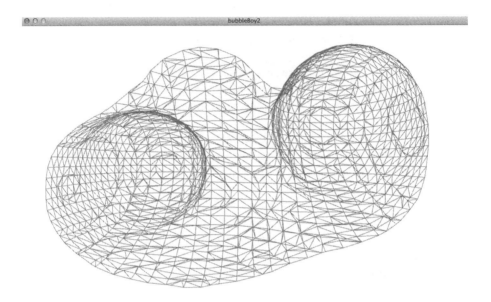

Figure 3-9.
Bubbleboy sketch

If you like this sketch, be sure to drop by Mike Newell's blog at *http://iwearshorts.com/blog* and say hi!

HACK 22 Create a Hairy Effect

In this openFrameworks app created by Kris Temmerman, a hair effect is applied to everything in the view of the Kinect. This hack aims to show you how you can convert the raw Kinect data into a triangle mesh and calculate normal vectors (the vector perpendicular to the surface). With this data, you can create all kinds of visual effects by manipulating the 3D surface or by adding new geometry to it—hairs, in this case.

Before you begin, you will require the following software and libraries to use KinectHair:

- Xcode

- openFrameworks V.007 (OS X)

- ofxKinect add-on: *https://github.com/ofTheo/ofxKinect*

To get the KinectHair app up and running, download KinectHair from *https:// github.com/neuroprod/kinectHair*.

Extract the contents of the ZIP file and place the folder into the *apps/examples* directory within openFrameworks. Plug your Kinect into a power source and into your Mac via USB. Then open the *furryKinectApp.xcodeproj* file within the *KinectHair* folder located in the *examples* folder.

You'll have to change your Base SDK from current to 10.6. You do this within the Build Settings for the Project and the Targets. For an example, see Figure 2-3.

I had to obtain the Mac 10.6 SDK for Xcode 4.4 (Mountain Lion), as it appears Apple is no longer including the 10.6 SDK with the latest version of Xcode. For more on how I achieved this, see http://forum.openframeworks.cc/index.php/topic, 10391.msg47150.html#msg47150.

If you receive the Clang LLVM 1.0 error with the following reason, create a new *of_v007* folder wherever it is trying to look:

```
clang: error: no such file or directory: '/Users/jaredstjean/Desktop/
of_preRelease_v007_osx/apps/examples/kinectHair/../../../addons/ofxKinect/
src/../../../../of_v007/addons/ofxKinect/src/ofxKinect.cpp'
```

In this case, that would be four levels deep in relation to my *addons/ofxKinect/src/* path. Create an *addons* directory and place *ofxKinect* in there—should work like a charm after that.

If all goes according to plan, you should now be staring at a black furry version of yourself (or whatever is in the path of the Kinect's viewing range, as shown in Figure 3-10). Here are some of the key commands you can now use while checking it out:

s

> Create a screenshot.

1–2

> Change the minimum depth.

3–4

> Change the maximum depth.

Space

Switch between single color/camera color mode.

Arrow up/down

Change the Kinect angle.

Figure 3-10.
KinectHair visual effect

The hair effect is created in three separate steps. Those steps are initialized in the `FurryKinect` app class, which is the main class of the project.

In the first step, the raw Kinect depth data is converted into a mesh, and the normals of the surface are calculated. We do this with the `KinectDepthTriangulation` class, which uses a marching squares algorithm to triangulate the depth pixels.

To initialize the class, we pass the minimum and maximum depth it needs to triangulate and the number of horizontal and vertical divisions of the triangulation grid:

```
KinectDepthTriangulation triangulate;
int gridSubII =128;
```

```
int gridSubW = 96;
int minDistance =600;
int maxDistance = 2000;
triangulate.setup(gridSubH,gridSubW, minDistance,maxDistance);
```

You can also set the depth range at runtime.

```
void KinectDepthTriangulation::setDepthRange
    (float minDepth,float maxDepth);
```

In the update of the **FurryKinect** class, we pass the raw depth data to the **KinectDepthTriangulation** class. It takes a 640×480 **float** array with the depth in millimeters, so you can use it with other Kinect frameworks.

```
void KinectDepthTriangulation::setRawPixels
    (float *depthPixels);
```

After that, you can access the vertices and indices of the mesh, or you can get the triangles separately.

```
vector<TriPoint > vertices;
        vector<int> indices;
    vector<TriTriangle > triangles;
```

In the second step, we calculate the start points and growing direction of the hairs. For this, we use the **KinectHairPoints** class. In the setup method, you set the amount of hairs you want for each triangle.

```
hairPoints:setup(in numHairs);
```

In the update, we set the triangles of the mesh we have just created.

```
hairPoints.setTriangles( triangulate.triangles);
```

We can pass a single color for the hairs.

```
void setHairColor(red,green,blue);
```

Or pass the Kinect webcam data to extract the hair colors from the webcam.

```
void setHairColors(kinect.getPixels());
```

In the final step, we pass these points to the **HairRenderer** class. This class is a wrapper around the shader that is responsible for calculating and drawing the final hairs.

```
hairRenderer.draw ( hairPoints.data,hairPoints. numIndices);
```

The shape of the hairs is created in a geometry shader (*ShaderHair.gsh*), which converts the start point and the normal of each hair to a triangle strip. After that, some basic shading is added with the fragment shader (*ShaderHair.fsh*).

With the mesh you get from the `KinectDepthTriangulation` class, you can do all kinds of cool stuff. You can also change the output geometry of the geometry shader to add other features to the surface of your Kinect view.

If you enjoyed this hack, be sure to check out Kris Temmerman's site at *http://www.neuroproductions.be*.

HACK 23 Create Hand Tracking Trails Using Cinder

This program uses Cinder (*http://libcinder.org/*) and its Open Computer Vision (OpenCV) (*http://opencv.willowgarage.com/*) Cinder Block to track a user's motions. A red ball will follow a region specified by a few simple parameters.

There is no actual recognition of the hands per se; rather, the program is simply using the Kinect's depth image to identify shapes of a certain size at a particular distance from the camera, exploiting the fact that people stand with hands outstretched when gesturing at the sensor. It was developed by Andrew Berg (*http://andrewberg.com*).

First, get all the software you'll need:

- libfreenect: *http://openkinect.org*
- Xcode: *https://developer.apple.com/xcode*
- Cinder: *https://github.com/cinder/Cinder*
- Kinect Cinder Block: *https://github.com/cinder/Cinder-Kinect*
- OpenCV Cinder Block: *https://github.com/cinder/Cinder-OpenCV*

The setup steps are as follows:

1. Make sure you have Xcode and its command-line tools installed.
2. Install the libfreenect driver: *http://openkinect.org/wiki/Getting_Started*.
3. Install Cinder from GitHub: *http://libcinder.org/docs/welcome/GitSetup.html*.
4. Clone the Kinect and OpenCV blocks listed previously into the *Cinder/blocks* folder.
5. Create a new project with TinderBox: *http://libcinder.org/docs/welcome/MacNewProject.html*.
6. Add the OpenCV block to the project: *http://forum.libcinder.org/topic/how-to-use-cinderblocks-in-xcode*. For this project, we need the *libopencv_core.a* and *libopencv_imgproc.a* files.
7. Add the Kinect block in the same way. In addition, we need to add the *Kinect.cpp* file in the *src* folder of the block to our project's source files.

8. Add the OS X native *IOKit.framework* file in Target → Build Phases → Link Binary With Libraries: *http://bit.ly/VFeS7t*.

9. Switch your compiler to LLVM/GCC.

The header files to include are all from Cinder for a basic app using OpenGL and textures. The **Params** header provides methods for tweaking the settings.

```
#include "cinder/app/AppBasic.h"
#include "cinder/gl/gl.h"
#include "cinder/gl/Texture.h"
#include "cinder/params/Params.h"
```

These are the OpenCV and Kinect blocks to include:

```
#include "CinderOpenCV.h"
#include "Kinect.h"
```

We use convenience namespacing so we don't have to prepend function calls.

```
using namespace ci;
using namespace ci::app;
using namespace std;
```

The following code block is responsible for the constructor function, which defines properties and methods for the app. Cinder apps automatically call, prepare, and set up during startup, and then update and draw every frame.

```
class TestApp : public AppBasic {

    void prepareSettings( Settings* settings );
    void setup();
    void update();
    void draw();
```

Here are the settings for the app that define what to track and add the Kinect instance and the textures to display what the program is seeing:

```
    float mThreshold, mBlobMin, mBlobMax;
    float mKinectTilt;

    Kinect mKinect;

    gl::Texture mColorTexture, mDepthTexture, mCvTexture;
```

The following represents a surface to store the depth image that gets passed to OpenCV, and the position being tracked along with the parameters pane so settings can be adjusted.

```
        Surface mDepthSurface;

        Vec3f mTargetPosition;

        params::InterfaceGl mParams;

    };

    void TestApp::prepareSettings( Settings* settings )
    {
        settings->setWindowSize( 640, 720 );
    }


    void TestApp::setup()
    {
```

Here, we define the default setting values and add them to our parameters pane for tweaking:

```
        mThreshold  = 70.0f;
        mBlobMin    = 20.0f;
        mBlobMax    = 80.0f;
        mKinectTilt = 10;

        mParams = params::InterfaceGl( "Hand Tracking", Vec2i( 250, 100 ) );
        mParams.addParam( "Threshold", &mThreshold,
            "min=0.0 max=255.0 step=1.0 keyIncr=s keyDecr=w" );
        mParams.addParam( "Blob Minimum Radius", &mBlobMin,
            "min=1.0 max=200.0 step=1.0 keyIncr=e keyDecr=d" );
        mParams.addParam( "Blob Maximum Radius", &mBlobMax,
            "min=1.0 max=200.0 step=1.0 keyIncr=r keyDecr=f" );
        mParams.addParam( "Kinect Tilt", &mKinectTilt,
            "min=-31 max=31 keyIncr=T keyDecr=t" );
```

Get the Kinect and set the target to zero:

```
        mKinect = Kinect( Kinect::Device() );

        mTargetPosition = Vec3f::zero();


    }
```

Image processing takes place for every frame via the **update** method. If the app has received a depth frame from the Kinect, get the current depth image from the Kinect. Make a texture to use for display along with a surface for OpenCV.

```
void TestApp::update()
{

    if( mKinect.checkNewDepthFrame() ){

        ImageSourceRef depthImage = mKinect.getDepthImage();

        mDepthTexture = depthImage;
        mDepthSurface = depthImage;

        if(mDepthSurface){
```

Once the surface is available, pass it to OpenCV. Even though the depth image is gray-scale, it still has a 16-bit depth, which is too high for OpenCV. The image surface is therefore converted to an 8-bit channel and then to an OpenCV image.

In addition, three other empty images are allocated for the processing and output.

```
cv::Mat input( toOcv( Channel8u( mDepthSurface ) ) ), blurred,
    thresholded, thresholded2, output;
```

First, the depth image is blurred to minimize noise.

```
cv::blur(input, blurred, cv::Size(10,10));
```

Make two thresholded images from the blurred image, one to display and one to pass the FindContours function since its process alters the image. By thresholding the depth image, the program is isolating a slice of space to look for contours in.

Adjusting the threshold value in the parameters pane will alter that slice's depth. The 2D vector to store the found contours is represented at the end.

```
cv::threshold( blurred, thresholded, mThreshold, 255,  CV_8U );
cv::threshold( blurred, thresholded2, mThreshold, 255,  CV_8U );
vector<vector<cv::Point> > contours;
```

Pass the thresholded image to OpenCV's FindContours function. The two constants passed as the third and fourth arguments ask the function to look only for outer contours that have been simplified (see *http://bit.ly/PQXjik*).

```
highlight=findcontours#cvFindContours
    cv::findContours(thresholded, contours, CV_RETR_EXTERNAL,
    CV_CHAIN_APPROX_SIMPLE);
```

We convert the threshold image to color for output so we can draw blobs on it, loop the stored contours, and return the center and radius for the current blob. Last but not least, convert the contour points to a matrix.

```
cv::cvtColor( thresholded2, output, CV_GRAY2RGB );
for (vector<vector<cv::Point> >::iterator
    it=contours.begin() ; it < contours.end(); it++ ){

    cv::Point2f center;
    float radius;

    vector<cv::Point> pts = *it;
    cv::Mat pointsMatrix = cv::Mat(pts);
```

Pass the matrix to **minEnclosingCircle** to make the blob. This function looks at the current contour's set of points and returns the radius of the minimum enclosing circle; see *http://bit.ly/PQXjik*.

```
highlight=findcontours#minenclosingcircle
            cv::minEnclosingCircle(pointsMatrix, center, radius);

            cv::Scalar color( 0, 255, 0 );
```

If the radius is within the specified range, draw the circle and update the target position.

```
            if (radius > mBlobMin && radius < mBlobMax) {

                cv::circle(output, center, radius, color);

                mTargetPosition.x = 640 - center.x;
                mTargetPosition.y = center.y;
                mTargetPosition.z = 0;
            }


        }

        mCvTexture = gl::Texture( fromOcv( output ) );

    }

}
if( mKinect.checkNewVideoFrame() )
        mColorTexture = mKinect.getVideoImage();

if( mKinectTilt != mKinect.getTilt() )
    mKinect.setTilt( mKinectTilt );

}
```

The **draw** method uses fixed-function OpenGL to draw the program output and clear the last frame.

```
void TestApp::draw()
{

    gl::clear( Color( 0.5f, 0.5f, 0.5f ) );
```

Disable depth for drawing video frames and push a new matrix to the top of the stack mirror by inverting x, and draw the color video frame.

```
    gl::disableDepthWrite();
    gl::disableDepthRead();

    glPushMatrix();
    gl::scale(Vec3f(-1, 1, 1));
    if( mColorTexture )
        gl::draw( mColorTexture, Vec2i( -640, 0));
    glPopMatrix();
```

Push a new matrix scale down and mirror it in order to draw the depth image along with the result of OpenCV processing below the main image, then reenable depth.

The image on the right will reflect the changes made to the settings; try adjusting the threshold and minimum and maximum blob size to see the results.

```
    glPushMatrix();
    gl::scale(Vec3f(-0.5, 0.5, 1));
    if( mDepthTexture )
        gl::draw( mDepthTexture,Vec2i( -640, 960 ));
    if ( mCvTexture )
        gl::draw( mCvTexture,Vec2i( -1280, 960 ));
    glPopMatrix();

    gl::enableDepthWrite();
    gl::enableDepthRead();
```

Draw the red dot at the target position and update the parameters pane.

```
    gl::color(Colorf(1.0f, 0.0f, 0.0f));
    gl::drawSphere(mTargetPosition, 10.0f);
    gl::color(Colorf(1.0f, 1.0f, 1.0f));

    params::InterfaceGl::draw();
```

```
}

CINDER_APP_BASIC( TestApp, RendererGl )
```

4

Gestural Interfaces for Making Music

Fancy yourself a bit of a music aficionado? Always keeping up to date on the latest sounds and advancements in music creation and engineering? If that's the case, then this chapter will be right up your alley. The Kinect's genius shines when integrating a natural user interface into just about every component of our lives. One of the most surprising and impressive implementations of the Kinect's NUI functionality is the integration and control of digital music components.

Using applications such as Ableton's Live and Max/MSP, you can transform yourself into a living, breathing dubstep master or a hands-free digital DJ. There's even a hack that lets you rock out on a virtual keyboard that can placed anywhere! Leave your audiences stunned and amazed as you use nothing more then your own natural gestures to create a symphony of incredible sounds.

In this chapter, you will learn what musical applications are available to use with the Kinect and how to configure and control them to your liking. You'll learn the basics of how to add customized sounds and how to seamlessly switch between samples based on preset custom gestures.

HACK 24 Install OSCeleton

OSCeleton is a wrapper that allows us to send OpenNI skeletal data in the form of open sound control (OSC) messages from one application to another. It's a great way to bridge the gap between two applications that serve different purposes. For example, if you want to use OpenNI skeletal joint information and pass that into a Processing sketch using pbox2d, you would take advantage of the OSCeleton wrapper to send that skeletal joint data over OSC. The nice part about OSCeleton is that it works with all programming languages and frameworks that use OSC events.

For this example, we'll be using OSCeleton with Processing to demonstrate how to run one of the *OSCeleton-examples* files. This will ensure that OSCeleton is working in the background, passing OpenNI skeletal data over OSC to the pbox2d Processing sketch.

Before you begin, you will need to ensure that OpenNI and Processing are both installed on your Mac OS X machine. Please refer to Hack #13 from Chapter 2 along with Hack #02 from Chapter 1.

To start off, download the latest version of Sensebloom's OSCeleton from *https:// github.com/Sensebloom/OSCeleton/downloads* and place it in any directory.

I always like to place libraries, frameworks, and applications that I know will be primarily used for Kinect-related projects into a Kinect *folder in my* Home *directory. You'll find it's much easier to keep track of things, especially if you plan on exploring all the different options the Kinect has to offer.*

Extract the *osceleton-v1.2.1_OSX.zip* file and then open your Terminal application.

The version number may very well change from v1.2.1 to something else by the time you read this. If so, replace the version number just listed with the latest version you just downloaded.

```
unzip osceleton-v1.2.1_OSX.zip
```

Change the read/write permissions of the file.

```
chmod a+x osceleton-v1.2.1_OSX
```

Before we run OSCeleton, we'll need to download the *OSCeleton-examples* Processing sketches along with a few Processing libraries.

Download *OSCeleton-examples* from *https://github.com/Sensebloom/OSCeleton-examples*.

Extract the contents of the *.zip* file and place the entire directory into your Processing *sketches* folder, located in *~/Documents/Processing/sketches* (see Figure 4-1).

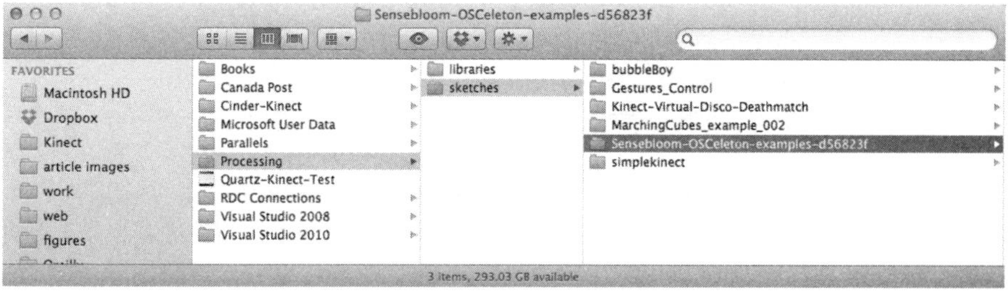

Figure 4-1.
Place the OSCeleton-examples directory in your Processing sketches folder

There are two libraries that need to be imported for some of the sample Processing sketches to work properly. Download *pbox2d* and *oscP5* and place the extracted contents of the files into your *Processing/libraries* directory:

oscP5

> http://www.sojamo.de/libraries/oscP5/

pbox2d

> https://github.com/shiffman/PBox2D/downloads

The Stickmanetic example is a little out of date, so we'll need to perform a few search-and-replace actions to correct some of the code (see Table 4-1). Launch the *Stickmanetic.pde* example. You should now see all the code in the scripting area, or Processing. To do a search and replace, press Command+F, or go to Edit → Find.

Table 4-1. Search-and-replace code changes for OSCeleton Stickmanetic example

SEARCH	REPLACE
`Vec2 pos=box2d.getScreenPos(body);`	`Vec2 pos = box2d.getBodyPixelCoord(body);`
`bd.position = box2d.screenTo World(x,y);`	`bd.position = box2d.coordPixelsTo World(x,y);`
`cd.radius = box2d.scaleScreenTo World(r);`	`cd.radius = box2d.scalarPixelsToWorld(r);`
`worldVertex = box2d.screenToWorld (screenVertex);`	`worldVertex = box2d.coordPixelsToWorld (screenVertex);`

Once that's done, plug your Kinect into your Mac. Navigate back to the location of *osceleton-v1.2.1_OSX* and run the file in a Terminal.

```
sudo ./osceleton-v1.2.1_OSX
```

Stand a few feet away from the Kinect and perform the Psi pose to calibrate.

Continue to run OSCeleton in the background and then run the Stickmanetic Processing example. If you feel so inclined, check out the *MotionCapture3D.pde* example (shown in Figure 4-2) as well.

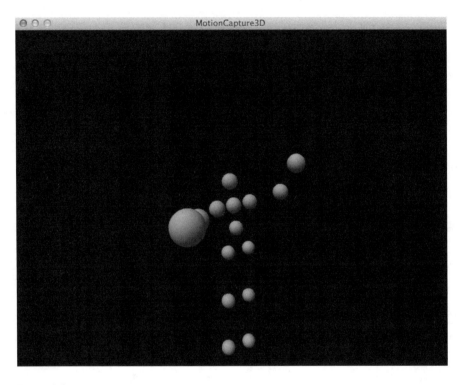

Figure 4-2.
MotionCapture3D OSCeleton example

Congrats, you now have OSC events being passed to Processing using OpenNI skeletal data. We'll also be using OSCeleton in the next hack, which involves passing OSC events through the Kinectar musical application.

HACK 25 Install Kinectar

Kinectar was developed as a complete solution for electronic musicians wanting to utilize the power of Microsoft Kinect as a hands-free Musical Instrument Digital Interface (MIDI) controller. It is a highly customizable and configurable toolkit designed for music, dance, and visual performers/artists.

Kinectar is designed to run alongside music production/performance software such as Ableton Live, providing an interface for the user to output MIDI notes, MIDI Control Change (CC), and OSC data in configurations that can change dynamically to suit an evolving performance. It receives joint position information from the Kinect and allows a large amount of advanced conditioning to be performed on the data before it leaves the program, ready for controlling synthesizers, drum machines, DAW functionality, or anything else that can be controlled using MIDI or OSC.

Kinectar doesn't communicate with the Kinect; it requires a skeleton tracker proxy to feed it the data it uses. At the time of writing, Kinectar is configured to receive information from two different proxies: OSCeleton and Synapse. Both are free, were created by independent developers, and run using the OpenNI framework (thus, they require the OpenNI drivers, PrimeSense NITE middleware, and SensorKinect Module to be installed).

For simplicity's sake, this installation guide will focus on using OSCeleton; however, you will find full installation notes for Synapse on its website, if that is your preferred method of skeletal tracking (*http://synapsekinect.tumblr.com*).

The simplest solution to installing the necessary components is to use the Zigfu developer bundle installer. This will install all three required modules so that your chosen Kinect → OSC proxy can communicate with the Kinect.

If you're using Kinectar on Windows to control a program like Ableton Live, Reason, or any other digital audio workstation (DAW), another program I highly recommend is MIDI Yoke (again, totally free). MIDI Yoke, once installed, will create up to 16 virtual MIDI devices on your computer that allow routing of MIDI messages between different programs. This will allow you to get the most out of Kinectar, since one of its important features is full-duplex control between itself and your chosen DAW via MIDI—the more virtual MIDI devices, the better.

Here's what you'll need to install Kinectar for Windows:

1. Download and install MIDI Yoke (optional; *http://www.midiox.com*)
2. Download and install Zigfu Development Bundle (*http://zigfu.com*)
3. Download and install Kinectar (*http://kinectar.org*)
4. Download and extract OSCeleton to any chosen folder (*https://github.com/Sensebloom/OSCeleton*)

Create a batch file for OSCeleton (e.g., *osceleton-kinectar.bat*) with the following switches/commands:

```
osceleton.exe -w -r
pause
```

You should now have all the required programs installed to run Kinectar and use all of its features. Here's what you'll need to install Kinectar for Mac.

1. Download and install Zigfu Development Bundle (*http://zigfu.com*)

2. Download Kinectar (*http://kinectar.org*)

3. Download and extract OSCeleton to any chosen folder (*https://github.com/Sensebloom/OSCeleton*)

Run OSCeleton from Terminal with the following commands:

```
sudo ./osceleton
```

Making sure your Kinect is plugged into both your computer and power, run the OS-Celeton batch. You should be presented with two windows: the DOS-style text window and the visual window showing the Kinect's grayscale depth image.

If OSCeleton is not loading at this point, or is showing an error message, you've missed a step along the way. Double-check the installation steps and, if necessary, check the OSCeleton website for more information.

Once you have OSCeleton working, launch Kinectar. Perform the lock-post to allow OSCeleton to detect your skeleton (see Figure 4-3). You will see "Calibration complete, start tracking user [x]" (in the OSCeleton text window). Kinectar should then jump to life, with the visual feedback modules reflecting your hand movements.

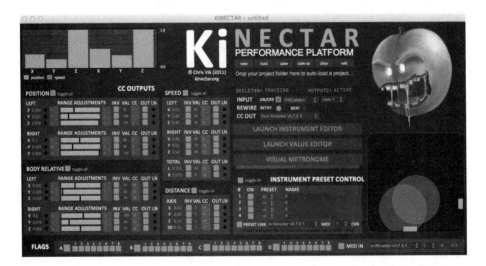

Figure 4-3.
Kinectar successfully receiving OSC signals

By default, Kinectar selects OSCeleton as its source of OSC input. However, if Kinectar is still not receiving data after a successful OSCeleton calibration, in the Setup section on the main page of Kinectar, make sure the Input box is checked and that OSCeleton is selected in the drop-down menu. At this point, you'll be looking at what's called the Tracking Page; however, it's worth pointing out here that Kinectar is split up into three main areas:

- The Tracking Page is the first screen you are presented with after opening Kinectar. It has visual displays representing the incoming and outgoing values, and allows the user to scale and adjust the hand position data, which can then be output as MIDI CC. The data is split up into four main data types:
  - Absolute hand positions
  - Body-relative hand positions
  - Hand speeds
  - Distance between hands

- The Instrument Editor is used to build graphical condition statements using flags and/or data conditions (i.e., if the <speed> of <left hand> <x-axis> is equal or greater than 0.5, then true else false) to activate actions. Actions can include outputting single MIDI notes or chords, or turning internal flags on and off to enable the creation of more complex triggers by allowing the sequencing of multiple events.

- The Value Editor section is dedicated to performing basic mathematical functions and scaling using any of the internal values (including raw position data, scaled position data, body-relative position data, speed, and distance). The resultant values can then either be output from Kinect via OSC or MIDI CC, or used to control parameters within Kinectar itself (such as velocity, pitch, or tempo of notes output within the Instrument Editor).

The Instrument Editor implements a method of switching between instrument presets on the fly, called the Preset Control System. This system allows up to 12 presets for each of the 4 instruments within a single project. To save a preset, simply hold Shift and left-click on the small nodes in the bottom-left corner of each instrument. You can recall the preset with a single left-click, or more excitingly, by using incoming MIDI notes, either via a hardware MIDI controller (such as a foot switch device) or sequenced within the DAW containing the musician's set of music. So, by simply sending a note to Kinectar, you can set up a simple way to automatically change which preset is to be used depending on its position within the piece.

Map Parameters in Ableton Live with Kinectar

Our goal in this hack is to use Kinectar's MIDI CC Output section to control specific audio units within Ableton Live via MIDI CC. Although this tutorial assumes the use of both OSCeleton as the proxy and Ableton Live as the audio program, you can easily translate it over to your preferred audio/music application, as most DAWs function in a similar manner when it comes to mapping parameters with MIDI.

The use of Kinectar assumes you have at least a basic level of knowledge in working with digital audio workstations (DAWs) and MIDI.

Because we'll be bouncing from one application to another, I've preceded each step with the appropriate piece of software or operating system in bold. If you do not see an application in bold, proceed in the application from the previous step. First up, we'll prepare Kinect for use with Ableton Live.

Open both Kinectar and Live (the order isn't important). Run OSCeleton (as described in Hack #24) and perform the lock-pose until your body is being tracked. Verify that **Kinectar** is receiving data with a simple check that the interface is responding to your movements. Set the MIDI CC Output device drop-down menu to a MIDI device on which Live is able to receive.

Mac users should be able to add communication ports for MIDI by using interap-plication communication (IAC). Go to Applications → Utilities → Audio MIDI Setup. Click the Window options in the toolbar and then Show MIDI Window. Ensure that "Device is online" is checked. You can also add a new port and rename it to some-thing more specific if you'd like, such as Kinectar <> Live. Restart Kinectar, and the option should be available under CC OUT.

In **Live**, check your MIDI preferences by going to the following menu:

Mac
> Live → Preferences → MIDI

Windows
> Options → Preferences → MIDI

Ensure that the MIDI device you've just selected as the CC Output device in Kinectar has both the Active and Remote buttons selected. This will allow MIDI messages to control parameters directly within the Ableton Live interface. Close the preferences window to return to the main page of Ableton Live.

In **Kinectar**, within the CC Output section on the left half of the main interface, locate the [position], [left hand], [y] value; this should be the second CC Output parameter from the top of the interface. Turn on the OUT toggle box (On is indicated with an X) toward the end of the parameter strip. This will enable the *y* position of your left hand to stream out of Kinectar via the MIDI CC Output device previously selected.

Ensure that the apricot is orange, not gray. This is the MIDI "mute" button, which will prevent ALL MIDI and Open Sound Control (OSC) from being output from Kinectar. At the moment, we wish to send MIDI out, so if the apricot is gray, click it to disable the mute function. This function is important to remember.

If all these steps were performed correctly, back in Ableton **Live**, we should notice a small solid yellow light in the top-right corner of Live's interface called *MIDI indicator*. This signifies that Live is receiving MIDI.

MIDI will not stream unless the proxy has a lock on a user. This is because Kinectar uses streaming data to perform its calculations for maximum resolution. If there is no streaming data going in, there will be no streaming data going out.

Now that we have MIDI streaming between programs, we can start mapping CCs (in this case, our hand position) to control parameters in Live. This tutorial can be altered and repeated to map many values from Kinectar to any number of parameters within Live and will commence from where the previous section left off (i.e., with Live, Kinectar, and OSCeleton running, and MIDI currently being streamed into Ableton Live).

If Kinectar stops responding at any point while building your patch, your proxy has most likely lost the lock on your body. Simply perform the lock-pose again and resume where you left off.

In **Kinectar**, turn MIDI mute on by clicking the apricot (it will turn from orange to gray).

This is a necessary step prior to performing any MIDI mapping functions within your DAW, as multiple streaming MIDI values into your DAW will confuse it during the mapping process.

In **Live**, ensure that the MIDI input indicator in the top-right corner of Live's interfaces is not lit up yellow, indicating that Kinectar's MIDI mute is on and there is no streaming data being received by Live. Click on the MIDI map button in the top-right corner of Live's interface. This will turn MIDI mapping mode on in Live, and parts of the interface will turn blue, indicating that these parameters can be mapped.

Now click the blue interface object you'd like to control with the Kinect. As an example, you can simply click on the master volume fader. You will notice small, white handles around the parameter you've selected, meaning it is ready to be mapped by a MIDI controller (i.e., Kinectar).

In **Kinectar**, pick an axis to use to control the selected parameter in Live. In this tutorial, we'll again use [position] [left hand] [y]. Click on the LN (or MIDI learn) button at the end of the parameter strip. This is the only feature that overrides the MIDI mute option, and sends a single MIDI value out for use with the MIDI learn feature common in all DAWs and software synths, samplers, etc. You will use this a lot.

In **Live**, you should now notice that a white box appears in the top-left corner of the master fader (or whichever parameter you've decided to map) with the numbers 1/1 or similar. This signifies that the parameter has been mapped to a CC value. The first number is the MIDI channel (1–16), and the second number is the CC number (0–127). Turn MIDI map mode off by clicking the MIDI button again. The interface should return to normal.

In **Kinectar**, ensure that the OUT toggle box at the end of [position] [left hand] [y] is turned on (with an X in it). Turn off MIDI mute (click apricot so that it turns orange).

In **Live**, move your left hand up and down (y-axis) and notice the master fader moving with it.

In **Kinectar**, alter the range needed to move your hand to achieve minimum/maximum CC values by clicking and dragging your mouse pointer over the Range Adjustment slider of the corresponding value you wish to adjust. Similarly, you may make adjustments by clicking on the min or max value and dragging up and down to alter it. By reducing the range of an output, you're maximizing the efficiency of your movements. Make sure to explore this feature heavily for the best performance results and maximum comfort while using the Kinect as a MIDI controller.

HACK 27 Set Up a Drum Kit with Kinectar

In this tutorial, we'll go over the steps needed to play a basic drum kit (kick and snare) with Kinectar and Ableton Live. It will introduce the concept of Kinectar's Instrument Editor for use with event triggering. We'll start off by opening up Kinectar. You may want to reference Hack #26 before going forward.

Turn on MIDI mute by clicking the apricot (it will turn from orange to gray).

This is a necessary step prior to performing any MIDI mapping functions within your DAW, as multiple streaming MIDI values into your DAW will confuse it during the mapping process.

Our first steps will cover how to configure Ableton Live for Kinectar.

In **Live**, create a new project. While in Session view (press Tab to switch between Arrangement and Session view), open the Live Devices Browser tab on the left side of the screen. Expand the Instruments menu, then expand the Impulse menu and drag Backbeat Room over into the session grid to create an instance of the module.

Make sure the I.O button is selected to show the MIDI From settings on the mixer panel. This button is located in the far right of Ableton Live's interface, next to the Master channel fader. In the mixer section of the newly created Backbeat channel, locate the MIDI From options and select MIDI Yoke 3 for the device and Ch. 1 for the channel. Then select In under the word Monitor, arming the channel to accept MIDI from Kinectar.

Next up, we'll configure the Kinectar Instrument Editor.

Back in **Kinectar**'s main interface, click Launch Instrument Editor to open the unit. Turn on the first unit of the Instrument Editor by clicking the option in the top-left corner of the unit and name the unit Kick.

Underneath the name, you'll notice four *condition strips*. Click the On toggle button on the first condition so that a cross appears in the box. Under Type, select "Coords (body rel.)"; then, select your right hand under the Hand title and select Y as the axis. Move right over the strip, just past the blue bar that shows the min and max selections for the trigger, and drag the Max number box down until it reaches about halfway down, or 0.500.

You've now set up a condition so that if your hand moves half way down your body, you will trigger the event. However, we want to make that trigger a little more robust. You don't want the kick triggering when you move your hand slowly, so let's add another trigger event that is related to the speed of your hand.

Still in **Kinectar**, in the next condition strip down, click the On box to enable the condition. Set its Type to "speed (w dir)." This will then let us set up a trigger that depends not only on the speed of our hand, but also on the direction in which it is moving. Select the same hand as before (right) and choose Y again for the axis.

Now you'll notice the value of this trigger sitting in the middle (around 0.500) when your hand is at rest. Moving your hand up and down will move the value above and below the 0.500 mark, respectively. The more sharply you move your hand, the further the value will move away from the center.

Next, bring the Max value of the condition down to 0.300 by either clicking and dragging down on the Max value number box, or by highlighting the area between 0.000 and 0.200 with the blue range selection bar in between the min and max number boxes. Now when you test the trigger, it should turn to True only when you strike your hand down at a faster rate—perfect for drums.

> *To the right of the Triggers section you'll see the Actions area. You'll notice that Static note mode is active. This is perfect for setting up single hit zones for drum triggers.*
>
> *Just to the right of the blue Static button is a drop-down menu that defaults to Off; this is the trigger mode of the static note output. It allows you to set up how the output is handled by the True/False messages it receives from the triggers.*

Remaining in **Kinectar**, set the Static mode to Once. This means the note will occur only on the upward edge of the trigger becoming True. For more information about the trigger modes for each note mode, hover your mouse over the trigger selection boxes.

> *You can select the note to play by clicking on the keyboard in the Static section. Leave this to C for now; it's safe to assume the kick drum of a sampler will always be triggered by the C note.*

The impulse racks in Ableton default to listening to MIDI octave 3, so for our notes to trigger the drums, we have to set that octave in our Instrument Editor. Under the Static mode keyboard, click the number 3 on the octave selection bar, lighting up the number in blue. By default, this is set to the lowest octave, −2.

Finally, just under the octave setting is the "MIDI output device" settings. Change this to the MIDI From device we set earlier in Live, which was "Out to MIDI Yoke 3." Then make sure 1 is selected for the channel.

> *Due to the Kinect's poor detection of quicker movements, there may be some unintended flam triggers (a note being triggered multiple times very quickly). We can remove the chance of this happening by moving our attention to the right of the Instrument where we have the buttons off, ms, clk, and midi. These are the timing modes of the note outputs. To see a description of these modes, hover your mouse over the buttons.*

For the moment, we will simply select ms.

To the right of this setting is the amount of milliseconds required between triggers. The default value is 100 ms, which is perfect for drum triggers. Generally, the unintended flams occur within 50 ms of each other; however, it's unlikely your hands can move fast enough to trigger notes intentionally more than once every 100 ms, so this setting is perfect for tightening up the sound.

Back in the main screen of Kinectar, click the apricot to disable MIDI mute and allow notes to be output from the Instrument Editor into Ableton Live.

Stand back and strike your hand downward to trigger the kick. You may have to adjust the instrument's trigger condition ranges slightly (position and speed conditions we set up previously) to get a better feel for the kit.

Turn the MIDI mute on again by clicking the apricot while we build the snare instrument.

Following the same principle, we will quickly set up a trigger and action for the snare drum for our other hand in the Instrument Editor.

Turn on the next Instrument unit and give it the name *Snare*. Next, turn on the first condition strip, set the type to "Coords (body rel.)," select the opposite hand to what you're using for your kick, and then set the axis to Y. Adjust the range to the same as the first strip in your kick unit.

Turn on the next condition strip to set up the speed condition, set the type to "speed (w dir)," select the correct hand, and then set Y for the axis, again adjusting the range as with the previous instrument. Set the static trigger mode to Once and then set the note to D, which will be the snare sample.

Still in **Kinectar**, set the octave again to 3 and change the output device to "Out to MIDI Yoke 3" and the channel as 1. Again turn the timing mode to ms with a value of 100 ms for our safety buffer, and then turn off MIDI mute by clicking the apricot.

Stand up and try your snare drum.

When everything is set up, the Instrument Editor should match what you see for both the Triggers and Actions sections shown in Figure 4-4 and Figure 4-5, respectively. You've now set up a basic drum kit with Kinectar. Experiment with different sounds to set up your own gesture-based drum kit using Live and Kinectar.

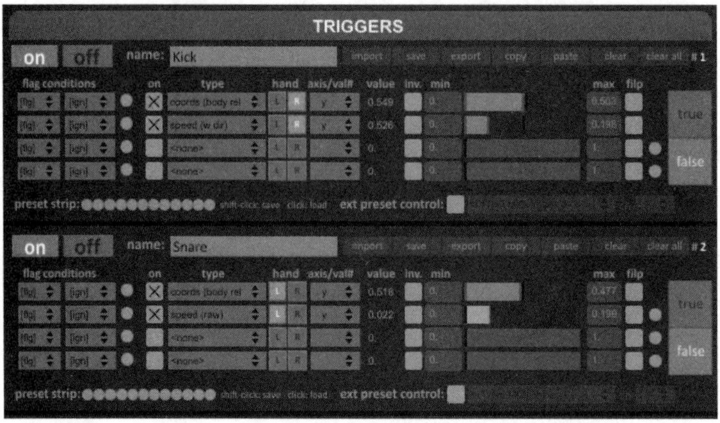

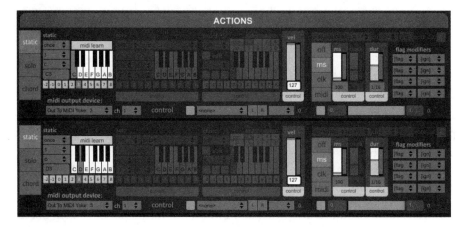

Figure 4-4.
Triggers setup for Kinectar drum kit Instrument Editor

Figure 4-5.
Actions setup for Kinectar drum kit Instrument Editor

HACK 28 Create a Dubstep Wobble Bassline with Kinectar

In this tutorial, we'll be learning how to create a simple dubstep bassline wobble. You can view an example on YouTube in the video "Dubstep Bassline using Kinect" (*http://youtu.be/325AhauQJCU*). The parameters we'll be mapping to our hands to get this sound are: Filter Cutoff, the low frequency oscillator (LFO) amount applied to the Filter Cutoff, and LFO speed. We'll also be using Kinectar to output the notes necessary to play the melody of the bassline.

I'll be using MASSIVE by Native Instruments to create the bassline; however, this tutorial can be applied to any synth with an LFO that can be attached to the filter. For simplicity's sake, I'll continue the tutorial assuming the use of MASSIVE (see Figure 4-6). The tutorial will also change software frequently from Kinectar to Live to the Synth, so it's important to pay close attention here.

It is best to go through Hack #26 *before beginning this tutorial.*

In **Kinectar**, turn on MIDI mute by clicking the apricot (it will turn from orange to gray).

This is a necessary step prior to performing any MIDI mapping functions within your DAW, as multiple streaming MIDI values into your DAW will confuse it during the mapping process.

In **Live**, create a new project in Live. While in Session view (press Tab to switch between Arrangement and Session view), open the Plug-in Devices tab on the left side of the screen. Drag over an instance of MASSIVE (or whichever synth you'll be using) onto the grid to create a new channel for the synth to reside in.

In **Synth**, with MASSIVE open, we'll quickly build a bassline patch. With the default preset open (this will load upon instrument creation), starting from the top left, set the OSC1 pitch to −24.00 and the OSC2 pitch to −12.06. Click the box next to OSC2 that says Squ-Sw1 and change the oscillator type to Dirty Needle and turn its Amp setting to 100%. Leave the other oscillators as they are. Locate the filter faders of both OSC1 and OSC2 (you'll find these faders just to the right of their Amp parameters), and bring the faders both to the top (to where it says F1 in light gray).

Now, to create the filter characteristics that we'll use to make the wobble, bring your attention to the Filter 1 section in the top-middle section of the synth. Where it says None, click and select Lowpass 4. Bring the Resonance 1/4 of the way up. Now bring the Mix fader to the right of the filter sections all the way up to the top so that the Filter 1 is mixed 100%.

Click the blue tab called 4 Env in the center of MASSIVE. This will change the center section of the synth to reflect the Envelope settings that are set to the Amplitude of the synth. Bring the knob called Level—located to the right of Decay—to 100%.

We'll create the wobble by first clicking the green tab in the middle called 5 LFO; the middle section of the MASSIVE interface will now show the LFO settings. On the left side of this section, click the Sync button to synchronize the LFO with the tempo of the track. Then ensure that the Restart button is not active. Click and drag the green cross (to the right of the 5 LFO tab) and drop it onto the Cutoff knob on the Filter 1. This will attach the LFO to the filter to give the synth the wobble characteristic.

Still in **Synth**, click and drag upward on the green 5 that appears under the Cutoff knob so that it applies around 60% of the LFO to the filter, signified by the green circle around the filter knob. In preparation for testing the sound with Kinectar in a later step, move the Filter 1 Cutoff to 50%, and the Amp in the LFO section to 0.

Figure 4-6.
MASSIVE plug-in interface

Moving back to **Live**, locate the MASSIVE device box at the bottom left of the screen. You'll notice it has three buttons to the left of the title MASSIVE. Click on the Unfold Device Parameters button, which is the gray arrow pointing down in between the on/off and wrench buttons.

The device will now unfold with the message "To add plug-in parameters to this panel, click the Configure button." Follow these instructions and click the Configure button in the top-right corner of the MASSIVE device. This will turn the button green, signifying you are ready to select parameters in the synth to map with Kinectar.

Back in **Synth**, in MASSIVE, click the following parameters to add them to the mappable parameters section in Live:

- Cutoff in the Filter 1 section (Filter Cutoff)
- Amp in the 5 LFO section (LFO amount applied to the Filter Cutoff)

- The second box down under the word Ratio in the top-left corner of the 5 LFO window; by default, this will be 1 (LFO/wobble speed)

Returning to **Live** now that we have the parameters we wish to control with Kinectar selected, click again on the green Configure button to get out of Parameter selection mode. Move your attention to the mixer section of Ableton Live's session view, where you've placed the instance of MASSIVE. In the boxes under MIDI From, select "In from MIDI Yoke 2," and 1 for the channel. Then click the In selection under the word Monitor. The synth is now armed to be played by MIDI notes that go through the MIDI Yoke 2 device under channel 1, which is what we'll now set up Kinectar to do.

In **Kinectar**, open the Instrument Editor by pressing the Launch Instrument Editor button (Figure 4-7). On the first Instrument unit, click the On button in the top-left corner and give the instrument a name like Bassline. We'll now set up a condition for the note to be played (e.g., if our hand is above our waist, then the note will be played). Make note of the four condition strips.

Figure 4-7.
Sections of the Kinectar Instrument Editor screen

Click the On box on the first condition strip so that it contains an X. Under Type, select the option "Coords (body rel.)"; this means we will use a value of our hand that is relative to our body, so no matter where you are standing, the position of your hand will always be relative to the position of your torso.

Select a hand (I'm left-handed and accordingly choose left, but you may wish to use your right). Select the axis Y, which is our movement up and down. Click and drag upward on the number box under the title min. (You may instead click on the box, type a number, and then press Enter.) For this example, use 0.360. Note that if you're dragging over the box, the farther to the right of the number box you click, the finer the adjustment.

Make sure OSCeleton is open and tracking your body by performing the lock-pose.

While still in **Kinectar**, if you stand back from your computer in front of the Kinect and move your hand up and down near your waist, you'll notice the blue box displaying TRUE/FALSE, changing states as you trigger the condition. This is what will trigger our notes. Just to the right of the TRUE/FALSE box, the ACTIONS section starts. This is where we'll set up which notes are output to play the synth.

Click the SOLO note mode button, which will now light up the Solo mode section. In the Solo section that you've just enabled, under the word SOLO there is a drop-down box that will read OFF; change this to HOLD. With the hold mode active, the note will play continuously while the condition is true.

Select a few notes to play by simply clicking on the keyboard. The selected notes will turn blue. Under the keyboard, click and drag to highlight the numbers 0, 1, and 2. This selects which octaves the notes will be played over.

Underneath the octave selector is the word CONTROL inside a gray tab. Click this to set the control strip at the bottom of the instrument to adjust which Kinect input we wish to use to control the pitch of our synth. The words SOLO NOTE will appear to the left of the control strip. Click on the gray box to the right to enable its control.

To the right of this box, we will select an input to control the notes we output. In the first box, select "Coords (body rel.)," then choose the same hand you chose earlier for the condition strip. This time, however, use the axis X, which is your lateral hand movement (left and right).

Still in **Kinectar**, adjust the blue range bar to the right of these selections on the control strip to adjust how far you have to move your hand to reach the highest and lowest note. For the moment, use the range of 0.100 to 0.730. You can adjust this later.

Above this section is the Sync Mode button. By default, OFF will be selected, signified in blue. Change this to CLK. This will synchronize the movement between notes to the tempo of your Ableton Live session.

To the left of the control strip are the "MIDI output device" settings. Set this to the device and channel that we set up in Ableton Live to play the synth—namely, "Out to MIDI Yoke 2" for the device and 1 for the channel.

Back in the main screen of **Kinectar**, click the apricot to enable MIDI out.

In **Live**, with Ableton Live in focus, press the spacebar or click the Play button at the top of the screen (Figure 4-8).

Figure 4-8.
Ableton Live with MASSIVE

Now stand back and move your hand up and down to hear the note triggering, then move your hand left and right to change the note being played. You're now playing a synth by waving your hand around in the air. Congratulations, and welcome to the future!

Return to **Kinectar** and mute the MIDI output of Kinectar by clicking the apricot again. With the MASSIVE channel selected in the mixer of Ableton Live, click the MIDI button in the top-right corner of the Live window to enable MIDI mapping. We'll now attach outputs from Kinectar to control the three synth parameters: Filter Cutoff, LFO Amp, and LFO Speed.

In **Live**, with mapping mode on (interface features should be blue), in the MASSIVE device unit (bottom-left corner of Live), click on the FILTER1-CUT parameter. It should now have black handles around the parameter. This parameter is now armed and ready to receive a Learn message from Kinectar.

In the main screen of **Kinectar**, locate the Body Relative section under the title Quick Outputs. Locate the y-axis of the hand you are using to control the pitch; then, on the far right of that section, click the empty OUT box so that it contains a cross, and click the LN button. This will now map the y-axis to the filter cutoff.

In **Live**, repeat the preceding two steps for the following parameters/inputs:

- Y-axis of the opposite hand to MOD5-DEN
- Z-axis of the opposite hand to MOD5-AMP

Click the MIDI mapping button to turn mapping mode off. The screen should now return to normal.

Now in **Kinectar**, enable the three body relatives you've just mapped by clicking the OUT box next to the LN button. Click the apricot to turn MIDI mute off.

Now step back and work out how your movements are now affecting the synth.

To get better articulations from your movements, you will have to tweak the *range adjustments* of each of the outputs that are controlling the filter and LFO (Figure 4-9).

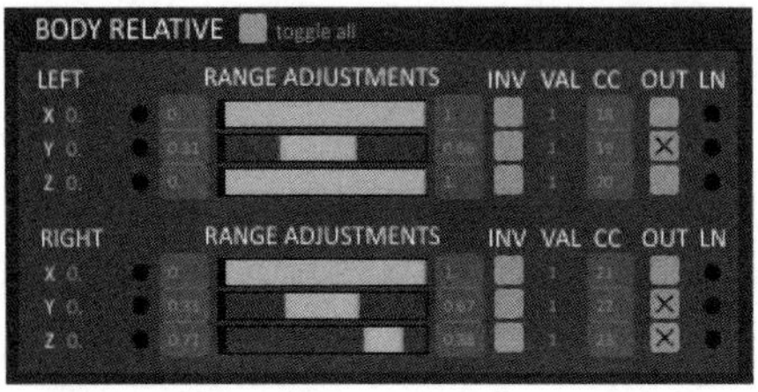

Figure 4-9.
Body relative activity

5

Motion Capture and Animation

Traditionally, if you wanted to reconstruct and capture the realistic motions of a 3D model, you would need to set up an elaborate rig involving sensors connected to every joint of the person being tracked. This technique, known as *electromechanical motion capture*, is not exactly the best way to capture realistic human movement for the average hobbyist with an interest in mocap. With the introduction of the Kinect's full skeletal tracking capabilities, we can now extract skeletal joint tracking data and import it into widely used motion capture software solutions such as MotionBuilder, Animata, Blender, Maya, Daz3D, and more!

In this chapter, we'll be using NI mate from Finnish startup Delicode. NI mate is a small but powerful software platform that takes real-time motion capture data from a Kinect and turns it into two industry-standard protocols: Open Sound Control (OSC) and Musical Instrument Digital Interface (MIDI). NI mate is available for both Windows and Mac OS X (with a Linux version pending). NI mate offers users easy installation and a powerful yet user-friendly configuration interface. Keeping to standard protocols for output makes NI mate a flexible piece of software that can be applied in a vast number of scenarios.

By downloading free add-ons and templates made available for a number of 3D and audio software packages, you can instantly transform your Kinect into a powerful performance interface (see an example in Figure 5-1). The list of supported software is constantly updated, and if your favorite software is not yet on the list, you can always request a plug-in for it on the NI mate user forums. Once you start using the software, you're encouraged to share your configurations, tutorials, use cases, and add-ons with others on the NI mate user forum.

NI mate's built-in MIDI support offers immediate integration for most audio software and many synthesizers. For deeper integration and more control, NI mate supports OSC. Upon launch, the first officially supported add-on has been made available for

Blender, the world's most popular open source 3D suite. Since then, a second official add-on has been released for Maxon's Cinema 4D. More add-ons and templates for a number of other 3D and audio software packages will be made available in the coming months.

Visit the NI mate Downloads page for Mac OS X and Windows versions along with installation instructions at *http://www.ni-mate.com/*.

Figure 5-1.
NI mate Kinected Bunny demo from *http://youtu.be/wNSMgX5t1RQ*

HACK 29 Use Blender and NI Mate for Motion Capture

We'll begin the setup process by importing the Blender add-on. Open up Blender and go to File → User Preferences. Click the Add-on tab and then Install Add-on. Locate the *animation+delicode_ni_mate.py*, and then click Install Add-on (see Figure 5-2).

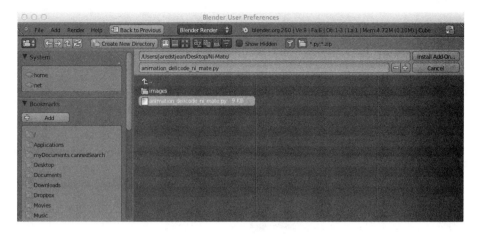

Figure 5-2.
animation_delicode_ni_mate.py Blender add-on

The Animation Delicode NI mate add-on should now be visible under the User Preferences/Addons tab. Enable it by clicking the checkbox to the right of the plug-in.

Close the windows, and you should notice the Delicode NI mate panel to the left.

Make sure the Kinect sensor is plugged into the computer and run Delicode NI mate. Click the OSC tab and remove the checks from the Quantized Data and Exact Data options. Leave the IP address as the default local host (127.0.0.1) and the port as 7000, matching up with the Blender Delicode NI mate panel. Click Apply Changes to save the configuration (see Figure 5-3).

We can now start interacting with Blender using NI mate OSC integration. In Blender, click the Start button in the NI mate panel to initiate communication between Blender and NI mate. In the NI mate configuration window, click the Skeleton tab and change the /Right_Hand value to Cube in the default Blender Object Mode. You should now be able to control the placement of the Blender cube.

If you want to control the camera, copy the /Left_Hand value and paste it into the name of the camera object. Now you're able to control the cube with your right hand and the camera with your left. See Figure 5-4.

Figure 5-3.
NI mate configuration window

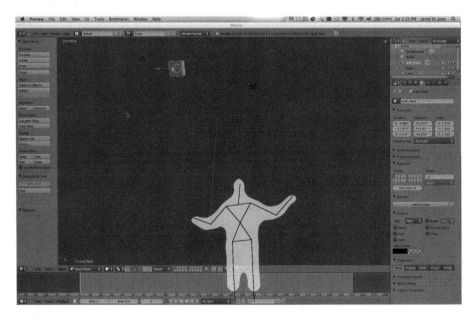

Figure 5-4.
Control the Blender camera and cube with NI mate

KINECT HACKS

HACK 30 Record Motion Capture with Blender and NI Mate

Download the *mocap.blend* file from *http://www.ni-mate.com/use/blender/* and open it up in Blender. The file contains a premade skeleton with all the necessary track points. Open up Delicode NI mate, import the Mocap and Bunny configuration profile, and save it from the Profile menu. Click the Start button in the Delicode NI mate Blender panel to begin sending OSC messages between Blender and NI mate. You should now be able to control the imported skeleton in Blender once NI mate is calibrated and tracking your motions. See Figure 5-5.

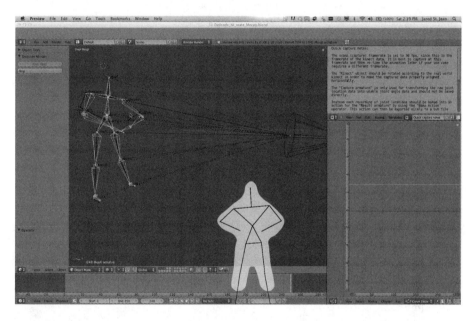

Figure 5-5.
NI mate controlling Blender skeleton

To begin recording the motion capture session, set the end frame to whatever you'd like. Click the automatic key frame insertion button and then the Play button. At this point, the recording session has started. Calibrate with NI mate by standing in front of the Kinect, and the skeleton should jump to action. Once you're done, pause the session to end recording.

We can now inspect and edit the motion capture data. See Figure 5-6.

Once you're finished fine-tuning the mocap data, you can export the motion capture recording. Go to File → Export. Select Motion Capture (bvh) and give it a name. When you're finished, click Export BVH.

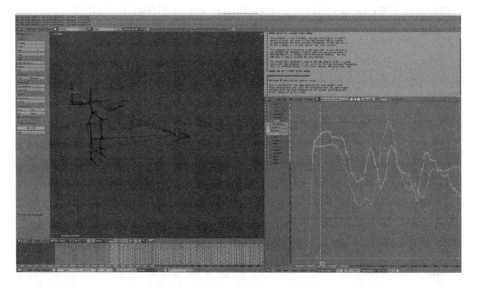

Figure 5-6.
Blender motion capture Data Editor

Open a new Blender project and import the recently saved *.bvh* file. In the bottom-left Import BVH Panel, select Y Forward for the Forward setting, and set Z Up for Up in the lefthand panel before importing the *.bvh* file. See Figure 5-7.

Figure 5-7.
Final imported motion capture

KINECT HACKS

Control a Rig in Blender with NI Mate

For the purposes of this hack, we'll be using bendansie's rig from *http://blend swap.com*. If you don't have an account on Blendswap.com, create one and download the rig from *http://www.blendswap.com/blends/characters/sintel-lite-2-57b/*. Save the file in a convenient place.

Open the *Sintel_Lite_Ni_mate_final.blend* file in Blender. We'll begin by pruning a few rig layers, as we won't be using them for this tutorial. From the Outliner view in the upper-right corner, select the rig as your active target. You'll now be in Pose Mode, which allows you to remove and edit some of the rig's values. Begin by setting the inverse kinetic (IK) left and right knee_target bone weights to 0.

Remove the root rig layer along with the IK layers for both the Leg.R and Leg.L while enabling the FK controls for Leg.R and Leg.L by clicking their respective buttons. The final results should look similar to Figure 5-8.

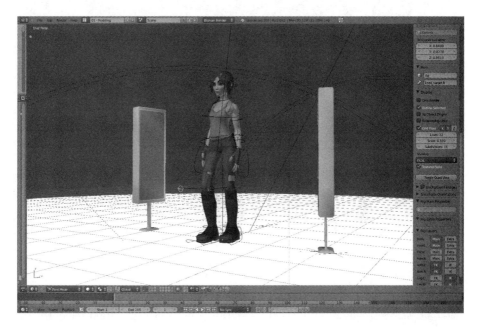

Figure 5-8.
Editing the rig layers in Pose Mode

We now need to append the *Delicode_Ni_mate_Mocap.blend* file. Do so by pressing Shift+F1 or going to File → Append. Navigate into the *Objects* directory and select all items except for Result Armature. When you're ready, click the Link/Append Library button in the upper-left corner.

Once the skeleton has been appended, you'll notice a huge difference in terms of the scale of the rig in comparison to the skeleton. You'll need to select the Kinect value from the Outliner view in the upper-right corner and start playing around with the Transform values.

I found that changing the X, Y, and Z values from 1 to 0.1 scaled things down appropriately. You'll then want to position the skeleton slightly behind the rig. Do so by editing the Location and Rotation values for X, Y, and Z under Transform. See Figure 5-9.

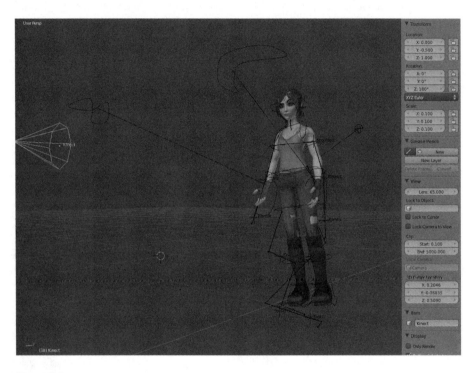

Figure 5-9.
Transform scale and location values

Now we can add the capture armature values that allow us to sync up the rig with the NI mate Kinect skeleton. Click the rig from the Outliner view and then select the rig pelvis ring directly on the rig in the main view. The pelvis ring should turn light blue if it's currently selected. Click the Bone Constraint option in the Properties view below the Outliner view to the right. Click Add Constraint and then Copy Location. For Target, select Capture Armature and for the Bone value, select Torso. The rig and skeleton should now *literally* be attached at the hip.

If you don't see the values right away, you can begin typing the name, which will autocomplete if the value is present.

KINECT HACKS

Next, add a Copy Rotation bone constraint to the same pelvis joint on the rig. Set the Target as Capture Armature and the Bone as Torso just like in the previous Copy Location constraint. You'll notice the lower half of the rig will point straight up into the air behind the rig's upper torso. To remedy this, click the Invert option below the x-axis for the Copy Rotation constraint. See Figure 5-10.

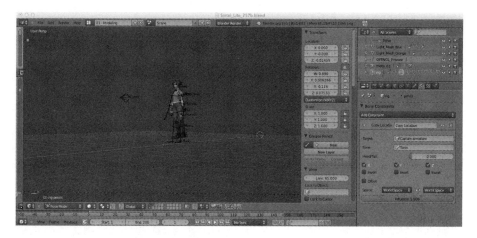

Figure 5-10.
Rig and skeleton torso/bone constraints

Continue adding the same copy rotation values (minus the copy location) for the rig's torso along with the left and right upper arms and forearms. Next up are the thigh and leg values. Create a Copy Rotation Constraint, beginning with the rig's right thigh or Thigh.R value. Set the Target as Capture Armature and the Bone as Thigh.R. You'll notice that the leg is now twisted at a horrific angle that reminds me of a brutal skateboarding video I once watched. If you have a weak stomach like I do, you'll want to address this immediately.

Change from Pose Mode to Edit Mode and select the Capture Armature value under Kinect from the Outline view. Set the bone as Thigh.R and change the Roll value under Tail to 180 degrees. Change back to Pose Mode, and the problem should be fixed. Do the same for the right leg, left thigh, and left leg.

Your rig model should now be all synched up, ready to receive OSC commands from NI mate. If you haven't done so, download the Blender add-on from *http://www.ni-mate.com/use/blender* called *animation+delicode_ni_mate.py*. Import it by going to User Preferences → Install Add-on. Enable the plug-in under the Animation menu item by selecting the checkbox for the Animation: Delicode NI mate option.

In the newly added Delicode NI mate panel, ensure the port is set to 7000 and click the Start button. Launch NI mate and click the OSC tab, then the Skeleton tab. Make sure that OSC is enabled, that your IP is 127.0.0.1, and that OSC is listening on port 7000. Uncheck the Quantized Data and Exact Data options and click Apply Changes.

With everything in place, step in front of the Kinect's line of view; NI mate should successfully calibrate, enabling skeletal tracking. Your rig should now mirror your arm and leg movements. See Figure 5-11.

If you're having trouble setting things up, be sure to check out NI mate's video tutorial at *http://youtu.be/EogegvTG3Po*.

Figure 5-11.
NI mate and Blender rig control

HACK 32 Use NI Mate with Animata

This hack involves using NI mate to control a puppet in Animita. Animata is a great application, which you can download for free, that allows you to create real-time animation and interactive backgrounds. For more on Animata, visit *http://anima ta.kibu.hu/*.

We'll begin by loading up an example *.nmt* file called *indonesian.nmt*. It can be found in the *.dmg* you downloaded from Animata's official site. See Figure 5-12.

Delete the animated bones by clicking on the third tab in Animata called Skeleton. Click the Delete option and then individually delete each colored bone (Figure 5-13). You'll also want to select the green anchor point at the bottom of the example. Under the Skeleton tab, choose Select/Move and uncheck the fixed option.

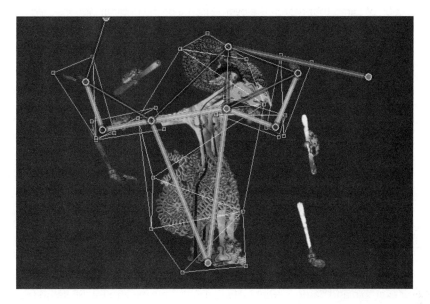

Figure 5-12.
Animata Indonesian example

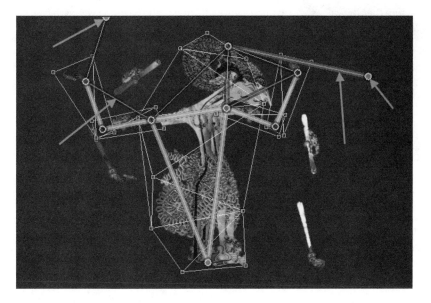

Figure 5-13.
Delete the colored bones

Create a new layer in Animata. Click the Layer tab and under Preferences, name the layer "NI mate." Use the Alpha slider bar under Layer to fade out the character as well. This makes it easier to see all the skeletal joints that we'll be editing shortly.

Create a series of joints that match the overall frame of the original *indonesian.nmt* file by selecting Create Joint under the Skeleton tab. Connect all the joints by creating bones from one joint to the next from the right hand to the left hand joint. Reduce the stiffness in each bone by clicking Select/Move under Skeleton. Drag the stiffness bar to 0 for each bone.

With the Kinect sensor plugged in, open up NI mate. We can now begin mapping the names of the NI mate joints to the Animata joints. In NI mate, select File → New to load the new profile and then click Apply Changes.

When using Animata, ensure the OSC controller port is set to 7110 in NI mate.

Under the Format drop-down in the Full Skeleton tab, ensure Animata Joint is selected. This is crucial for Animata to understand what signals are being sent from NI mate.

Now go back to Animata. Select the joint that represents the right hand in the *indonesian.nmt* example and name it /Right_Hand. Do this by going to the Skeleton tab, clicking Select/Move, selecting the joint, and then filling in the Name field.

Make sure that the values you assign to the joints match the Skeleton values in NI mate.

Under the Full Skeleton tab under Skeleton Settings, invert the scale values by changing the X and Y values from 1.000 to −600.000.

Click the Enable Skeleton OSC button under the Full Skeleton tab in NI mate, and your newly created joints should spring to life. You may notice the arm joints and bones will be way up in the corner. If this is the case, you need to adjust the Post offset values in NI mate in Full Skeleton and Skeleton settings. I was able to line things up nicely using Post offset values of 600 and 300 for X and Y, respectively. See Figure 5-14.

Scaling values under the Tracking tab in NI mate should match the X and Y joint values in Animata. Coordinate values are also inverted, so be sure to apply negative values in NI mate.

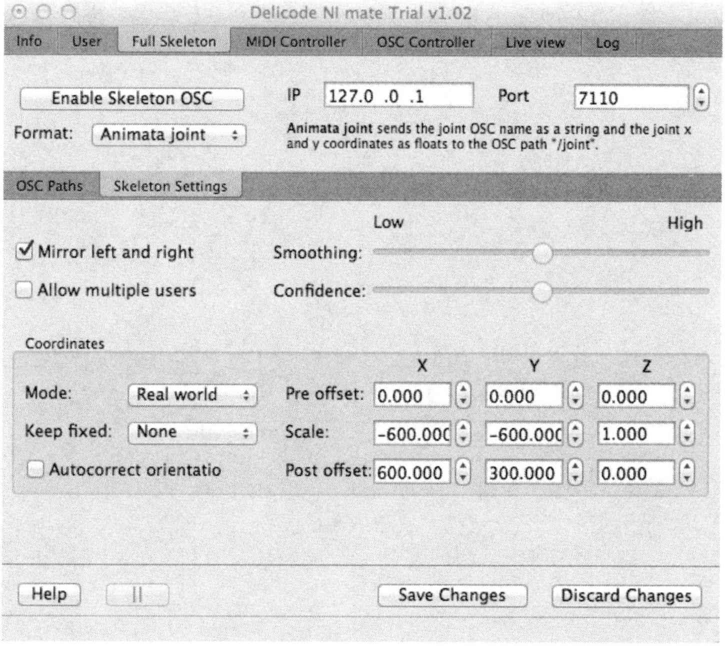

Figure 5-14.
Scale and Post offset calibration for NI mate

That's all well and good, but I'm sure you'd like to see the actual NI mate example move around. To control the puppet, delete the NI mate layer we created and start naming the joints of the *indonesian.nmt* example exactly like the joints we created earlier.

> You might want to disable Skeleton OSC in NI mate; otherwise, you may have a
> hard time just clicking the joints to rename them. Once they've all been named to
> match the NI mate OSC paths, click Enable Skeleton OSC.

And there you have it. If all sailing was smooth, you should be controlling the arm movement of the Animata Indonesian puppet example (Figure 5-15). Try out some of the other examples to see what sort of cool real-time, gesture-based animation you can come up with.

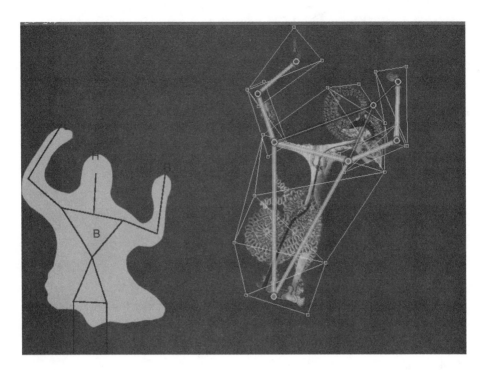

Figure 5-15.
NI mate–controlled Animata puppet

3D Object and Scene Reconstruction

Kinect's ability to accurately recreate the dimensions of any room in real time lends itself to multiple purposes and opens up several new DIY simultaneous location and mapping (SLAM) solutions. Having this information converted to a digital wireframe using a Kinect sensor saves a huge amount of time and money. In the past, most people would have to purchase a light detection and ranging (LIDAR) camera, which costs anywhere from $10,000 to $200,000. Now all you need is a Kinect and your choice of a wide variety of 3D scanning software solutions from the free multiplatform RGBDemo to the Windows-only Brekel Kinect to other full environmental mapping tools like RGBDEMO-6D-SLAM.

With a $150 Kinect camera in hand along with a PC and some free software, it's now possible to accomplish things that would set back professionals using high-end equipment tens of thousands of dollars. We can now easily venture into remote locations without fear of damaging expensive equipment while maintaining a high degree of quality in terms of the 3D scene recreation.

HACK 33 Install RGBDemo and Skanect

RGBDemo is a great open source toolkit written by Nicolas Burrus that allows you to start playing with Kinect data to develop standalone computer vision programs without the hassle of integrating existing libraries. It's simple in design, it's easy to use, and it produces great results (see Figure 6-1). It comes with loads of demos that you can use to import mesh files into 3D software solutions such as MeshLab and Blender.

RGBDemo includes the following features:

- The ability to grab Kinect images and visualize/replay them
- Support for libfreenect and OpenNI/NITE backends
- The ability to extract skeleton data/hand point position (NITE backend)

- Integration with OpenCV and PCL
- Multiple Kinect support and calibration
- The ability to calibrate the camera to get point clouds in metric space (libfreenect)
- The ability to export to MeshLab/Blender using *.ply* files
- Demo of 3D scene reconstruction using a freehand Kinect
- Demo of people detection and localization
- Demo of gesture recognition and skeleton tracking using NITE
- Demo of 3D model estimation of objects lying on a table (based on PCL table-top object detector)
- Demo of multiple Kinect calibration
- Linux, Mac OS X, and Windows support

To install RGBDemo, simply download the appropriate packages (Windows or Mac) from *http://labs.manctl.com/rgbdemo/index.php/Main/Download* and follow the installation instructions.

Figure 6-1.
RGBDemo capture interface

Skanect was developed from the groundwork laid down by RGBDemo. This application allows you to easily move the sensor around while capturing new views of an object or a room and automatically computes a metric 3D model, in real time. It can also detect planes, such as floors and walls, and perform automatic ground alignment. Skanect's output can be imported into popular 3D software such as MeshLab or Blender for further examination, measurement, and refinement.

Skanect will eventually by distributed as a commercial product and will not be open source. For the time being, hobbyists are encouraged to download the free version by going to *http://manctl.com/products.html*.

To install Skanect on a Mac, simply download the *.zip* package located at *http://manctl.com/products.html*. Extract the files and move the *skanect.app* file to the *Applications* folder. Plug in your Kinect and launch the app. See Figure 6-2.

Figure 6-2.
Skanect for Mac

Further instructions for Windows 32 and 64 are located at *http://manctl.com/prod ucts.html*.

HACK 34 Import RGBDemo Output into Blender

For this hack, I'll be demonstrating how you can easily import Kinect-captured models into Blender using Nicolas Burrus's RGBDemo. This great tool brings a wide assortment of options to the table in terms of capturing Kinect depth data and saving the point cloud representation as a mesh. A few key features include:

- Support for both libfreenect and OpenNI
- Multiple Kinect support
- Ability to export *.ply* files into Blender and MeshLab
- Support for Linux, Mac OS X, and Windows

For a full feature listing, be sure to check out the Kinect RGBDemo official site at *http:// labs.manctl.com/rgbdemo/*.

For the purpose of this tutorial, I'll be importing a *.ply* file generated by RGBDemo that will be imported into Blender and then texture-mapped using a MacBook Pro running OS X Lion 10.7.2.

> *You will need to have either libfreenect or OpenNI/NITE installed before you can use RGBDemo. See Chapter 1.*

Download the RGBDemo Binary dmg installer from *http://labs.manctl.com/rgbde mo/index.php/Main/Download*.

To install RGBDemo, just drag the *RGBDemo* folder into the *Applications* folder. Go into the *RGBDemo* folder and launch the rgbd-viewer application.

Using some of the options available in RGBDemo, you can fine-tune the depth threshold to eliminate any background the Kinect is picking up. You'll essentially want to place a solid object in front of the Kinect camera that doesn't have too many gaps or holes. The more structured and complete the object, the better it will translate into a 3D model.

Click the Show option and check the 3D Viewer and the Filters options (Figure 6-3).

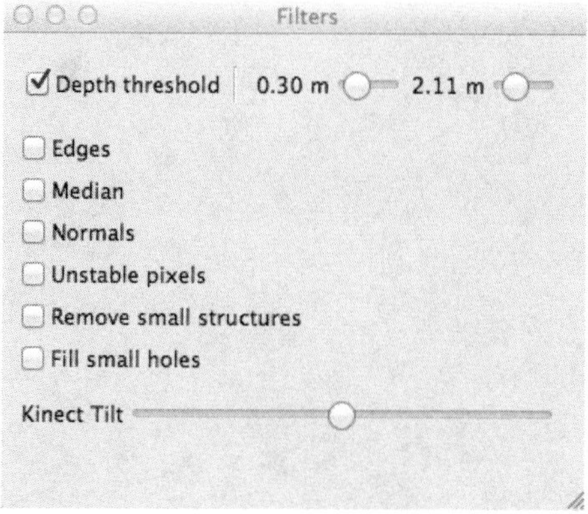

Figure 6-3.
RGBDemo rgb-viewer Filters option

Adjust the filter Depth threshold until the object you plan to capture appears in either blue or green and any background has been filtered out. Experiment with the other options—such as Edges, Median, and Normals—as you see fit.

The Kinect Tilt option will work only if you are using the libfreenect backend.

Switch over to the 3D Viewer window and click the Triangles button. When you have your object set, click the SaveMesh button. Two files, *current_mesh.ply* and *current_mesh.ply.texture.png*, will be placed in your */Applications/RGBDemo* directory.

We'll now go ahead and import the RGBDemo output into Blender. Open up Blender and import the *current_mesh.ply* file located in the *RGBDemo* folder. You can do this by going to File → Import → Stanford (.ply). See Figure 6-4.

Once the file loads, it may appear as though nothing happened. The 3D object you just imported is probably hanging out inside or just below the big gray box in the center of the world map. You'll need to continuously zoom in until you've located it. It may look very strange at first as well. You'll need to continue altering the perspective in relation to the x-, y-, and z-axes. This may include rotating the image around and tilting the vertical alignment. You can perform these camera orientation techniques by holding the Option key and moving two fingers either vertically or horizontally on the trackpad.

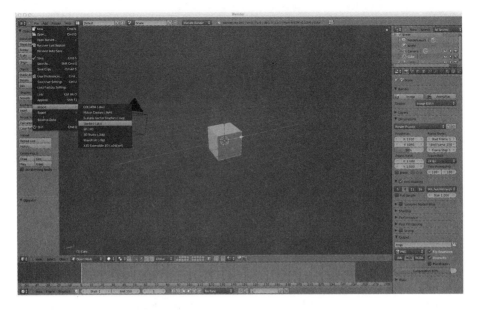

Figure 6-4.
Import current_mesh.ply into Blender

Hopefully, you have the 3D object facing you in the same manner it was when you took the original capture using rgb-viewer. Our next task is to import the *current_mesh.ply.texture.png* file and overlay it onto the 3D object. We'll accomplish this by creating a new material and then applying our imported *.png* file as a texture to that material.

Begin by splitting your screen into two sections. One screen will remain as our 3D Object view, while the other will need to be changed to the UV/Image Editor type. You will also need to change your original window mode from Object Mode to Edit Mode.

To the right of the screen, there are some important editing tools and options that we'll reference from time to time. For this guide, we'll be using the orb and plaid square icons labeled Material and Texture, respectively.

Click the Material icon. We'll need to create a new material. Currently you should see a *Material.001* filename. Change this to whatever you see fit. Then follow these steps:

1. Click the checkered Texture icon. We're going to create a new texture, so you'll want to give it a unique name. Anything descriptive enough to know what you're selecting down the road should suffice.

2. Click the + icon when you're finished labeling it.

3. Change the Type drop-down menu to Image or Movie.

KINECT HACKS

4. Import the *current_mesh.ply.texture.png* file by clicking the Open button under the Image category. The file is located in */Applications/RGBdemo*.

5. Change the Mapping Projection drop-down menu to UV as opposed to the default, Flat.

Now we'll need to add the newly created texture to the UV/Image Editor window pane.

1. Click the icon of the image (not the word *Image* or the + icon in the same field).

2. Select *current_mesh.ply.texture.png* (or whatever you have renamed it to).

Hold down the Option key and click the original 3D object that's currently in Edit Mode. You should see an outline that matches the 3D object overlapping the texture visible in the secondary window.

Switch from 3D Edit Mode to Object Mode and then change the Viewport Shading to Textured. The texture should now be wrapped around the 3D object.

HACK 35 Use Skanect to Create a Scene Mesh

For this hack, we'll be using Manctl's Skanect application to scan an area that produces a 3D model of the environment in real time. We'll then import this mesh file into the 3D modeling software MeshLab (*http://meshlab.sourceforge.net/*).

It's assumed that you've already installed Skanect for your OS of choice. If you haven't done this yet, please refer to Hack #33.

The first thing you'll need to do is determine the amount of space you want to capture. Position your body in a central location about five to eight feet away and hold the Kinect sensor in a static place. I had great success holding the sensor in my lap on a swiveling office chair.

To begin capturing mesh data, click the Start button in Skanect. Begin by pointing your Kinect in the upper-left corner of the environment you'd like to capture.

Slowly start to move the angle of the sensor downward, always watching the output window to ensure that the mesh points are properly capturing the scene. As you reach the bottommost point of the captured area, move the Kinect slightly to either the right or left and begin to scan in an upward direction.

Depending on the size of the area you're trying to capture, take your time when scanning the environment with the Kinect. The longer and slower you move it, the more data will be captured, thus producing a more detailed final mesh when imported.

Continue to do this until you feel the environment has been captured to your liking (Figure 6-5). To see if things shaped up properly, you can edit the viewing perspective of the scene by using your mouse to control the angle of the Output view from within Skanect.

Figure 6-5.
Scanning an environment in real time with Skanect

Pause the program and then click the Save button. Save the *.ply* file in a convenient, easy-to-find place. We'll now import the newly created *.ply* scene into MeshLab.

Open up MeshLab and click File → Import Mesh. Depending on the amount of mesh points you captured, the import process may take anywhere from a few seconds to a minute. You're now able to manipulate the data from within MeshLab. Try using the Measuring tool to gauge the distance from one point to another (Figure 6-6).

Figure 6-6.
MeshLab import using the Measurement tool

HACK 36 Use Processing to Create a 3D Scanner with Mesh Viewer

Another great means of producing a 3D mesh model using the Kinect comes to us in the form of a Processing sketch developed by Javier Garcia Carpio.

This hack requires the use of two sketches. The Kinect 3D Scanner sketch allows you to take a scan of an object or area, and the Mesh Viewer sketch displays the results of the scan.

Download the required sketches from the following locations:

- Kinect 3D Scanner (*http://www.openprocessing.org/sketch/62534*)
- Kinect Mesh Viewer (*http://www.openprocessing.org/sketch/62533*)

The libraries used include:

- SimpleOpenNI
- controlP5
- Hemesh

Start by making sure the libraries just listed are snug and cozy in the *Processing/ libraries* directory. Begin by opening up the Kinect 3D Scanner (shown in Figure 6-7).

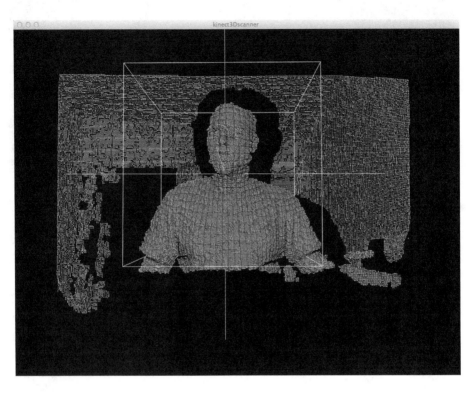

Figure 6-7.
Kinect 3D Scanner interface

You'll need to tweak the Kinect 3D Scanner control panel (Figure 6-8) to place the box around the subject you're trying to scan. In my case, I was sitting about two and a half feet away from my Kinect sensor. I had to bring the box Z value down to almost nothing to bring it close enough to capture my upper body.

Once the box area has been set properly, smile for the 3D volumetric depth sensing camera, click the Take Scan checkbox, and say, "CHEESE!" It may take a moment or two before the scan is completed. Once the live video feed returns to the Kinect 3D Scanner sketch, your mesh should be ready to check out. It's waiting for you in the *Procssing/sketches/Kinect3DScanner/* folder. The scans will be labeled *face0.col* and *face0.hemesh*, with the exact number depending on how many you've taken.

To view your scan, you'll now need to move the files into the *meshViewer/data* folder. Feel free to replace the ones that are already there courtesy of Javier.

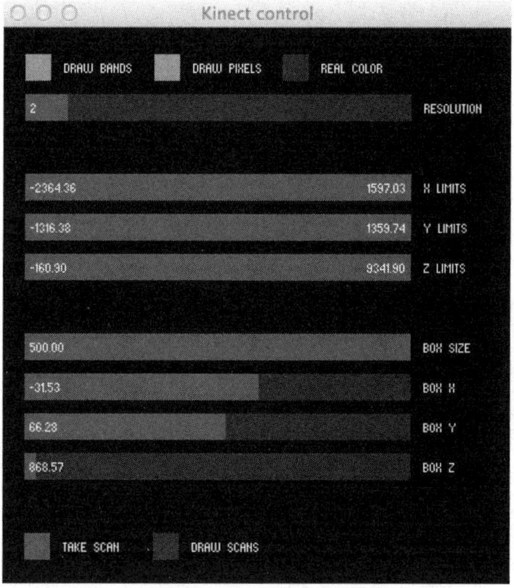

Figure 6-8.
Kinect 3D Scanner control panel

The following code, located in the *meshViewer.pde* file, determines where and what to look for when importing your scans.

```
// Read the mesh files
mesh1 = loadMesh(file+"0"+".hemesh");
mesh2 = loadMesh(file+"1"+".hemesh");
mesh3 = loadMesh(file+"2"+".hemesh");
mesh4 = loadMesh(file+"3"+".hemesh");
mesh5 = loadMesh(file+"4"+".hemesh");

// Read the color files
col1 = loadColors(file+"0"+".col");
col2 = loadColors(file+"1"+".col");
col3 = loadColors(file+"2"+".col");
col4 = loadColors(file+"3"+".col");
col5 = loadColors(file+"4"+".col");
```

Feel free to change these values depending on your desired end results. See Figure 6-9 for a sample scan.

Figure 6-9.
Kinect 3D scan in Mesh Viewer

That's it. Take as many scans as you'd like and create your own gallery of scanned objects. You can use your mouse to rotate and adjust the viewing angle of your scan. If you dug this hack, check out Javier Garica Carpio's OpenProcessing portfolio page at *http://www.openprocessing.org/user/16300*. Be sure to also check out his Vimeo video demos at *https://vimeo.com/jagracar*.

HACK 37 Import a Scanned Object for Printing with MakerBot

Brian Jepson, an editor for O'Reilly, was kind enough to lend his talents for this great hack, which uses Kyle McDonald's KinecToStl app and Blender to create a 3D mesh capable of being imported into MakerBot. This guide will explain how to scan something using the Kinect, and then print it on the MakerBot.

It's very easy to scan something with the Kinect, but the models that you get from it are quite complex. This guide focuses on simplifying those models while retaining as much detail as possible, with the goal of making it faster to slice and print your designs.

These instructions were tested on the Mac.

KINECT HACKS

First, you'll need to download and install Kyle McDonald's KinectToStl from *https://github.com/kylemcdonald/Makerbot/tree/master/KinectToStl*. Plug the Kinect into a wall outlet for power, and plug the USB cable into your Mac.

Run KinectToStl and have someone (or something) stand in front of the screen. Drag the mouse in the view to rotate around and adjust the zCutoff to set the depth of the scan (rotate the mouse around to get a sense of how deep the scan is).

Use fovWidth and fovHeight to adjust the width and height of the field of view. Say cheese, then click the checkbox to the left of exportStl to capture the subject (Figure 6-10).

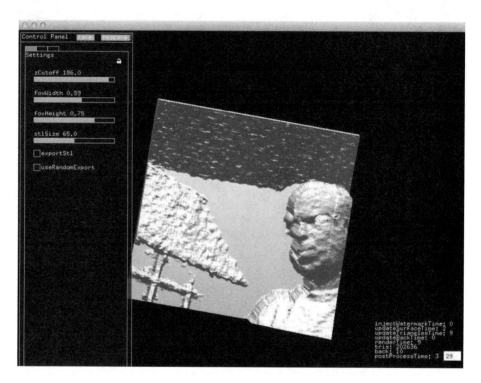

Figure 6-10.
KinectToStl scanned image

There is a *data/* subdirectory in the same location that the KinectToStl app lives. Look in this directory for the most recent file. The file will have a name like *Kinect Export 2011-08-13 at 16.51.53.stl*. Move this file to another folder (wherever you want to save it for future use) and give it a meaningful name.

You've got your scan, but if you try to print it now, it's going to take forever. Let's simplify it. Download and install MeshLab, an open source program for working with 3D meshes, from *http://meshlab.sourceforge.net* (as described previously).

Quit MeshLab if you already have it running, then right-click the STL file you got from KinectToStl, and choose Open With → MeshLab. When MeshLab opens, it will pop up a dialog box with an option to Unify Duplicated Vertices; select it and click OK. You should see your subject appear in the MeshLab window, as shown in Figure 6-11.

Figure 6-11.
Scanned object in MeshLab

Now you'll need to click the Filters menu, then open the "Remeshing, simplification, and reconstruction" menu and find Quadric Edge Collapse Decimation. Hover the mouse over the option, think about what an awesome name it has, and then click it. This will simplify your 3D model. You want to reduce the number of faces to around 20,000. Now set the Percentage Reduction to .75 and click Apply.

Drag in the model to rotate it and inspect it. If it looks good, click Apply until you're close to 20,000 faces and still looking good.

Now it's time to export the model. Click Close to dimiss the Quadric Edge Collapse Decimation dialog and then click File → Export Mesh As…. Give it a new filename (don't overwrite your original, since you've decimated a lot of original information), select the STL file format, and click Save.

KINECT HACKS

You could print what you have now, but it's likely that it's too deep, and what's more, there's also a big platform at the bottom of it. To solve this problem, download and install Blender from *http://www.blender.org*.

Run Blender, and marvel at how complicated the user interface is. Then ponder the fact that it's much simpler than it used to be!

Right away, you'll notice a cube. We'll use this cube to chop away at the STL file. First off, let's make the cube really big. In Blender, zoom out until the cube is a tiny dot. On the Mac, you can zoom in and out by pinching. Move the cursor close to the cube and press S (to scale it). Drag until the cube fills the screen, and then press Enter or Return.

Next you need to import the STL file. Click the File menu and choose Import → STL. In the file chooser that appears, navigate to wherever you saved the STL file and choose it. You won't be able to see the STL file, but if you right-click-drag (or Control-click-drag), you'll be able to move it to the top of the cube.

If you absolutely can't figure out where the heck the STL file is after you import it, right-click (or Control-click) once on the cube, then right-click-drag (or Control-click-drag) the cube around instead of the STL.

Your goal is to mask out all the parts of the STL that you don't want, as shown in Figure 6-11.

Now it's time to erase the parts you don't want. Right-click (or Control-click) on the cube to select it. Shift-right-click (or Shift-Control-click) on the STL file. Now both objects should be selected. On the right side of the window, look for a tiny wrench icon and click it.

Click the menu that says "Add modifier" and choose Boolean; then, under Operation, choose Difference. Click the box-shaped icon under Object, and click Cube. Wait, possibly a minute or more, for Blender to think. Once that's done, click Apply.

Right-click (or Control-click) and right-click-drag on the cube to pull it away from the STL you imported. Press Return or Enter. If you followed these steps exactly, you should have successfully cropped the STL file (it will be shorter, without a platform). Right-click (or Control-click) the STL you just cropped to select it, and choose File → Export STL. Give it a new name, and save it somewhere.

Now you're pretty much ready to print. Open the cropped file in Replicator G, select the Move option, click Center, and then click "Put on Platform." If you want to, select the Scale option and make your object bigger. Click Generate GCode (save changes when prompted to do so), generate your GCode, and when you're ready, print your scan. See Figure 6-12 for the end result.

Figure 6-12.
3D MakerBot printout

Now that you've simplified and cropped your 3D scan, you can print it on your MakerBot in much less time than if you'd simply tried to print the raw scan!

HACK 38 Set Up PCL and OpenCV

Before we start aligning as many point clouds as your computer's memory can hold, creating complex 3D worlds from gazillions of pixels, we'll align just a single pair of overlapping point clouds. And even before we can do that, we need to learn how to associate points found in both images. To achieve all this, we will build upon existing libraries to save us tons of work, so the first step is to set up the libraries that will provide us with the powerful tools we need.

I have tried to keep the code as readable as possible, sometimes sacrificing a performance gain for code clarity. The code is just a template for you, so feel free to tweak it to your heart's content.

Fusing the stream of RGB-D images to a high-quality world model while you brandish the Kinect through your living room requires sophisticated algorithms. But fear not: to keep our efforts to a minimum, we will make extensive use of existing, freely available tools that have been crafted and extensively tested by highly skilled programmers. For image analysis in 2D, we will use OpenCV (*http://opencv.itseez.com/*). For 3D-related processing, we employ PCL (Point Cloud Library; *http://pointclouds.org/*). PCL uses algorithms and data types from the Eigen library (*http://eigen.tuxfamily.org*), so we'll make use of Eigen too. All three are written, at least partly, in C\++, which is a good language to process heaps of data as fast as possible.

To understand what's happening under the hood, you will need a fairly good grasp of this language. In particular, Eigen and PCL make heavy use of C++ advanced features, which sometimes is detrimental to the clarity of the code. Where I feel things are getting too arcane, I will provide explanation, but a good C++ reference will nevertheless be an invaluable companion for less experienced C++ programmers.

All of the mentioned libraries are available as open source projects with permissive libraries (BSD, BSD, and LGPL). All of them are also available for Linux, OS X, Windows, and even Android (which, in fact, is just another Linux). Linux is freely available for everybody, so I'll explain the system-specific setup for Ubuntu Linux~11.10, which you can download at *http://www.ubuntu.com/download*.

For the installation of the libraries, we will go the easy route and pick binary packages. Eigen is included in the Ubuntu repositories, so it can be effortlessly installed. Open a terminal (e.g., gnome-terminal or xterm) and run the following commands.

```
sudo apt-get update
sudo apt-get install libeigen3-dev
```

For PCL, we follow the appropriate installation instructions located at *http://point clouds.org/downloads/linux.html*.

```
sudo add-apt-repository ppa:v-launchpad-jochen-sprickerhof-de/pcl
sudo apt-get update
sudo apt-get install libpcl-all
```

OpenCV binary packages are somewhat hidden, but if you know where to look, OpenCV is just as easily installed. We partly follow the installation guide from *http://www.ros.org/wiki/electric/Installation/Ubuntu* for the Robot Operating System (ROS) on ros.org. The first command is too long for a single line here, but in your terminal, you should not break the line.

```
echo "deb http://packages.ros.org/ros/ubuntu oneiric main"
  |sudo tee /etc/apt/sources.list.d/ros-latest.list
wget http://packages.ros.org/ros.key -O - | sudo apt-key add -
sudo apt-get update
sudo apt-get install libopencv2.3-dev
```

Everything else we need will automatically be installed through the dependencies of these three packages.

Display a Colored Point Cloud

Continuing on from the previous hack, it's time to get some data out of your Kinect. There are several ways to get RGB-D images or point clouds. The most convenient seems to be the OpenNIGrabber framework of PCL, which you can download at *http:// bit.ly/TfZGKQ*. To get data from the grabber, we need to give it a function to call with said data. In this function, we can do with the data whatever we please. So, in this section, we write a small piece of code that defines a function to obtain a colored point cloud and, when called, displays the point cloud using the CloudViewer of PCL's visualization module.

Think of a good name for the project and create a new directory for it using a terminal application:

```
mkdir _<project-name>_
```

I will use the name *nicv*, mostly because it is short and I am not the creative type. Feel free to choose a better name. After creating the project, open your favorite editor (or use gedit if you are new to Ubuntu and don't want to spend much time choosing an editor) and create a new file called *main.cpp* in the fresh project directory.

First, we will include the required header files for PCL's OpenNIGrabber.

The API specification for the OpenNIGrabber can be found at http://bit.ly/SiBEOl.

This link should always point at the latest version. If you followed the earlier installation instructions, you will find the API documentation locally at */usr/share/doc/libpcl-1.5-doc/doc/pcl-1.5/html/index.html*, along with CloudViewer at *http://bit.ly/XgsoN2*. Also, since PCL is heavily templated and we will be using only one specific type of point cloud, we'll save some time in the future and define a new type name as a shortcut to a PCL point cloud with color information.

```
#include <pcl/io/openni_grabber.h>
#include <pcl/visualization/cloud_viewer.h>
typedef pcl::PointCloud<pcl::PointXYZRGBA> cloud_type;
```

Next, we define the function the OpenNIGrabber should call with the data. And since the data should be shown in the CloudViewer, it also gets a pointer to the viewer it will use to display the cloud.

```
void cloud_callback(cloud_type::ConstPtr cloud,
                    pcl::visualization::CloudViewer* cloud_viewer)
```

```
    {
      if(!cloud_viewer->wasStopped())
        cloud_viewer->showCloud(cloud);
    }
```

So, whenever new data is available (and no previous invocation of the cloud_callback is running), we'll get a call by the driver. We then check whether the viewer is alive and, if so, command it to display the fresh point cloud.

The rest of the code is the obligatory main function. It instantiates an object of the CloudViewer class, which will create a nice window with the specified title. In the next line, we create an instance of the OpenNIGrabber.

```
int main (int argc, const char** argv)
{
  pcl::visualization::CloudViewer cloud_viewer("World Viewer");

  pcl::OpenNIGrabber grabber;
```

Then a strange thing happens: we use the boost library to create an object that acts like a regular function pointer, but keeps a hidden treasure.

```
boost::function<void (const cloud_type::ConstPtr&)> f =
boost::bind(cloud_callback, _1, &cloud_viewer);
```

The syntax is confusing, to say the least, and is hardly understandable without reading it several times. The template parameters (in the angle brackets) specify the signature of the function—that is, the return type and (in parentheses) the data type(s) of the arguments. So here we create an object that can be called like a function, returns void (i.e., nothing), and takes one reference to a constant: cloud_type::ConstPtr.

Now what comes next? It's one of the two forms—the point cloud we defined will occur in our code. This form is used often in the PCL code and is a typedef to a reference-counting (constant) pointer implemented in the boost library. So, if you see this, think of it as no more than a constant pointer that deletes the object it points to, when the last pointer goes out of scope. So, the left side of the assignment means we want to get an object that acts like a function, and it will be called f. The type of the function is precisely defined so that the OpenNIGrabber can call it.

The next line (i.e., the right side of the assignment) creates this function object using boost::bind, which will create a function mimicry object from the callback function we just defined. More magic follows: the function object will be called with one parameter, represented by _1. It should call the cloud_callback with both the cloud it gets when called and a pointer to the cloud viewer. So we specify _1 and the address of our cloud_viewer object, in that order.

I hope you are still here, because the remainder is fairly straightforward. Having created the boost function object, we register it with the grabber, start the latter, and sleep until the viewer is stopped.

```
grabber.registerCallback (f);

grabber.start();
while (!cloud_viewer.wasStopped()) {
  sleep(1);
}
grabber.stop();
return 0;
}
```

Now let's compile, link, and run this! A quick, convenient, and portable way to build our project is provided by CMake. Create a new file, *CMakeLists.txt*, next to your *main.cpp* and put the following content in it:

```
cmake_minimum_required(VERSION 2.8 FATAL_ERROR)

project(nicv)

# Activate this for use with a debugger
# SET(CMAKE_BUILD_TYPE RelWithDebInfo )

find_package(PCL 1.2 REQUIRED)

include_directories(${PCL_INCLUDE_DIRS})
link_directories(${PCL_LIBRARY_DIRS})
add_definitions(${PCL_DEFINITIONS})

add_executable (nicv main.cpp)
target_link_libraries (nicv ${PCL_LIBRARIES})
```

This will mainly search for PCL, find it, and set the correct include and linker paths. The three occurrences of **nicv** can be replaced with a name of your choice; this will be the name of your project and executable. From the command prompt, first execute **cmake .** (the dot signifies the current directory). This checks your software setup and creates a makefile containing precise information for the build process. Second, use the command **make** to run the compiler and linker with the information stored in the makefile. As long as you made no typos, you can now start your program like this: **./<name>** (you'd use **./nicv** if you didn't come up with a name replacement yet).

Figure 6-13 shows the final product.

Figure 6-13.
Display cloud

HACK 40 Use Features to Track Camera Image Motion

Now the 3D information is cool, but there are powerful algorithms we can apply to the 2D data that allow us to track the motion of the camera image. Tracking requires that we store information about the images and keep it between the calls to our callback function. Object orientation is definitely overused, but this is a good opportunity to create a class. The project setup is quick: create a new directory and put the header file *tracker.h* in it. This will give us a good idea of what the class should do and should contain:

```
#include <opencv2/opencv.hpp>
#include <vector>

class Tracker
{
  public:
    Tracker();
    std::vector<cv::DMatch>
    match_and_filter(const cv::Mat& descriptors);
    void new_image(cv::Mat& gray_img);
```

```
private:
    cv::Ptr<cv::FeatureDetector> featureDetector_;
    cv::Ptr<cv::DescriptorExtractor> descriptorExtractor_;
    cv::Ptr<cv::DescriptorMatcher> descriptorMatcher_;
    std::vector<cv::KeyPoint> last_keypoints_;
};
```

First we include the main header from OpenCV, which takes care of including all the individual headers for us. We also use the vector from the standard template library.

The class itself has a constructor, two methods, and some private member variables. The first three variables contain the elements for finding, describing, and matching small image patches. For the latest image, the positions and descriptions of these *image features* will be stored in the last two member variables. If you wonder about the trailing underscore, it is a technique that helps you distinguish the member variables from local variables at a glance.

So let's implement the constructor and methods. Create the file *tracker.cpp* next to the header file. And, of course, we directly include it.

```
Tracker::Tracker()
{
    featureDetector_ = cv::FeatureDetector::create( "SURF" );
    descriptorExtractor_ = cv::DescriptorExtractor::create( "SURF" );
    descriptorMatcher_ = cv::DescriptorMatcher::create( "BruteForce");
    if(featureDetector_.empty()
        || descriptorExtractor_.empty()
        || descriptorMatcher_.empty() )
      std::cerr << "Error creating detector, extractor or matcher.\n";
}
```

The constructor sets up the feature processing. There are several algorithms implemented in OpenCV. We are using **SURF** for detection and description, because the generated features are very stable over appearance variations, which is an important quality for tracking. Feel free to try out the (much slower) **SIFT** or the (much faster and less stable) **ORB** descriptors as well.

Now let's define the entry point for new data.

```
void Tracker::new_image(cv::Mat& gray_img)
{
    std::vector<cv::KeyPoint> keypoints;
    featureDetector_->detect(gray_img, keypoints);
    std::cout << "Found " << keypoints.size() << " keypoints\n";
    if(keypoints.size() == 0)
      return;
```

```
//Compute descriptors for keypoints
cv::Mat descriptors(1, keypoints.size(), CV_32FC3);
descriptorExtractor_->compute(gray_img, keypoints, descriptors);

cv::drawKeypoints(gray_img, keypoints, gray_img);

if(!last_keypoints_.empty()) //First Frame
{
  std::vector<cv::DMatch> matches = match_and_filter(descriptors);
  std::cout << "Matches:\n" << matches.size() << std::endl;
  if(matches.size() > 0)
  {
    for(int i = 0; i < matches.size(); i++){
      cv::Scalar color(255);
      cv::line(gray_img,
               last_keypoints_[matches[i].trainIdx].pt,
               keypoints[matches[i].queryIdx].pt,
               color, 2);
    }
  }
}
std::vector<cv::Mat> tmp;
tmp.push_back(descriptors);
descriptorMatcher_->clear();
descriptorMatcher_->add(tmp);
last_keypoints_.swap(keypoints);

  }
}
```

The method gets a `cv::Mat` as parameter, which is OpenCV's matrix data type used for images. In the first block, keypoints are detected in that image. For each keypoint, a description is stored. The description is a bunch of numbers, and `cv::Mat` can contain any numbers in a 2D (i.e., row and column) layout. So each description is stored as a row.

Having extracted the descriptions, we draw the keypoints to the image, so we can see them later.

The big `if` block checks whether we have previous data to compare against. If so, the new features are compared to the old by a function yet to be written. Matches, if any, are drawn as lines, connecting the position of the current feature with the position of the one it has been matched with. In the end, we prepare the next run of the method by replacing any previous information with the freshly extracted features.

The class is nearly complete, lacking only the matching of features. Matching is a little challenging, so we employ a little trick: we can compute the difference between two feature descriptions, but we don't know what the difference means! The difference is a distance—not spatial, but rather an appearance distance. There's not even a unit for that. But even though the appearance of something will change from one image to the next, we can usually rely on the fact that it doesn't change so much that it looks as different as the most similar thing. For example, if I took pictures of your family, you won't look the same in every picture, but you will still look more similar to yourself than to your parents. So here it goes:

```
std::vector<cv::DMatch>
  Tracker::match_and_filter(const cv::Mat& descriptors)
{
  std::vector<cv::DMatch> result;
  if(last_keypoints_.empty()) { //First frame
    return result;
  }

  //For each keypoint of the new image
  //get two matches in the database
  std::vector<std::vector<cv::DMatch> > pairs_of_matches;
  descriptorMatcher_->knnMatch(descriptors, pairs_of_matches, 2);

  for(unsigned int i=0; i< pairs_of_matches.size(); i++){
    float ratio = pairs_of_matches[i][0].distance /
      pairs_of_matches[i][1].distance;
    if(ratio < 0.5){
      result.push_back(pairs_of_matches[i][0]);
    }
  }
  return result;
}
```

The call to knnMatch fills pairs_of_matches. For every descriptor, it searches for the two most similar descriptors stored in the DescriptorMatcher. These two "neighbors" are put in a vector, which is itself put in a vector. So, to filter for the good matches, the for loop goes through the outer vector and compares the two nearest neighbors against each other as just described. Play with the threshold value for the ratio, and you will see how the amount of bad matches will increase rapidly when the value approaches 1.

The next part is very similar to the previous hack: create a main.cpp file in your project directory. We again use the OpenNIGrabber, but not the CloudViewer, so the includes are a little different. We explicitly need includes for the PointCloud and Point classes. Yet our point_type and cloud_type typedefs are the same as before.

```
#include "tracker.h"
#include <pcl/point_cloud.h>
#include <pcl/point_types.h>
#include <pcl/io/openni_grabber.h>

typedef pcl::PointXYZRGBA point_type;
typedef pcl::PointCloud<point_type> cloud_type;
```

Before defining the callback, we need to take a little detour this time that converts the point cloud to a monocular 2D image, so we can use it as the parameter for the **new_image** method. The function is pretty straightforward: it uses the **create** method of **cv::Mat** to make the second parameter a grayscale image that fits to the cloud given in the first parameter. Then the color value of each point is combined to a grayscale value. Now, this is, of course, not the most efficient way of getting the image, but it is also not as bad as it seems. There is no way to directly get a grayscale image out of the Kinect driver, so we might as well flatten a 3D point cloud.

```
void convert_to_img(const cloud_type& cloud, cv::Mat& gray_img)
{
  gray_img.create(cloud.height, cloud.width, CV_8UC1);
  for(int row = 0; row < cloud.height;row++){
    for(int col = 0; col < cloud.width;col++){
      const point_type& pt = cloud.at(col, row);
      gray_img.at<unsigned char>(row, col) =
        0.3*pt.r + 0.6*pt.g + 0.1*pt.b;
    }//for col
  }//for row
}
```

The callback function again gets a cloud and a pointer to something else. This time it's a pointer to the **Tracker** object that is given the image extracted from the cloud. Afterward, we use OpenCV's **imshow** to display the image with the keypoints that are drawn within **new_image**. The call to **waitKey** is more important than it seems. Without it, the window of **imshow** wouldn't be updated. When you press a key while the window is focused, it will return the (positive) ASCII value of the key, in which case the callback will activate the ejection seat.

```
void cloud_callback(cloud_type::ConstPtr cloud,
                    Tracker* tracker)
{
  cv::Mat gray_img; //Create a grayscale image for feature extraction
  convert_to_img(*cloud, gray_img); //Extract 2D information
  tracker->new_image(gray_img);
```

```
  cv::imshow("Current View", gray_img);
  if(cv::waitKey(200) > 0)
    exit(0);
}
```

The obligatory **main** function is just as in the last hack, except with the **CloudViewer** being replaced by the **Tracker**.

```
int main (int argc, const char** argv)
{
  Tracker tracker;

  boost::function<void (const cloud_type::ConstPtr&)> f =
    boost::bind(cloud_callback, _1, &tracker);

  pcl::OpenNIGrabber interface;
  interface.registerCallback (f);

  interface.start();
  while(true)
    sleep(1);
  interface.stop();
  return 0;
}
```

The last piece missing is the file *CMakeLists.txt*, again very similar to the one in the previous hack. In addition to the optional name changes, there is a new line to find OpenCV. There are two C++ files to compile now, so the **add_executable** line mentions both. And to let the linker know about OpenCV, we add a variable containing its whereabouts to the last line.

```
cmake_minimum_required(VERSION 2.8 FATAL_ERROR)

project(motion_tracker)

# Activate this for use with a debugger
# SET(CMAKE_BUILD_TYPE RelWithDebInfo )

find_package(PCL 1.2 REQUIRED)
find_package( OpenCV REQUIRED)

include_directories(${PCL_INCLUDE_DIRS})
link_directories(${PCL_LIBRARY_DIRS})
add_definitions(${PCL_DEFINITIONS})
```

```
add_executable (motion_tracker main.cpp tracker.cpp)
target_link_libraries (motion_tracker ${OpenCV_LIBS}
   ${PCL_LIBRARIES})
```

Great—you are ready to go! As before, the command **cmake** executed in your project directory will generate a makefile. Execute **make** to generate the program from source according to the information in the makefile. The executable name in the preceding *CMakeLists.txt* is **motion_tracker**, so if everything went well, go ahead and start it. Unless you point the Kinect at a blank wall or cover it in darkness, you should see many colorful circles indicating points of salient appearance. Move the Kinect to see your movement visualized by lines indicating where the features were found in the last frame. See Figure 6-14.

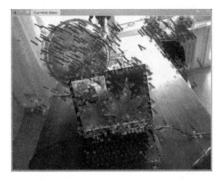

Figure 6-14.
Motion tracker

HACK 41 Fuse Point Clouds into a Consistent 3D Model

Tracking the motion of image features as in the previous hack is fun, but we want to tap the potential of this technique some more. Every recent digital camera offers some functionality for stitching panorama shots. And if the onboard functionality is not sufficient, there is plenty of software available to do a magnificent stitching job, in 2D. Wouldn't it be great to have this functionality for our 3D images? Yes, it would, and so we set out on the mission to establish this (as of today) not-yet-commonplace 3D-stitching software.

In 2D, stitching is mostly done with the assumption that the camera motion was either in parallel to the image plane or a rotation about the focal point; the latter is more common, but the software will still act as if the individual images were in a plane (or on a cylinder around the camera). In any event, the software performs the alignment by shifting and rotating the images in 2D, such that they overlap correctly. For 3D images, the shifting and rotating becomes a little trickier due to the three extra dimensions (one more shifting axis and two more for rotation), but we can cope with that. The result will be complex 3D worlds stitched together from images taken from arbitrary camera positions—well, almost arbitrary (of course, we still need the images to overlap).

How exactly do we achieve this? Based on feature correspondences, we can reidentify points in a set of images. We also know the full 3D position of these points with respect to the camera position. Knowing how these presumably fixed positions "moved" relative to the camera enables us to find out the motion of the camera itself, and thus align the point clouds to get a consistent model of the world. This alignment process is also called *registration*.

This hack will build on what you learned in the previous two, but the modifications needed are extensive, so we will write the new program from scratch. The complexity of the code will be slightly higher than before, but the principles stay the same. Our project will consist of four files. First, as before, we have a *CMakeLists.txt* file containing the project's build information. Second and third, *world_model.h* and *world_model.cpp*, contain the definition and implementation of the class for computing and managing the world state. The fourth file will be *main.cpp*, where all the setup will be done including an interface to the user.

Quickest job first: let's create a new directory and put *CMakeLists.txt* in it with the following content:

```
cmake_minimum_required(VERSION 2.8 FATAL_ERROR)

project(world_modelling)

# Activate this for use with a debugger
# SET(CMAKE_BUILD_TYPE RelWithDebInfo )

find_package(PCL 1.2 REQUIRED)
find_package( OpenCV REQUIRED)

include_directories(${PCL_INCLUDE_DIRS})
link_directories(${PCL_LIBRARY_DIRS})
add_definitions(${PCL_DEFINITIONS})

add_executable (world_modelling main.cpp world_model.cpp)
target_link_libraries (world_modelling ${OpenCV_LIBS}
  ${PCL_LIBRARIES})
```

As you can see, there is not much different from the previous hack's file. The only changes are the project and executable name, and of course the referenced source files. This is kind of boring, so let's proceed.

The class for computing and storing the world still has similarities to the `Tracker` class, but the increased functionality is already evident in the `private` section of the interface description. Next to OpenCV and the STL vector, we now also include the "core" of Eigen. Eigen being a library mainly for linear algebra, this preludes the usage of some heavy math. But happily Eigen and PCL will make things easy for us. Again, we find the PCL includes and typedefs of the heavily used `cloud_type`.

The public interface is very clean. Aside from the constructor, there are only two public methods. The method `add_cloud` takes 3D and 2D data from the Kinect and incorporates it to the world model. So here the bulk of the work is done (or delegated). The other public method simply provides access to the point cloud representation of the world. Everything else is hidden under the hood.

Here is the content of *world_model.h*.

```
#include <opencv2/opencv.hpp>
#include <vector>
#include <Eigen/Core>
#include "pcl/point_cloud.h"
#include "pcl/point_types.h"

typedef pcl::PointXYZRGBA point_type;
typedef pcl::PointCloud<point_type> cloud_type;

class WorldModel
{
  public:
    WorldModel();
    void add_cloud(cloud_type::ConstPtr cloud, cv::Mat& gray_img,
        cv::Mat& mask);
    cloud_type::ConstPtr get_world_cloud();
  private:
    ///Store 3D position for each feature in <new_keypoint_coords_>
    void keypoints_in_3d(const cloud_type &cloud,
                         std::vector<cv::KeyPoint>& keypoints);

    ///Find and store matches with good nearest neighbor ratio
    void match_and_filter(const cv::Mat& descriptors);

    ///Run RANSAC for robust motion estimation from matches
    void ransac(Eigen::ArrayXi& inliers,
                Eigen::Affine3f& motion_out,
                int ransac_iterations = 100);

    ///Randomly set <sample_size> elements of <inliers> to 1
```

```
void sample_matches(int sample_size,
                    Eigen::ArrayXi& inliers);

///Compute the <motion_candidate> from the <inliers> flag
void motion_estimate(const Eigen::ArrayXi& inliers,
                     Eigen::Affine3f& motion_candidate);

///Flag matches as inliers based on the <threshold>
void compute_inliers(const Eigen::Affine3f& motion_candidate,
                     float threshold,
                     Eigen::ArrayXi& inliers);

///Compute the root mean squared error for given inlier match
float compute_rmse(const Eigen::Affine3f& motion_candidate,
                   const Eigen::ArrayXi& inliers);

///World representation
std::vector<Eigen::Vector3f> world_keypoint_coords_;
std::vector<cv::Mat> world_descriptors_;
Eigen::ArrayXi inlier_counts;
cloud_type world_cloud_;

///Information about the newest data, used by RANSAC
std::vector<Eigen::Vector3f> new_keypoint_coords_;
std::vector<cv::DMatch> new_matches_;

///Feature processing stuff
cv::Ptr<cv::FeatureDetector> featureDetector_;
cv::Ptr<cv::DescriptorExtractor> descriptorExtractor_;
cv::Ptr<cv::DescriptorMatcher> descriptorMatcher_;
};
```

For the implementation of the class, we create the file *world_model.cpp*. Of course, we include the respective header and two more from PCL: one that provides the functionality to compute the motion from point correspondences, and one for the functionality to transform a point cloud using such a motion. We'll need that because all clouds, except for the first, will need to be moved such that they fit together nicely. The constructor is almost the same as before, yet with one important update: we use the `FlannBased` matcher instead of the `BruteForce` one we used in the previous hack. What's the difference? We are searching for good matches between image features. Depending on the scene, a couple hundred features are found per image.

To find the best match for one new feature, you can compare it one by one to all the previous ones; this is known as the brute force method. However, the structure of the feature storage needn't be a simple list that we search one by one—we can sort the images into a tree structure, which quickly leads us to the best match at each branch based on the feature to be matched. Building this structure takes time, but for a huge number of features, this cost pays off quickly. And building 3D models from many images piles up quite a heap of features.

The following is the first part of *world_model.cpp*. (This file's content will be split into sections separated by brief explanations in the following pages.)

```cpp
#include <pcl/common/transforms.h>
#include <pcl/common/transformation_from_correspondences.h>
#include "world_model.h"

WorldModel::WorldModel () :
  world_descriptors_(1)
{
  featureDetector_ = cv::FeatureDetector::create( "SURF" );
  descriptorExtractor_ = cv::DescriptorExtractor::create( "SURF" );
  descriptorMatcher_ = cv::DescriptorMatcher::create( "FlannBased");
  if(featureDetector_.empty()
      || descriptorExtractor_.empty()
      || descriptorMatcher_.empty() )
    std::cerr << "Error creating detector
                  or extractor or matcher.\n";
}
```

Now comes the interesting part: the **add_cloud** method takes a point cloud and two OpenCV matrices. The first matrix should contain the monochrome image of the camera; the second one contains a flag for each pixel, indicating whether its distance could be measured. This mask is used directly in the feature detection. Detection of good image features is costly and we need the depth information for the later calculation, so masking areas where no depth was found speeds up the detection process.

Next, **keypoints_in_3d** fills the vector of **keypoint_coords** with the corresponding 3D positions. If there are fewer than 10 keypoints, getting a reliable motion estimate is highly improbable, so we rather skip.

```cpp
void WorldModel::add_cloud(cloud_type::ConstPtr cloud,
cv::Mat& gray_img, cv::Mat& mask)
{

  //Compute keypoints and get their 3D coordinates
  std::vector<cv::KeyPoint> keypoints;
  featureDetector_->detect(gray_img, keypoints, mask );
  std::vector<Eigen::Vector3f> keypoint_coords;
  keypoints_in_3d(*cloud, keypoints, keypoint_coords);
```

```
std::cout << "Found " << keypoint_coords.size() <<
          " usable keypoints\n";
if(keypoint_coords.size() < 10)
  return;
```

If things are more promising, we continue by computing the feature description for the keypoints. Then, for the first shot we take, we store the information gathered so far in the class's member variables. The as-yet empty descriptor matrix in the world_descriptors_ vector is assigned the descriptors; the keypoint_coords_ vector swaps its data with world_keypoint_coords_ (which may seem weird, but avoids copying of the data); and the current cloud is appended to the empty world_cloud. In addition, we initialize a one-dimensional array to keep statistics about the image features. We want to know, for each one, how often it has been successfully used for a motion estimation.

```
cv::Mat descriptors(1, keypoints.size(), CV_32FC3);
descriptorExtractor_->compute( gray_img, keypoints, descriptors);

if(world_descriptors_[0].empty()) //First Frame
{
  world_descriptors_[0] = descriptors;
  world_keypoint_coords_.swap(keypoint_coords);
  world_cloud_ += *cloud;
  inlier_counts = Eigen::ArrayXi::Zero(descriptors.rows);
}
```

For the first iteration, the bulk of the work is done. All that follows is the training of the descriptor matcher, which builds the search structure mentioned previously. Now, before we get there, we need to specify what happens after the first frame (in the else block). It starts straightforward, by calling match_and_filter to get—hopefully correct--matches to the descriptors found in earlier images. We then throw the matches into the function ransac_motion_from_matches, which we will implement later in *tools.cpp*. For now, we just trust it to compute the motion, or return false, in which case we take the quick way out.

In the successful case, we use the computed motion to revert the motion of the camera, so all the keypoint coordinates from the new image are moved to the coordinate system of the world_keypoint_coords_. And since we stored the keypoint coordinates for the first image as-is, we will always transform the new keypoints to the coordinate system of the first camera image.

```
else
{
  std::vector<cv::DMatch> matches = match_and_filter(descriptors);
  std::cout << "Matches:\n" << matches.size() << std::endl;
```

```
Eigen::ArrayXi new_inliers(descriptors.rows);
Eigen::Affine3f motion = Eigen::Affine3f::Identity();
if(!ransac_motion_from_matches(matches, world_keypoint_coords_,
    keypoint_coords, new_inliers, motion, 100))
{
  return;//no valid motion
}
std::cout << "Motion:\n" << motion.matrix() << std::endl;
```

In the successful case, we use the computed motion to revert the motion of the camera, so all the keypoint coordinates from the new image are moved to the coordinate system of the **world_keypoint_coords_**. And since we stored the keypoint coordinates for the first image as-is, we will always transform the new keypoints to the coordinate system of the first camera image. This is done separately for keypoints that could be matched and those that couldn't. The keypoints in our world model with matching keypoints in the new image are updated with the new motion information.

We use the information in **inlier_counts** to recursively compute the new position as the average of all computed positions. If we keep the old positions, only the new (i.e., unmatched) keypoints include this error as an offset to the "real" positions, while the old ones keep their value. This inconsistency would make it increasingly difficult to determine the correctly matched features in the next images, in the worst case to the point where no consistent motion estimate could be found.

```
//Correct positions of matched features
for(unsigned int i=0; i< matches.size(); i++)
{
  if(new_inliers[matches[i].queryIdx])
  {
      int count = ++inlier_counts[matches[i].trainIdx];

      Eigen::Vector3f v1 =
        motion * keypoint_coords[matches[i].queryIdx];
      Eigen::Vector3f& v2 =
        world_keypoint_coords_[matches[i].trainIdx];
      v2 =  (float)count * v2;
      v2 =  v2+ v1;
      v2 /= count+1.0f;
  }
}
```

The handling of unmatched descriptors and their coordinates is easier: they are transformed to the world coordinate system and appended to the world model representation. After that, the inlier count statistics are extended to include the yet-unmatched-but-added new features.

```
//Preparations for next call: copy unmatched features to storage
for(unsigned int i=0; i< new_inliers.rows(); i++)
{
  if(!new_inliers[i]) { //New Feature
    world_keypoint_coords_.push_back
        (motion * keypoint_coords[i]);
    world_descriptors_[0].push_back
        (descriptors.row(i));
  }
}


//add inlier counts for new features
int unmatched_count = descriptors.rows - new_inliers.sum();
inlier_counts.conservativeResize(inlier_counts.rows()+unmatched_count);
inlier_counts.bottomRows(unmatched_count).setZero();
```

And while the feature descriptors, their coordinates, and the inlier statistics are crucial parts of our algorithm, our set goal is still to stitch the point clouds together. This works the same as for the keypoints: transform to world coordinates and append.

```
//Use the motion to "revert" the motion of the camera
cloud_type transformed_cloud;
pcl::transformPointCloud(*cloud, transformed_cloud, motion);
//Append to current world model
world_cloud_ += transformed_cloud;


}
```

We conclude the method by adding the feature descriptors to the search structure. Actually, we reconstruct the structure from scratch. You may rightfully ask why we don't append the new descriptor matrix to the **world_descriptors_**, given that it is a **std::vector**. Unfortunately, looking under the hood of the **add** function reveals that the tree structure for the fast nearest neighbor search is created from scratch anyway. Therefore, we can save ourselves some hassle with the indexing of the descriptors by packing them into one big matrix.

```
///Reconstruct descriptorMatcher from scratch
descriptorMatcher_->clear();
descriptorMatcher_->add(world_descriptors_);
std::cout << world_descriptors_[0].rows <<
" descriptors in the Database\n\n";
descriptorMatcher_->train();
}
```

The second and last public method of our class provides a constant pointer to our world point cloud so that it can be visualized.

```
cloud_type::ConstPtr WorldModel::get_world_cloud()
{
  return world_cloud_.makeShared();
}
```

The first private method we find under the hood is **keypoints_in_3d**. We now want
to make use of the real-world 3D position of each feature; however, since the Kinect
does not necessarily provide a depth value for every pixel, we need to throw out the
keypoints located at such depthless pixels. The 3D positions of the remaining keypoints are then stored in the member variable **new_keypoint_coords_**. Since we
also need the 2D keypoints, we accumulate the valid ones in another STL vector and
eventually swap its content with the original keypoint vector.

```
///Get 3D coordinates for keypoints from cloud.
///Filter out keypoints with invalid coordinates
void WorldModel::keypoints_in_3d(const cloud_type &cloud,
std::vector<cv::KeyPoint>& keypoints)
{
  std::vector<cv::KeyPoint> valid_keypoints;
  new_keypoint_coords_.clear();
  for(unsigned int i=0; i< keypoints.size(); i++){
    const cv::Point2f& pt2d = keypoints[i].pt;
    const point_type& pt3d = cloud.at(pt2d.x, pt2d.y);
    if(isnan(pt3d.z)){
      continue;
    }
    valid_keypoints.push_back(keypoints[i]);
    new_keypoint_coords_.push_back(pt3d.getVector3fMap());
  }
  std::swap(valid_keypoints, keypoints);
}
```

The next private method, **match_and_filter**, selects good matches of features in
the new image to previously seen features. This method is a nearly unmodified copy
of the **Tracker** class from the previous hack. Even though we have changed the underlying data structure for matching, OpenCV exposes a consistent interface, so the
method **knnMatch** will be used just as before. The only change is that it puts the resulting matches into a member variable instead of the return value.

```
///Computes descriptor matches. Filters by nearest neighbour ratio
void WorldModel::match_and_filter(const cv::Mat& descriptors)
{
  new_matches_.clear();
  if(world_descriptors_[0].empty()) { //First frame
    return;
  }
```

CHAPTER 6: 3D OBJECT AND SCENE RECONSTRUCTION

```
//For each keypoint of the new image
//get two matches in the database
std::vector<std::vector<cv::DMatch> > pairs_of_matches;
descriptorMatcher_->knnMatch(descriptors, pairs_of_matches, 2);

for(unsigned int i=0; i< pairs_of_matches.size(); i++){
  float ratio = pairs_of_matches[i][0].distance /
      pairs_of_matches[i][1].distance;
  if(ratio < 0.8){
    new_matches_.push_back(pairs_of_matches[i][0]);
  }
}
}
```

All the rest of the private methods implement a procedure called RANSAC, which computes the 3D motion estimation from the matches. So what is this RANSAC and why do we need it? RANSAC (RANdom SAmple Consensus) is a procedure applicable to any problem where a solution can be computed from data points, but data is noisy, and some data points might even be completely off. This is often the case with sensor data, but data from, for example, medical surveys often exhibits the same properties.

Back to motion estimation: we can easily compute a motion hypothesis from our feature matches. Since the measured position data for the features is not perfect, we want to find a motion that minimizes the distance between matching features, if all the features are aligned using that motion. Imagine a spring between each pair of features that pulls the matching features toward each other. Due to the inaccurate positions, not all springs will be able to fully contract to an optimal (and only theoretical) zero length, but the feature positions will converge to a state that minimizes the energy of the springs.

The math of both problems is indeed equivalent (assuming a linear spring model, that is). However, if some of the points are mismatched, their spring may have an exorbitant high tension in the state where the good matches would converge. This greatly distorts the motion estimate, so we better take some care. With a potentially distorted estimate, it is hard to tell which ones are the bad matches; many springs would be under strong tension now.

So, first we use a small random sample from the matches. If we are lucky and all of them are good, the motion estimate will be good too, and the good matches in the remainder should "consent" to that estimate. We will survey that using a threshold on the spring tension and call the consenting matches *inliers*. The fewer samples we use for the initial estimate, the better the chances that no bad match is included. On the downside, few samples will lead to a coarse estimate. Therefore, it makes sense to iteratively refine the estimate by including the consenting samples into the computation—of course, only while things get better (the number of inliers goes up while the average spring tension does not). And, just in case we had bad luck with the initial set of matches, we repeat the whole process several times with a newly chosen set of initial matches.

So let's have a look at the methods belonging to RANSAC: `sample_matches` is rather unspectacular. It is called to initialize the computations with a random set of (yet-to-be-verified) inliers. The second method is `motion_estimate`. The given inliers are added to a `pcl` object, which internally employs the singular value decomposition to find the best rigid motion to align the matching points.

The newly computed alignment will be assessed by two criteria:

- The new number of inliers, computed in `compute_inliers` by applying the motion and accepting all matched pairs nearer to each other than the given threshold.
- The error described before by the spring tension analogy. It is determined in `compute_rmse` as the square root of the average squared distance between the matches that have been flagged as inliers.

So all that is left to do for the `ransac` method is to use `sample_matches` for initialization, evaluate as just described, and reiterate with the new set of inliers as long as the evaluation gets better. Should the result be unsatisfactory, we start the process over with a new initialization.

```
///Flag a random subset of the feature correspondences as inliers
void WorldModel::sample_matches(int sample_size,
                                Eigen::ArrayXi& inliers)
{
  while(inliers.count() < sample_size){
    int id = rand() % new_matches_.size();
    inliers(new_matches_[id].queryIdx) = 1;
  }
}


///Compute the <motion_candidate>
///from the matches flagged in <inliers>
void WorldModel::motion_estimate(const Eigen::ArrayXi& inliers,
                                 Eigen::Affine3f& motion_candidate)
{
  pcl::TransformationFromCorrespondences tfc;
  for(int i = 0; i < new_matches_.size(); i++)
  {
    if(inliers(new_matches_[i].queryIdx)){
      const Eigen::Vector3f& q = new_keypoint_coords_
```

```
        [new_matches_[i].queryIdx];
      const Eigen::Vector3f& t = world_keypoint_coords_
        [new_matches_[i].trainIdx];
      tfc.add(q, t, 1.0);
    }
  }
  motion_candidate = tfc.getTransformation();
}


///Flag matches as inliers based on the <threshold>
void WorldModel::compute_inliers
    (const Eigen::Affine3f& motion_candidate,
     float threshold, Eigen::ArrayXi& inliers)
{
  Eigen::Matrix3Xf from(3, new_matches_.size());
  Eigen::Matrix3Xf to(3, new_matches_.size());
  Eigen::Matrix3Xf delta(3, new_matches_.size());

  for(int i = 0; i < new_matches_.size(); i++)
  {
    from.col(i) = new_keypoint_coords_[new_matches_[i].queryIdx];
    to.col(i)   = world_keypoint_coords_[new_matches_[i].trainIdx];
  }
  //Apply to sample set and compute root mean squared error
  delta = (motion_candidate * from) - to;
  Eigen::Array<float, 1,
    Eigen::Dynamic> sq_norm(new_matches_.size());
  sq_norm = delta.colwise().squaredNorm();

  float sq_thresh = threshold*threshold;
  for(int i = 0; i < new_matches_.size(); i++)
  { //Use the casting definition in C++:
    //boolean true -> 1, false -> 0
    inliers(new_matches_[i].queryIdx) = (sq_norm(i) < sq_thresh);
  }
}


///Compute the root mean squared error for given inlier matches
float WorldModel::compute_rmse
(const Eigen::Affine3f& motion_candidate,
 const Eigen::ArrayXi& inliers)
{
  int inlier_count = inliers.sum();
  Eigen::Matrix3Xf from(3, inlier_count);
```

```
    Eigen::Matrix3Xf to(3, inlier_count);
    Eigen::Matrix3Xf delta(3, inlier_count);
    int j = 0;
    for(int i = 0; i < new_matches_.size(); i++)
    {
      if(inliers(new_matches_[i].queryIdx)){
        from.col(j) = new_keypoint_coords_[new_matches_[i].queryIdx];
        to.col(j) = world_keypoint_coords_[new_matches_[i].trainIdx];
        j++;
      }
    }
    //Apply to sample set and compute root mean squared error
    delta = (motion_candidate * from) - to;
    return sqrt(delta.colwise().squaredNorm().mean());
}


///Run RANSAC for robust motion estimation from matches
void WorldModel::ransac(Eigen::ArrayXi& inliers,
                        Eigen::Affine3f& motion_out,
                        int ransac_iterations)
{
  inliers.setZero();
  if(new_matches_.size() < 4) return;

  ///Matrices used to evaluate the motion estimate:
  Eigen::ArrayXi new_inliers(inliers.rows());
  Eigen::ArrayXi best_inliers(inliers.rows());
  int best_inlier_count = 0;
  Eigen::Affine3f best_motion;
  float best_rmse = 1e9; //evaluation criterion to be minimized

  std::cout << "Ransac iteration: ";
  //RANSAC Iterations
  for(unsigned int i = 0; i < ransac_iterations; i++)
  {
    //initialize this iteration
    new_inliers.setZero();
    sample_matches(4,inliers);
    int refined_inlier_count = 0;
    float refined_rmse = 1e9;

    while(true) //refine as long as things are getting better
    {
      Eigen::Affine3f motion;
```

```
      motion_estimate(inliers, motion);
      compute_inliers(motion, 0.10, inliers);
      int inlier_count = inliers.sum();
      if(inlier_count < 4) break;//while
      float rmse = compute_rmse(motion, inliers);

      if(rmse < refined_rmse && inlier_count
                           >= refined_inlier_count)
      {
        refined_rmse = rmse;
        refined_inlier_count = inlier_count;
        best_motion = motion;
        continue;//still improving: further refinement
      }
      else if(refined_rmse < best_rmse && refined_inlier_count >
                                       best_inlier_count)
      {
        best_rmse = refined_rmse;
        best_inlier_count = refined_inlier_count;
        best_inliers = inliers;
      }
      break; //not getting better: reinitialize
    }

    if(best_rmse < 0.1 && best_inlier_count > new_matches_.size()/3) {
      std::cout << "\nTook " << i+1 << " iterations to find motion\n";
      std::cout << "Evaluation (RMSE): " << best_rmse << "\n";
      motion_out = best_motion;
      inliers = best_inliers;
      return;
    }
  }//end ransac loop
  std::cout << "\nNo motion found.\nBest evaluation (RMSE): "
                                     << best_rmse;
  std::cout << "\nMost inliers: " << best_inlier_count << "\n";
}
```

Writing the `WorldModel` class was the bulk of the work. What is left to do is to put it to good use. Applying the separation of concerns, the functionality encapsulated in the class is to be kept agnostic to the source of data, so we still need to set up a means to get data from the OpenNI driver. As before, we will employ the PCL OpenNIGrabber interface in our **main** function to receive a point cloud in a callback function. From the point cloud, we then extract the grayscale image for feature computation in the function **get_img_and_mask**. It further computes the **cv::Mat** to flag the missing depth values, as used in **add_cloud**.

We've included no means for communication with the user, so this is also taken care of in the **cloud_callback**. An OpenCV window is used to show the current view of the camera. The keyboard events to that window will be used to trigger single snapshots, perform continuous capturing, or call it quits.

Here are the contents of *main.cpp*.

```cpp
#include <pcl/io/openni_grabber.h>
#include <pcl/visualization/cloud_viewer.h>
#include "world_model.h"

void get_img_and_mask(const cloud_type &cloud,
                      cv::Mat& gray_img,
                      cv::Mat& mask)
{
  gray_img.create(cloud.height, cloud.width, CV_8UC1);
  mask.create(cloud.height, cloud.width, CV_8UC1);
  for(int row = 0; row < cloud.height;row++){
    for(int col = 0; col < cloud.width;col++){
      const point_type& pt = cloud.at(col, row);
      mask.at<unsigned char>(row, col) = isnan(pt.z)? 0 : 255;
      gray_img.at<unsigned char>
        (row, col) = 0.3*pt.r + 0.6*pt.g + 0.1*pt.b;
    }//for col
  }//for row
}

void cloud_callback(cloud_type::ConstPtr cloud,
                    WorldModel* nicv,
                    pcl::visualization::CloudViewer* cloud_viewer)
{
  static bool paused = true;
  bool unpause_once = false;
  //This Mat flags the pixels with valid depth
  cv::Mat gray_img, mask;
  get_img_and_mask(*cloud, gray_img, mask);
  cv::imshow("Current View", gray_img);
  //cv::imshow("Mask View", mask);
  switch(cv::waitKey(20)) {
    case 'c': paused = !paused;
              break;
    case ' ': unpause_once = true;
              break;
    case 'q': exit(0);
  }
```

```
    if(paused && !unpause_once)
      return;

    nicv->add_cloud(cloud, gray_img, mask);
    if(!cloud_viewer->wasStopped() &&
      !nicv->get_world_cloud()->empty())
      cloud_viewer->showCloud(nicv->get_world_cloud());

}


int main (int argc, const char** argv)
{
  WorldModel nicv;

  pcl::visualization::CloudViewer cloud_viewer("World Viewer");

  boost::function<void (const cloud_type::ConstPtr&)> f =
    boost::bind(cloud_callback, _1, &nicv, &cloud_viewer);

  pcl::OpenNIGrabber interface;
  interface.registerCallback (f);

  interface.start();
  while (!cloud_viewer.wasStopped()) {
    sleep(1);
  }
  interface.stop();
  return 0;
}
```

Finally, let's build the project and build a world model. Because we already created *CMakeLists.txt*, you just need to issue the following commands in your project directory: `cmake .` (mind the dot, as it represents the current directory), `make`, and `./world_modelling`. A window should appear displaying the—as-yet empty—world model. Another window is created shortly after to display the current image from the camera. You can take single shots with the space bar (make sure the latter window is activated) and see how they add up in the world model window. (See Figure 6-15.) Have fun!

Some notes on how to get good results: as you will notice, it works best when the captured images have significant overlap. In other words, do not move the camera too much between shots. With a decent GPU and a lot of memory in your machine, you can also try continuous recording (press C). Be warned, this mode quickly slows down even modern machines. In contrast to the last hack, you also need to take care that the camera points at a scene where the Kinect provides depth information. You can easily visualize this by activating the second `cv::imshow` in `cloud_callback`. The quality of the alignments also depends strongly on the lighting conditions, as increased contrast and less noise in the image will increase the number of reliable features. Keep in mind that the Kinect automatically adjusts the white balance and exposure time. Both may change the appearance of the features beyond recognition, but the latter especially will change tremendously when a light source comes into view. Don't worry: the next hack will make things easier.

Figure 6-15.
Room model

HACK 42 Add Convenience Functionality to a 3D Model

After playing around with the previous hack, you probably find it quite clear that creating smooth models doesn't come easy. In this section, though, we will make things easier. The last shot(s) didn't fit well? We'll add an undo history! Want to start over? We'll code up a reset function. And, of course, we want to save our models to view later on. And while we are at it, we also want to load them, so we can continue our model of the whole building complex, which we couldn't finish in one session because the notebook battery went dry.

We'll start off with an undo feature. The undo functionality is straightforward. We just need to track the change of the world state. Have a look at the class definition in *world_model.h*: there is a block of four variables containing the world state. If we want to undo the latest additions, it suffices to keep track of how large these containers were before. And since the data structures for the keypoints, descriptors, and inlier counts always have an equivalent size, we need only one figure for those and another one for the point cloud. So we add two STL vectors to the class definition to store the counts for each step, and (of course) a declaration for the actual undo method.

world_model.h:

```
public:
  void undo();
private:
  ///Undo information
  std::vector<int> previous_feature_size_;
  std::vector<int> previous_cloud_size_;
```

We left them uninitialized in the constructor, so by means of their default constructor they are initially empty. Now, in *world_model.cpp*, the first thing we do for every call to **add_cloud** is to store the current state:

```
///This function is the entry point for the camera data
void WorldModel::add_cloud(cloud_type::ConstPtr cloud,
                           cv::Mat& gray_img, cv::Mat& mask)
{
  ///keep record for undo
  previous_cloud_size_.push_back(world_cloud_.size());
  previous_feature_size_.push_back(world_keypoint_coords_.size());
```

The actual undo function needs just a little thought. Of course, we can't undo more than we have done. Further, after resizing the descriptor container, we also need to retrain the search structure for matching. Apart from that, it is just a matter of resizing the world state containers and popping the undo information from the vectors.

world_model.cpp:

```
void WorldModel::undo()
{
  if(!previous_cloud_size_.empty())
  {
    ///Resize all containers to previous sizes
    world_cloud_.resize(previous_cloud_size_.back());
    world_cloud_.width = world_cloud_.size();
    previous_cloud_size_.pop_back();
    world_descriptors_[0].resize(previous_feature_size_.back());
    world_keypoint_coords_.resize(previous_feature_size_.back());
```

```
    previous_feature_size_.pop_back();

    ///Reconstruct descriptorMatcher from scratch
    descriptorMatcher_->clear();
    if(!world_descriptors_[0].empty()){
      descriptorMatcher_->add(world_descriptors_);
      descriptorMatcher_->train();
    }
  }
}
```

Finally, the callback function in *main.cpp* has to be modified to provide the undo feature to the user. A new **case** expression can trigger the undo method. To make the
change visible immediately, we add another Boolean: **update_display**. This will trigger the viewer update even if **add_cloud** is not to be called.

main.cpp:

```
void cloud_callback(cloud_type::ConstPtr cloud,
                    WorldModel* nicv,
                    pcl::visualization::CloudViewer* cloud_viewer)
{
  static bool continuous_recording = false;
  bool record_once = false;
  bool update_display = false;
  //This Mat flags the pixels with valid depth
  cv::Mat gray_img, mask;
  get_img_and_mask(*cloud, gray_img, mask);
  cv::imshow("Current View", gray_img);
  cv::imshow("Mask View", mask);
  switch(cv::waitKey(20)) {
    case 'c': continuous_recording = !continuous_recording;
              break;
    case ' ': record_once = true;
              break;
    case 'u': nicv->undo();
              update_display = true;
              break;
    case 'q': exit(0);
  }

  if(continuous_recording || record_once)
    nicv->add_cloud(cloud, gray_img, mask);

  if(continuous_recording || record_once || update_display)
```

```
    if(!cloud_viewer->wasStopped() &&
      !nicv->get_world_cloud()->empty())
        cloud_viewer->showCloud(nicv->get_world_cloud());
}
```

Next up, we'll create a reset function. While one might be tempted to write a reset method that loops over the undo history, it will be more efficient—and nearly as brief —to clear out all the state variables explicitly. So add one more method to the *World-Model* class and one **case** to the callback function.

world_model.h:

```
public:
    void reset();
```

world_model.cpp:

```
void WorldModel::reset()
{
    world_keypoint_coords_.clear();
    world_descriptors_[0] = cv::Mat();
    descriptorMatcher_->clear();
    inlier_counts = Eigen::ArrayXi::Zero(0);
    world_cloud_.clear();
    previous_cloud_size_.clear();
    previous_feature_size_.clear();
}
```

main.cpp, **cloud_callback**:

```
switch(cv::waitKey(20)) {
    case 'c': continuous_recording = !continuous_recording;
             break;
    case ' ': record_once = true;
             break;
    case 'u': nicv->undo();
             update_display = true;
             break;
    case 'r': nicv->reset();
             update_display = true;
             break;
    case 'q': exit(0);
}
```

Wouldn't it be nice to save this generated input? How about building a save feature? Now you should be able to conveniently generate a nice model, removing badly aligned clouds. But as nice as it is to look at it in the viewer, after some experimentation, you probably wondered how you could store your models. You can easily store the point cloud using the **savePCDFile** function from PCL's io module. Saving the keypoint coordinates and descriptors is trickier. We employ the OpenCV FileStorage API to accomplish this. It provides functionality to serialize and deserialize data to and from a YAML file.

ASCII-based storage is not very efficient; you might want to compress the YAML file after saving. On the pro side, it conveniently allows us to write and read all the image feature information to a single file and makes us independent of the platform and architecture of your system. For details about OpenCV's FileStorage API, see its documentation at *http://bit.ly/TV3L3A*.

Add the method declaration to the public section of *world_model.h*. In principle, you should also add an include for **string** at the top of the file. In practice, one of the other includes makes it available already.

```
    void save_world(const std::string& filename);
```

```
#include <pcl/io/pcd_io.h>
```

```
    ///Serialize the world state to
    ///"<filename>.pcd" and "<filename>.yaml"
    void save_world(const std::string& filename);
```

The method definition goes into *world_model.cpp*. After we open FileStorage, first the feature coordinates are stored individually in the loop. The feature descriptors can be stored in one go, as they are all in one big OpenCV matrix. The inlier counts are not crucial, so we omit them. The point cloud is saved at the end. The Boolean parameter sets the output format to ASCII.

```
#include <pcl/io/pcd_io.h>

void WorldModel::save_world(const std::string& filename)
{
  std::string yaml_filename = filename + ".yaml";
  cv::FileStorage fs(yaml_filename.c_str(), cv::FileStorage::WRITE);
  if(fs.isOpened()){
    std::cout << "Saving all features to " << yaml_filename << "\n";
    fs << "Feature_Locations" << "[";

    for(unsigned int i = 0; i < world_keypoint_coords_.size(); i++)
    {
      const Eigen::Vector3f& p = world_keypoint_coords_[i];
      fs << "{:" << "x" << p.x() << "y" << p.y()
        << "z" << p.z() << "}";
    }
    fs << "]";
```

```
    fs << "Feature_Descriptors" << world_descriptors_[0];
    fs.release();
  }
  else
  {
    std::cerr << "Error opening file " << yaml_filename << std::endl;
    return;
  }

  std::string pcd_filename  = filename + ".pcd";
  std::cout << "Saving point cloud to file '"
    << pcd_filename << "'\n";
  pcl::io::savePCDFile(pcd_filename, world_cloud_, false);

  std::cout << "Successfully saved world model.\n";
}
```

As before, we call the new method within the keyboard code switch statement in the **cloud_callback** function in *main.cpp*. Here we choose the filename, but since we have no fancy dialog, it is just set to **world**.

```
    case 's': nicv->save_world("world");
              break;
```

That's it! You can now save the current state of your models by pressing S in the window with the current camera view. Go ahead, try it. The output files will be saved as *world.pcd* and *world.yaml*. You can then easily visualize the point clouds using the program pcd_viewer, which comes with PCL. It is very similar to the viewer we embedded. An important note: pressing 5 will switch the colors on. Figure 6-16 shows it displaying my attempt at generating a model of some objects.

The logical next step is to reverse the save and load the model, so that you can continue the model creation. Things are very similar to the saving procedure. Put this right next to the definition of **save_world**:

```
    ///Deserialize the world state from
    ///"<filename>.pcd" and "<filename>.yaml"
    void load_world(const std::string& filename);
```

Figure 6-16.
Object model

Because the loaded scene has a fixed origin (the camera location of the first frame), it cannot easily be merged into another existing model. Therefore, the first step after opening the file is to reset the world state. Then the data from the YAML file is used to fill the feature coordinates and the feature description matrix. The PCD file is loaded as you would expect. Then we arbitrarily set the inlier count for each feature to one and build the search structure for the descriptor matching.

```
void WorldModel::load_world(const std::string& filename)
{
  std::string yaml_filename = filename + ".yaml";
  cv::FileStorage fs(yaml_filename.c_str(), cv::FileStorage::READ);
  if(fs.isOpened()){
    this->reset();
    std::cout << "Loading features from " << yaml_filename << "\n";

    cv::FileNode features = fs["Feature_Locations"];
    cv::FileNodeIterator it = features.begin(),
        it_end = features.end();
    int idx = 0;

    for( ; it != it_end; ++it, idx++ )
```

```
  {
    Eigen::Vector3f vec;
    vec << (float)(*it)["x"], (float)(*it)["y"], (float)(*it)["z"];
    world_keypoint_coords_.push_back(vec);
  }
  fs["Feature_Descriptors"] >> world_descriptors_[0];
  fs.release();
}
else
{
  std::cerr << "Error opening file " << yaml_filename << std::endl;
  return;
}
std::string pcd_filename  = filename + ".pcd";
std::cout << "Loading point cloud from file '"
  << pcd_filename << "'\n";
pcl::io::loadPCDFile(pcd_filename, world_cloud_);

//Assume all features to be matched once
inlier_counts = Eigen::ArrayXi::Ones(world_descriptors_[0].rows);

//Build the feature matching search structure
descriptorMatcher_->add(world_descriptors_);
descriptorMatcher_->train();

std::cout << "Successfully loaded world model'\n";
}
```

Analogous to the save method, the load method is called from the `cloud_callback`. Naturally, loading should trigger the update of the point cloud display. So add the following **case** to the switch statement, and you are ready to reuse your saved models:

```
case 'l': nicv->load_world("world");
          update_display = true;
          break;
```

HACK 43 Next Steps: SLAM, OctoMaps, Surface Reconstruction

So far, we have achieved a fully fledged application for creating 3D models with a Kinect, so this is a natural point to end the chapter. But first I offer this guide on registering point clouds. There are a lot of amazing things left to do, and I want to take the opportunity to point some of them out.

First are some suggestions for straightforward additions. If you want to manually edit your model, you can also save in PLY format (use `pcl::io::savePLYFile`, which can be downloaded from *http://docs.pointclouds.org/trunk/group__io.html*, and use a tool like MeshLab (*http://meshlab.sourceforge.net*). To reduce the memory footprint of the point cloud, you can switch to binary save mode or use `pcl::removeNaNFromPointCloud` (*http://docs.pointclouds.org/trunk/group__filters.html*) to throw out points with color, but no valid coordinates. There are plenty of them, and they are kept only to retain the 2D grid structure of the original depth and color images. Another very useful tool to reduce the size of the point cloud is the PCL `VoxelGrid` filter class.

For more on the `VoxilGrid` *class, visit* http://bit.ly/PQYpKR.

Our user interface at present processes keypresses only via OpenCV. If you want the CloudViewer window to react to the keys, you can use its method `registerKeyboardCallback`.

For more on `registerKeyboardCallback`, *visit* http://bit.ly/XgsoN2.

More advanced extensions include the introduction of a nonlinear graph optimization engine and the creation of memory efficient voxel maps. Graph optimization software computes the camera poses from the geometric constraints between the camera and the relative positions of the inlier features. This is more accurate than the method we used, in particular, since later observations can improve the position estimate of earlier ones. Nonlinear graph optimization libraries (*http://openslam.org/g2o.html*) are commonly used tools in robotics, to enable robots to autonomously record a world model. Also, Google developed and open-sourced such a library for street view, which can be downloaded at *http://code.google.com/p/ceres-solver*.

Voxel grid maps are to 3D what raster images are to 2D. The aforementioned voxel grid filter is one way to create such a map. Another technique coming from the robotics community is the use of probabilistic occupancy maps. In contrast to the application of the voxel grid filter, these maps not only care about the points, but also about the space between the points and the camera. Since this space must be unoccupied to see the point, this information can be explicitly used to rule out spurious points from badly aligned clouds. A very memory-efficient and easy-to-use library to create 3D occupancy maps is the OctoMap library (*http://octomap.sourceforge.net*). If you like MineCraft, you'll love it.

7

Web Applications and Gaming

The Kinect was designed for gaming—naturally, those who have hacked the Kinect wanted to see what types of games they could produce with motion controls. With wrappers for game building applications such as Unity, Processing, and Scratch, developers have taken the Kinect into their own hands and have created a wide variety of game experiences you can enjoy on your own PC.

HACK 44 Install the Zigfu SDK

Zigfu is a recent startup with a lot of promise that specializes in gesture-based gaming. The team comprises Kinect hacking gurus and an assortment of other specialists in fields such as robotics and software engineering. As an added bonus, two former employees of PrimeSense are a part of this gesture-based team whose primary goal is to deliver easy-to-use developer resources to simplify Kinect development.

Zigfu offers a free SDK that provides a set of motion-controlled user interface components, as well as access to the lower-level Kinect data, including hand-point controls, skeleton joint positions and orientations, and depth mapping. The SDK includes bindings to the Unity3D game engine, HTML5/JavaScript, and Flash, allowing developers to create Kinect games and apps either for the browser, using the cross-browser Zigfu browser plug-in, or as native applications.

With Zigfu bindings and libraries installed, you can develop Kinect integrated applications on a wide assortment of platforms, making it the perfect software solution for all your casual Kinect game development needs.

Go to the downloads section of *http://zigfu.com* to find detailed tutorials and examples to get started using Zigfu's platform!

Create an HTML User Radar Using Zigfu SDK

For this hack, I'll illustrate how to build your own gesture-controlled user radar function using Zigfu's great SDK. The radar is essentially a square box that will represent a tracked user in a web browser. Before we get started, download and install the ZigfuJS browser plug-in from *http://zigfu.com/en/downloads/browserplugin/*. This will install the latest versions of OpenNI, NITE, and SensorKinect along with ZigJS.

Once the installation process is complete, a browser should open up, bringing you to the motions.com examples and demo site. If your Kinect is plugged in and all goes according to plan, you should be able to navigate around the menu and try out some of the samples. Check out the punching bag demo from the Samples menu for a little fun before we get under way (Figure 7-1).

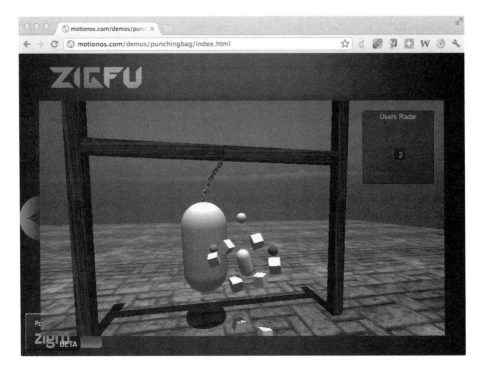

Figure 7-1.
Zigfu punching bag demo (*http://motionos.com//demos/punchingbag/index.html*)

Now that ZigJS has been installed properly, we're ready to get started on our first Zigfu Hello World web app.

The following simply displays an alert when the Zig plug-in loads.

```
<!DOCTYPE html>
<html>
<head>
<title>Zig Plugin Test</title>

<script src='http://cdn.zigfu.com/zigjs/zig.min.js'></script>

<script>

    function loaded() {
        zig.addEventListener('loaded', function() {
            alert('Hello motion world!');
        });
        zig.embed();
    }

    document.addEventListener('DOMContentLoaded', loaded, false);
  </script>
  </head>
<body>
</body>
```

Save the file with some naming convention like *zigfutest.html* and place it somewhere convenient. Right-click the file and open it with a browser. You should be presented with a pop up displaying the alert text "Hello motion world!" See Figure 7-2.

The included script from *http://cdn.zigfu.com*, *zig.js*, defines the `zig` object and all of the bindings you'll need to interact with the browser plug-in. `zig.embed()` embeds the plug-in object into the browser, which calls the `loaded` event upon finishing loading and initializing. Note that you don't have to have an event handler for the `loaded` event. It's a good way of testing the basic functionality of the plug-in, and for doing something different on your site based on whether or not the user has the plug-in installed.

The page at file://localhost/ says:
Hello motion world!

OK

Figure 7-2.
Hello World alert

For our next step, we'll introduce the Radar sample app. This function essentially displays where the users who are currently being tracked by the Kinect are located within the room. Alone, it's not exactly the most useful application, but when used in tandem with the Zigfu object model, it's a different story.

Begin by commenting out the **alert** function, as we won't need to be disrupted by its persistent loading every time we refresh.

```
<script>
/** function loaded() {
        zig.addEventListener('loaded', function() {
            alert('Hello motion world!');
        });
        zig.embed();
    }

    document.addEventListener('DOMContentLoaded', loaded, false);
    **/
</script>
```

Now that that's out of the way, we'll begin by creating a box that will represent the tracked users. We'll code up the user radar using a div for the box, and some JavaScript code that creates a div for each dot. Add the following code inside the head of the HTML:

```
<style>
    div#radar
    {
        width: 400px;
        height: 400px;
        border: 1px solid black;
        overflow: hidden;
    }
</style>
```

The following code can be placed anywhere between the **<body>** tags.

```
<div id='radar'></div>
```

This creates a box (the div called **radar**) with the dimensions of 400×400 pixels and a surrounding solid black border. The **overflow: hidden** directive ensures that users do not show up outside of the box.

We'll receive events from the **zig** object, and for the **onuserfound** callback function, we'll instantiate an object with that class and stick it in the box. Then each time there's new data from the Kinect, there will be an **onupdatedata** callback function. In that callback, we'll move the user to the appropriate position on the screen.

We'll now set up the receiving callbacks from the `zig` object and make sure that the callbacks are being run. Add the following `ZigPluginLoaded` function between the `<head>` tags like this:

```
<script>

function loaded() {
    zig.embed();
    var radardiv = document.getElementById('radar');

    // The radar object will respond to events from the
    // zig object and move the dots around accordingly.
    // It is also responsible for creating and destroying
    // the dots when users are added and removed.
    // Functions onnewuser(), onlostuser(), and ondataupdate()
    // are called by the zig object when those things happen.
    var radar = {
        onuserfound: function (user) {
            console.log('running onnewuser in radar');
        },
        onuserlost: function (user) {
            console.log('running onlostuser in radar');
        },
        ondataupdate: function (zig) {

        }
    };
    // Add the radar object as a listener to the zig object, so that
    // the zig object will call the radar object's callback functions.
    zig.addListener(radar);
}
    document.addEventListener('DOMContentLoaded', loaded, false);

<script>
```

At this point, you can open up the file in a browser and stand in front of the Kinect. If you open up the JavaScript console for your browser (in Chrome go to the wrench icon → Tools → JavaScript Console), you'll notice the output shown in Figure 7-3 once the sensor detects you.

```
html  body                                              ≡
  Zig: inited                                    zig.min.js:1
  Zig: inited                                    zig.min.js:1
  Zig: New user: 3                               zig.min.js:1
  running onnewuser in radar                     test.html:39
  Zig: Lost user: 3                              zig.min.js:1
  running onlostuser in radar                    test.html:42
>
```

Figure 7-3.
Chrome JavaScript console output

If you do see the New User message from the `zig` *object, but not the onuserfound*
message, then for some reason, **onuserfound** *is not being called. Double-check*
that the spelling of the functions is correct, because if it's not, the code will simply
fail silently. If you don't see anything in the console, then reload the page and try
again.

Now that the callback structure has been set up, the next step is creating the dot that
will go inside the box to represent a user. We want to create a new dot each time a user
is found, and remove the dot when the user is lost. Since the user dots should all look
the same, create a CSS class called **user** that we'll add to all the objects that we create
in the JavaScript code.

Add the following code within the same **<style>** tags as the **div#radar** div:

```css
div.user
{
    position: relative;
    width: 10px;
    height: 10px;
    background-color: blue;
}
```

Now we'll add the code that creates and destroys the dots depending on whether or
not the user has been found or lost. An elegant way of associating a div with each user
is to add a reference to a user div as a property of the respective **user** object. Here's
code that creates and destroys a div for each tracked user. Change the declaration of
the radar object to the following:

```javascript
var radar = {
    onuserfound: function (user) {
        var userdiv = document.createElement('div');
        userdiv.className = 'user';
        // add radarelement as a property of the user
        user.radarelement = userdiv;
        radardiv.appendChild(user.radarelement);
```

KINECT HACKS

```
        },
        onuserlost: function (user) {
            radardiv.removeChild(user.radarelement);
        },
        ondataupdate: function (zigdata) {

        }
    };
```

If you open the test file in a browser, you should now see a blue 10×10-pixel square in the upper-left corner of the box we created earlier once you stand in front of the Kinect. If you move out of its line of sight, the blue dot disappears.

Now we move to the final stretch: controlling the little blue dots. For this we'll use the **ondataupdate** callback, which gets called every time the sensor has new data, approximately 30 times per second. The data passed in the **zigdata** parameter is a reference to the **zig** object, which has a number of different pieces of data inside it. We're interested in **zig.users**, which is a hashtable of all the users currently being tracked. The **zig.users** hashtable has **userids** as keys for user objects, which are the values. Replace the definition of the **ondataupdate** callback with the following:

```
ondataupdate: function (zigdata) {
    for (var userid in zigdata.users) {
        var user = zigdata.users[userid];
        var pos = user.position;
        var el = user.radarelement;
        var parentElement = el.parentNode;
        var zrange = 4000;
        var xrange = 4000;
        var pixelwidth = parentElement.offsetWidth;
        var pixelheight = parentElement.offsetHeight;
        var heightscale = pixelheight / zrange;
        var widthscale = pixelwidth / xrange;
        el.style.left = (((pos[0] / xrange) + 0.5) * pixelwidth -
        (el.offsetWidth / 2)) + "px";
        el.style.top = ((pos[2] / zrange)
        * pixelheight - (el.offsetHeight / 2)) + "px";
    }
}
```

That's it! If you step in front of the Kinect's line of sight, you should now be able to move the blue dot by moving around. This represents your position in relation to the user radar!

Install Scratch and Kinect2Scratch

Scratch (Figure 7-4) is an integrated development environment (IDE). It is different from other IDEs, however, typing arcane computer language commands.

Figure 7-4.
Scratch official site

Scratch is aimed at younger programmers (and new programmers who are not so young), and it uses a building-brick approach. Each brick is a single command, and users can combine or snap together many bricks to achieve more complex commands. Scratch programming revolves around *sprites*, which are individual graphical characters or models in your program. In Figure 7-5, notice the main components of the Scratch user interface.

Kinect2Scratch is a Java application developed by Stephen Howell that allows you to take skeletal and joint data from your Kinect sensor, and use that information to develop applications in Scratch. What's great about this is that it is easily accessible; those who have little to no programming background can start building great musical and gaming applications using a Kinect sensor. If you're interested in teaching your kids—or yourself, for that matter—programming basics, this is a great way to start.

There are a few prerequisites you'll need to have before getting started with Kinect2Scratch. Depending on your operating system, there are slightly different steps to set up this hack.

On Windows (XP, Vista, Windows 7, and Windows 8), you need to install OpenNI, NITE, and the SensorKinect drivers (in that order). Download the 32- or 64-bit versions depending on your OS.

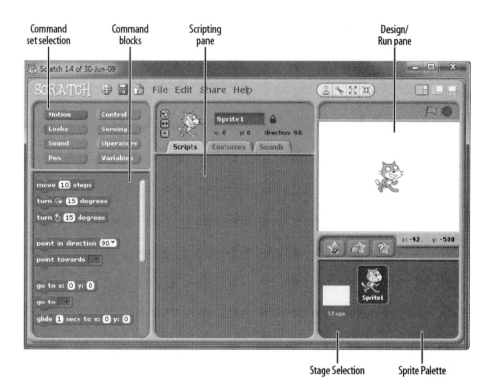

Figure 7-5.
Scratch user interface

This was tested on 64-bit, and the particular versions of the drivers used were:

- *openni-win64-1.5.2.23-dev.msi*
- *nite-win64-1.5.2.21-dev.msi*
- *SensorKinect091-Bin-Win64-v5.1.0.25.msi*

On Mac OS X, the procedure is different (as of this writing). The required installs are available in a handy SimpleOpenNI installer at *http://bit.ly/Rh8lvV*.

The steps are as follows:

```
unzip OpenNI_NITE_Installer-OSX.zip
cd ./OpenNI_NITE_Installer-OSX
sudo ./install.sh
```

Once the Kinect drivers and OpenNI are installed, download and install Scratch (*http://scratch.mit.edu*) for your OS. Finally, download Kinect2Scratch from *http://scratch.saorog.com*.

Choose the version that suits your OS. Kinect2Scratch is written in Java, so it should run on most operating systems that have OpenNI drivers. To install, simply unzip your download into a folder on your computer. Kinect2Scratch does not need a special install procedure.

Launch the Scratch application. This will create a *Scratch Projects* folder inside your *Documents* directory (depending on your OS, of course).

Download the Scratch Kinect examples from *http://bit.ly/VpnKsn* and place them in the *Scratch Project* folder.

Run one of the Kinect2Scratch applications and then click the Launch Kinect button.

Stand about six to eight feet in front of your Kinect until the skeletal tracking is initiated.

Go to your *Documents/Scratch Projects* folder and launch one of the Kinect Scratch examples. Once it has finished loading, click the green flag in the upper-right corner of the staging window and enjoy!

HACK 47 Create a Basic Tennis Game Using Scratch

Let's start out the gaming portion of this chapter by creating a Scratch game. We'll develop a very short (but playable) game of tennis. This type of game has existed on nearly every computer and console for decades. The design is very simple: the player(s) control paddles or bats on either side of the game window, and a ball bounces between them. Players lose a point if they fail to repel the ball, and the ball manages to touch the edge of the screen that they are protecting.

To make this game, you will need Kinect2Scratch installed (as described in Hack #46) and Scratch. There will be one background and three sprites in this project. All of them have short scripts, so you should be able to make this classic retro game in about five minutes.

Before we begin, make sure that only one instance of Scratch is running (Scratch won't talk to external peripherals like Kinect if more than one instance is executing). Once Scratch is launched, remove the default cat sprite by right-clicking it and selecting Delete, or clicking the scissors icon above the stage then clicking the cat. Finally, you will need to have the Kinect connected to your computer and Kinect2Scratch running in the background (as described previously). Click Launch Kinect in Kinect2Scratch. Switch to Scratch, click on Sensing, and ensure remote sensors are enabled (right-click on "slider sensor value" and select "enable remote sensor connections"). Now return to Kinect2Scratch and click Connect to Scratch.

To play a proper game of tennis, we'll need to include two bats in the game, each one controlled by a different hand (if you have more than two hands, please increase the number of bats as necessary). Let's do the left side bat first. Start by clicking on Paint New Sprite. When the Paint Editor appears, click the rectangle tool, pick any color you like, and then draw a vertical rectangle that is tall but narrow, like a lowercase L, anywhere on the canvas. Click OK when finished. See Figure 7-6.

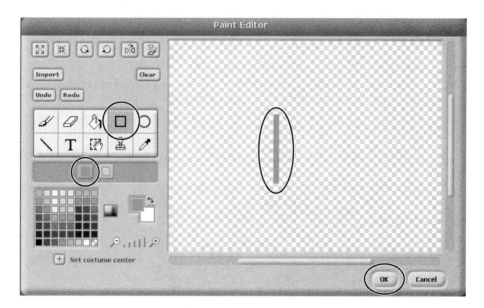

Figure 7-6.
Creating a tennis paddle in scratch paint editor

Name the new sprite "left bat" and create the script as follows.

We required two blocks from Control ("When [green flag] clicked" and "forever") and one from Motion ("go to x: y:"). Put the value −220 into the x: value box in the "go to" block. This is the left side of the stage and where we want the bat to stay.

Finally, the Kinect bit! Click Sensing, drag out "slider sensor value," and place it into the white y: value box in the "go to x: y:" block. Click the small down arrow beside "slider," and you should see the list of joints the Kinect is tracking. If not, check back on the setup instructions for Kinect2Scratch. If you do see the joints, select HandLeft_y. Now click the green flag, stand in front of your Kinect (keep back; it needs room to see you), and wave your left hand up and down. You may feel a little silly, but the left bat should instantly follow the height of your hand. Try jumping and touching the floor. If the Kinect can see you, the left bat will track your hand. See Figure 7-7.

Figure 7-7.
Scratch script for left hand bat movement

The next bit is easy. Right-click on the "left bat" Sprite in your sprite palette and select "duplicate." A new duplicate called Sprite 1 should appear. Select it by clicking on it in the palette. Rename it "right bat." Click the Scripts tab and make two changes: remove the minus sign in "go to x: -220" so that it reads "x: 220." Now change the HandLeft_y to HandRight_y. That's it! See Figure 7-8.

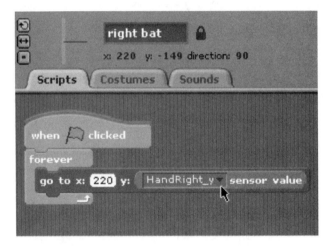

Figure 7-8.
Scratch script for right hand bat movement

Run the game again by clicking the green flag, stand in front of your Kinect, and wave your hands up and down. Hopefully, the bats move up and down for you, and no one sees you waving at your computer. What this script does is move the bats to the y position of your hands as detected by the Kinect. Kinect2Scratch is converting where your hand joint positions are in space to something Scratch can understand.

Next up, we'll work on creating a background for the game. The stage background needs to be done before the ball script is coded. The background should be plain white with two red bars along the left and right sides of the screen. The red bars should be the exact same color and should not be too wide.

KINECT HACKS

Click Stage and select the Backgrounds tab. Click the Edit button on background1. When the background Paint Editor appears, select the rectangle tool, ensure the filled rectangle option is selected, click any red color you like, and draw two rectangles along the entire left and right edges of the screen. Click OK when you've finished. See Figure 7-9.

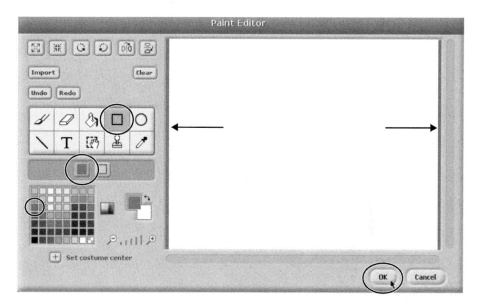

Figure 7-9.
Scratch background Paint Editor

The ball sprite does not have any Kinect-aware scripts, so it can be coded before you have connected your Kinect to Scratch. Start by clicking the Paint New Sprite button. When the Paint Editor appears, click the ellipse or circle tool, pick any color you like, and draw a circle or ball anywhere on the canvas. Try to make it a circle rather than an oval if you can. Click OK when finished.

Now let's write the script for the ball. You can copy the entire script you see for Figure 7-10.

As you can see, this script is a little more complicated than the last. Start by pulling out the "when [green flag] clicked" sprite from Control. In Motion, you will find the next two blocks, "go to x:0 y:0" and "point in direction: 90." Click the 90 and change it to 45 (you can type in this box; you don't have to use the drop-down menu). Go back to Control and add a "forever" block. Now add three "if" blocks inside the "forever" block. Make sure the "if" blocks are parallel to one other, not nested inside one another.

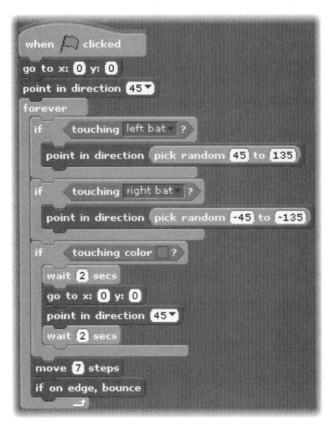

Figure 7-10.
Scratch tennis game ball script

The first and second "if" blocks will deal with what happens when the ball touches the left and right bats, and the third "if" deals with the ball touching the red sides of the screen. Select Sensing and add the diamond "touching" block to the empty diamond in the first "if" block. Click the drop-down in the "touching" block and select "left bat." Repeat this for the right bat in the second "if." Now select Motion and place "point in direction" blocks inside both the first and second "if" blocks. Now select Operators and drag out the "pick random 1 to 10" block and place it in the white 90 at the end of the "point in direction" block inside the first "if." Change the 1 and 10 to 45 and 135, respectively. These are the min and max angles at which we want the ball to bounce. Now do the same for the second "if," but change the angles to bounce off to −45 and −135.

For the last "if," there is a slightly different procedure. Select Sensing, and drag out a "touching color" block, and add it to the empty diamond of the third "if." The next bit can be tricky: click the color square beside in the diamond; your mouse pointer should change into an eye dropper. Click the red lines used on your stage. If the color in the diamond changes to red, you have successfully selected the right color. If it stays white or turns any other color, repeat the procedure until it is red. Return to Control and add two "wait 1 secs" blocks to the third "if." (One second is a bit too fast, so you can change it to two seconds like in Figure 7-10; however, this is a subjective value, so you can also leave it at one if you like.) Now go to Motion and add the same two blocks that you added originally, "go to x:0 y:0" and "point in direction: 90." Click the 90 and change it to 45 again. These blocks should be added in between the two "wait" blocks. Don't worry if you click them into the wrong place; you can pull them out and replace them any time.

Finally, after the three "if" blocks, place a "move 10 steps" block inside the "forever" loop. This is how fast the ball will move. Moving at a speed of 10 steps is quite fast, so 5 or 7 is a good alternative. The last block is "if on edge, bounce," which makes the ball bounce off the top and bottom edges.

Now make sure Kinect2Scratch is running, click the easel icon on the top right to go to full screen mode, and click the green flag to run the program and start playing tennis. Stand in front of your Kinect and raise both hands in front of you. When the ball starts moving, try to deflect it from the red edge. If you succeed, it will come right back at the other edge, where you must deflect it also. Although you might look like you've gone crazy and are waving with both hands at your computer, you have made a simple Kinect-controlled game!

So waving your hands at the computer is fun, but if you have a friend nearby, you might rather play tennis against her rather than playing by yourself (if you have no friends, go and make some before attempting this part). You can create a completely new game and follow all the previous instructions, or simply modify the tennis game you already have. You can create a copy of the game by clicking File and Save As... and giving it a new name, such as "Tennis Two Player."

Now return to Kinect2Scratch for a moment (assuming it is still running from when you played single-player tennis). Click on Configure Skeleton and then click "Two player mode enabled," as shown in Figure 7-11. Close the window by clicking the X in the righthand corner (your settings are saved automatically).

Return to Scratch now, and for this part, you will need that friend. Pick one of the bats to change. (In this example, the left bat will be changed, but it could be either one.) First, you both must stand in front of the Kinect for a moment so that Scratch knows there are two different skeletons to track. If the Kinect saw both of you, you will see a change in the sensor values available. Click on the left bat sprite in the Sprite palette and then select the Scripts tab. Click on the small down arrow in the sensor value block and change the HandLeft_y value to HandRight_y2. The trailing 2 means second player. If you can't see any values with a trailing 2, it just means the Kinect couldn't see both players at the same time or that two-player mode isn't enabled.

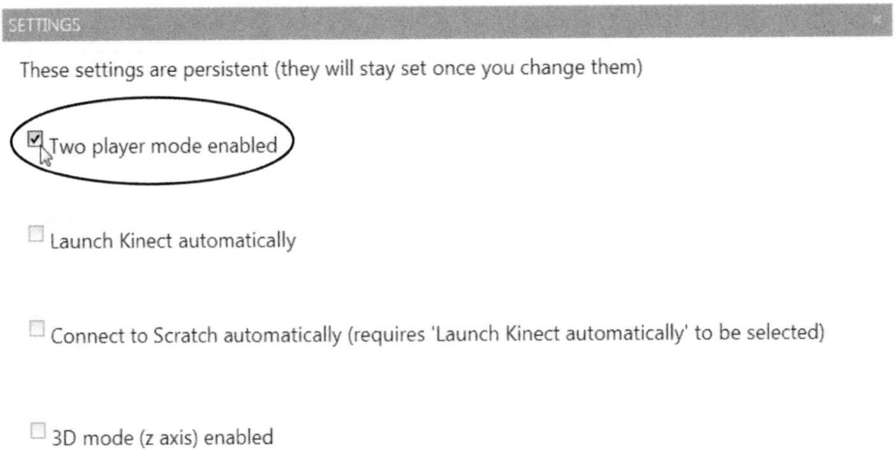

These settings are persistent (they will stay set once you change them)

☑ Two player mode enabled

☐ Launch Kinect automatically

☐ Connect to Scratch automatically (requires 'Launch Kinect automatically' to be selected)

☐ 3D mode (z axis) enabled

Figure 7-11.
Scratch two-player mode

Now run the game and stand with your friend in front of the Kinect. Both of you raise your right hand—player one will control the right side bat and player two will control the left side bat. You may not actually be standing on the same side as the bat you are controlling; this will be down to who the Kinect saw first. Play the game as before, only now each player controls just one bat. And that's all there is to making a two-player Kinect game with Scratch!

HACK 48 Build a Defender-Style Shooter Game with Scratch

This hack is a little more complicated than the previous Scratch tennis game, so you might prefer to download it and read through the explanations here. Hopefully you have learned enough Scratch now to recreate the scripts as shown, so rather than detailing each and every step of creating them, this hack will concentrate on explaining how and why they work. There are quite a few scripts, but stick with it—by the end, you will have a fun game.

The game itself is simple. You control an elephant that is hungry and anticipating some lovely bananas falling from the trees into his watering hole, where he will collect and eat them. However, a cheeky monkey lives in the trees and he will attempt to catch and eat the bananas before they touch the ground. The first animal to touch the bananas gets them, and the first to collect 10 bananas wins. Although the monkey moves very fast, the elephant can spray water from his trunk to splash the monkey and frighten him back into his den. The Kinect interaction in this game is based on head tracking for the elephant's position and detecting the gesture of both hands being raised above the player's head simultaneously to trigger a water launch.

The first thing we'll focus on is creating the stage. This will include four backgrounds: a title background, an instructions background, a game background, and a game-over background.

Make the first stage with any design you like and call it "title." Make sure to add some text with the name of the game, Elephant Defender.

For the next stage, again make any background you like (though make it different from the others) and call it "how to play."

Create another stage named "game" and select the photo of a watering hole with some jungle and a heron (or stork?). Ignore the crocodile; he's just having a rest. You can import this photo from the backgrounds included with Scratch; click on Import, select Nature, and scroll down to "lake."

The final stage is called "game over" and must have some text with "Winner:" positioned in the bottom third of the screen. This is important, as the winner will be displayed here at the end of the game.

See Figure 7-12 for the configuration of all four stage backgrounds.

The stage scripts mostly deal with the progression of when each screen is shown. Before creating these scripts, you will need to create two variables (click on Variables → Make a Variable). Call the variables Monkey Score and Player Score.

The green flag starting block sets up initial values and changes the stage to the title screen. It then loops forever, checking if either animal has accrued 10 points. If one has, it broadcasts a message. Broadcasting is a sprite's way of telling all other sprites something important has happened that they may want to respond to. To add a new broadcast message, click the small arrow in the "broadcast block," select "new," and add your new message.

The Boolean block "Monkey Score = 10 or Player Score = 10" can also seem tricky, but it's actually made up of three blocks. Start with an operator's "or" block and drop the two "=" blocks into the "or" block options. Then drop the variables and "10" into the "=" blocks.

The rest of the "hat" blocks, such as "When I receive start game," will each require taking a Control block "When I receive" and selecting the small drop-down arrow. Select "new" and type in the receive message. You have to do this only once per project; the other sprites will pick it up automatically.

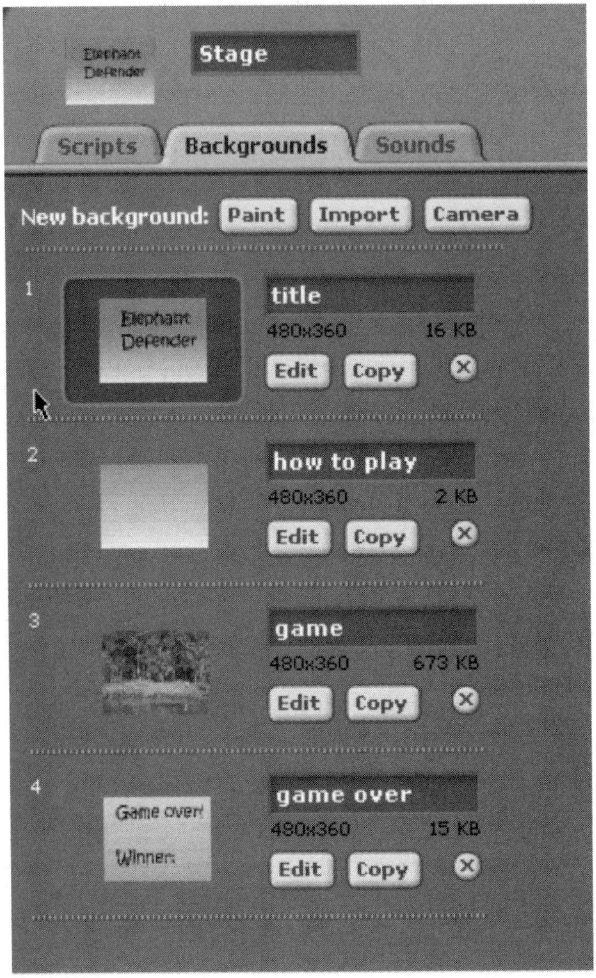

Figure 7-12.
Scratch stage backgrounds

Next up, create the sprites that you will use to play the game. Start with a new sprite, named Instructions. This sprite is text only, and has an important job: it detects when the user wants to start.

There's only one script, but it's a little complicated. This is where the Kinect functionality first shows up.

The first four commands (up to "repeat until") are necessary to avoid premature launch of the game. As the user may not be in view of the Kinect, we cannot assume that valid skeletal data is being received; it could be erroneous data or no data at all. To counter this, we wait until the user's right hand y-axis value begins to change. This means that the Kinect senses movement and is sending data that is (hopefully) valid. See Figure 7-13.

The next block, "wait until," is really useful for Kinect programming in Scratch. It allows you to detect simple gestures—in this case, your right hand being higher than your head. Then the script proceeds to broadcast a message "show instructions," which is picked up by other sprites, as we'll see later. The stage also hears this message, and it has a script to change the background to the "how to play" image. Finally, after waiting for the user to read the instructions, the script will launch the game by broadcasting "start game."

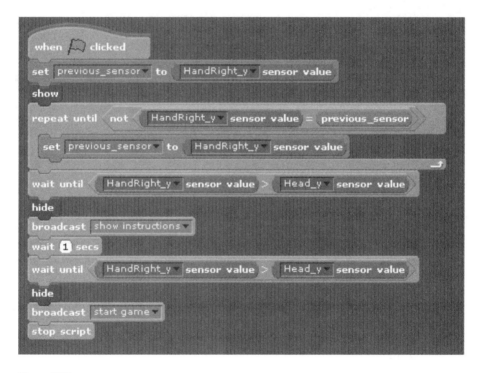

Figure 7-13.
Kinect instructions sprite script

This next step involves creating a How to Play sprite, which will display instructions to the user. Create a new sprite and name it How to Play. This sprite has only one costume, and it is all text, just like the previous sprite.

Figure 7-14 shows some suggested text, but it can be any instructions you like, as long as you remember the directive to raise your hand to start at the end.

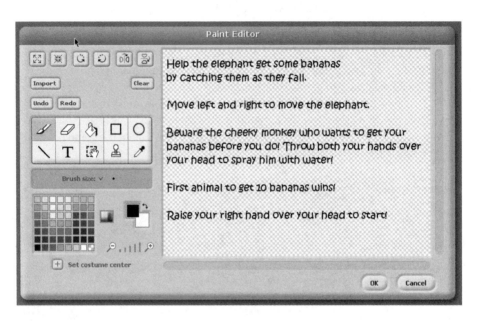

Figure 7-14.
Suggested text for instructions

The How to Play script is relatively straightforward, as it reacts only to messages from other sprites; it has no real functionality of its own. See Figure 7-15.

The next sprite up to bat is the Fruit sprite. You actually don't have to draw anything for this one. Click the "Choose new sprite from file" button under the stage and select the *Things* folder. The bananas should be the first sprite.

The script is a little trickier. We want the bananas to fall vertically from a random position along the x-axis, but always from the top of the stage. Name the sprite Fruit.

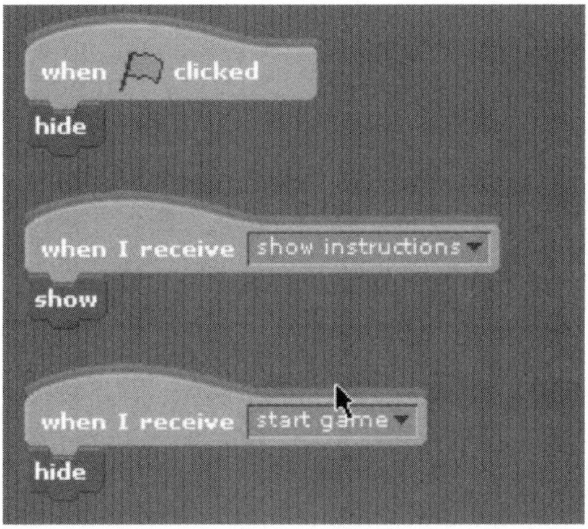

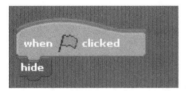

Figure 7-15.
Instructions script

When the program is first run, the bananas should be hidden. See Figure 7-16.

Figure 7-16.
Hide banana script

Once the game has started (when the "start game" message is received), the banana sprite will fall down the screen. See Figure 7-17. If it reaches the bottom, it will sit there (sprites are not allowed go beyond the stage limits in Scratch). However, if it detects that it has come into contact with the elephant sprite, it increments the player's score by one and broadcasts a message that someone has caught it and is eating the fruit.

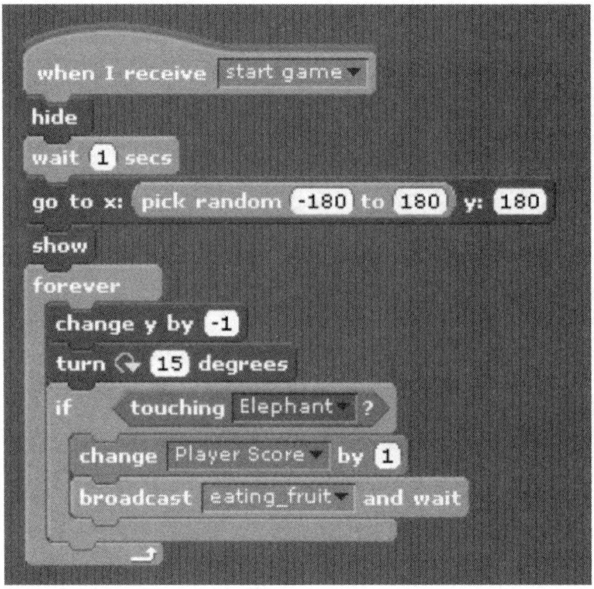

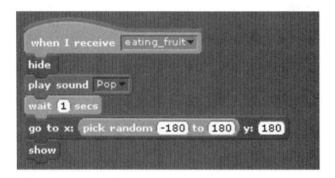

Figure 7-17.
Banana sprite start game script

Funnily enough, the banana sprite wants to know when someone is eating it too! See Figure 7-18.

Figure 7-18.
Bannana sprite eating fruit script

It makes a sound and restarts the falling process. To add a sound, select the banana sprite, click on the Sound tab (beside costumes and scripts) and click Import. The Pop sound is in the *Effects* folder. Finally, all bananas should disappear once the game is over. See Figure 7-19.

Figure 7-19.
Banana game over script

Next up is building the missile sprite. This is the only sprite that calls upon your artistic skills. Create a new sprite with the Paint New Sprite button under the stage.

Draw a water spray shape as you imagine it might look. Don't make it too big. Notice that Figure 7-20 is zoomed in at medium (or point 3 of 5) scale. You can optionally add another costume that slightly changes the water shape (perhaps to add some foam), but this is not necessary.

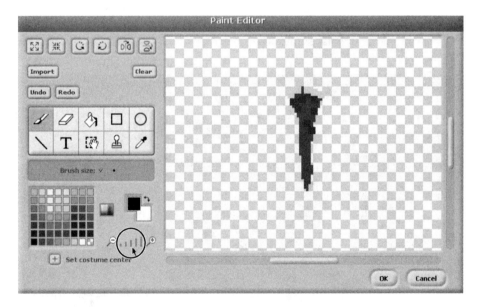

Figure 7-20.
Missile sprite image

An initial green flag block sets a variable "missile_in_flight" (create it in the "variables" section) to 0. This means we are using the variable as a Boolean—it is either 1 or 0 (true or false). In this case, it tells us whether a missile is already in flight. Our missile here is a water spray from an elephant, but it could be a missile from a spaceship or any projectile. See Figure 7-21.

Figure 7-21.
Missile flight script

Next, the sprite must react to receiving a "fire_missile" event. It immediately sets the "missile in flight" variable to 1 (so we can't accidentally launch two missiles) and then locates itself where the elephant is, shows itself, and starts flying upward.

It will continue moving upward until it reaches the edge of the screen. This resets the missile to a not-fired state. We will see later in the monkey script that the water may reset if it comes into contact with it.

Notice the "next costume" command. This will have no effect unless you added the optional costume earlier. Depending on how you good of an artist you are, this may look like an animated water spray. See Figure 7-22.

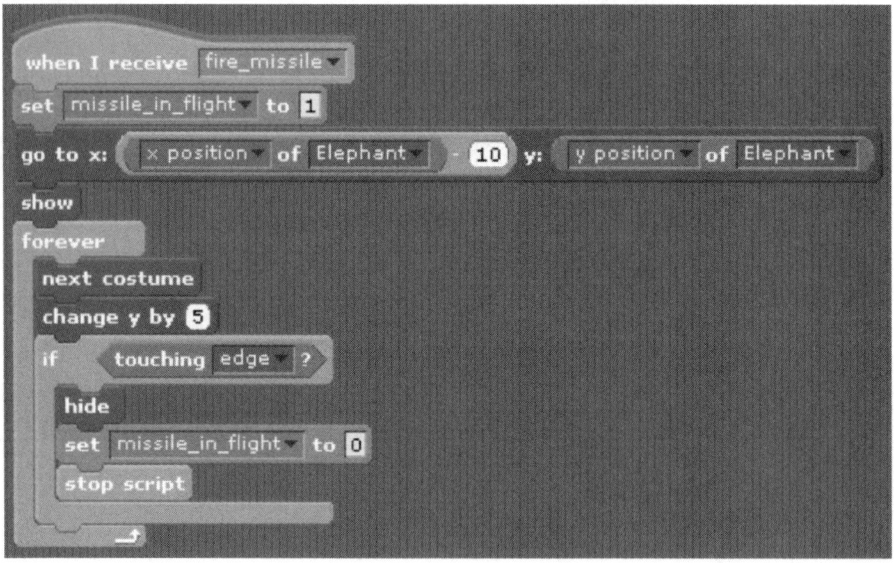

```
when I receive fire_missile
set missile_in_flight to 1
go to x: ( x position of Elephant ) - 10  y: ( y position of Elephant )
show
forever
    next costume
    change y by 5
    if < touching edge ? >
        hide
        set missile_in_flight to 0
        stop script
```

Figure 7-22.
Missile firing script

Finally, we need to respond to the missile hitting something (like the monkey) and then hide it when the game is over. See Figure 7-23.

Figure 7-23.
Missile impact script

Next up is the monkey sprite, which is completely made up of costumes and sounds that ship with Scratch. Start by clicking "Choose a new sprite from file," select the *Animals* folder, and scroll down to select "monkey1." Now go to the Sounds tab and import Plunge from the *Effects* folder. The first script is similar to other start scripts; it sets the monkey's score to 0 and hides him. See Figure 7-24.

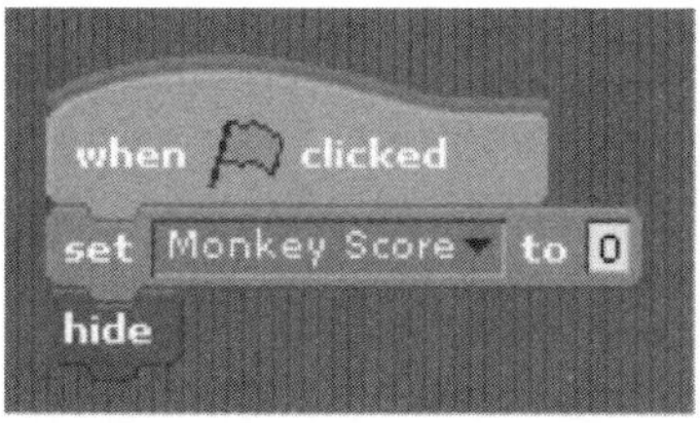

Figure 7-24.
Monkey score script

More complicated is the "start game" script, which starts the monkey off in his den (or nest) in the trees. A forever loop makes him point to wherever the fruit is and move in that direction. There are two "if" blocks that detect two possible events that we are interested in. The first is if the missile (water) has hit the monkey, then we play the plunge sound and he retreats momentarily to his nest. The other "if" deals with the monkey finding the fruit. Then he gets a score update, broadcasts to the other sprites that the fruit is being eaten, and retreats to his nest. See Figure 7-25.

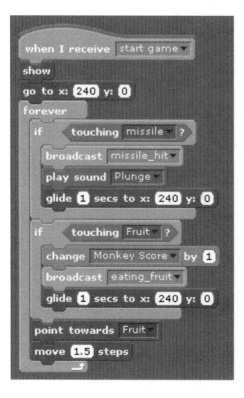

Figure 7-25.
Monkey start script

Finally, the script for when "game over" is received is a bit more complicated still. It checks if the monkey has the winning score; if so, it positions him after the "winner:" text to show he has won. His costume is stamped in place and then the sprite is hidden. Finally, we stop the entire game (see Figure 7-26).

Figure 7-26.
Monkey game-over script

The final sprite and script will involve our courageous and noble elephant, whose job is to fend off pesky monkeys looking to steal the banana stash! This is the most complex sprite, and also the one where most of the Kinect action happens. Create a new sprite by clicking "Choose new sprite from file," selecting the *Animals* folder, scrolling down, and selecting "elephant1-a." Then click on the Costumes tab, select Import, navigate back to *Animals*, scroll down, and select "elephant1-b." At this point, you should have two costumes for your elephant sprite.

Name them something similar to "normal" and "attack" (for instance, you could call them "relaxed" and "spraying"), but remember the names you gave them. See Figure 7-27.

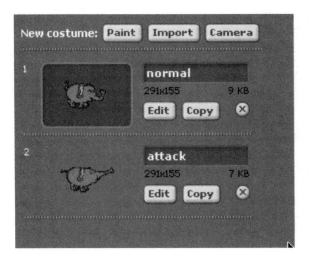

Figure 7-27.
Elephant costume sprite

The scripts are the most complex of the game, but should still be understandable. The first script deals with initialization; costumes and variables are reset and the sprite hides until the game starts. See Figure 7-28.

Figure 7-28.
Elephant initialization script

Following that, the script that runs during the game is the most complicated. If you look at Figure 7-29, you'll notice that it points in direction 0 (straight up) and an initial position (this can be anything on the x-axis as long as the y value is −123).

Then it shows the sprite and goes into a forever loop. The loop continuously moves the sprite to the player's head x position, keeping the sprite on its original y position. The next bit is a little tricky; it deals with firing the missile (or water spray). Notice that this script is actually several scripts merged into one.

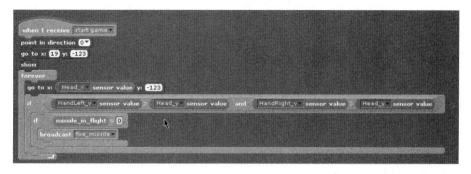

Figure 7-29.
Final elephant script layout

This script uses what is formally called a Boolean AND expression, which, simply put, ensures that two separate events are occurring at the same time to trigger a positive result. In this case, it's both the left hand and right hand being above your head at the same time. If only one of these conditions is true, no missile will be fired. Test this by raising only one hand above your head at a time and see if the missile is launched. It's deconstructed in Figure 7-30 to show you how to build it up yourself (you should have only the last item if you made it correctly).

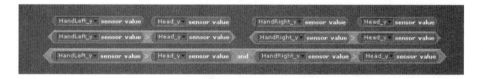

Figure 7-30.
Missile firing script

To read this out in English, we'd say, "If your left hand's *y* value is greater than your head's *y* value AND your right hand's *y* value is greater than your head's *y* value, then…" In this case, the positive result is to first check that another missile is not already in flight (you can have only one) and if not, broadcast the message "fire_missile."

The elephant sprite itself is a consumer of values represented in Figure 7-31; it changes the costume to a spraying or attack costume for a second when it receives this message, then it changes it back.

Figure 7-31.
Elephant costume switching script

All good things must come to an end. Similarly to the monkey sprite, when the elephant receives a "game over" message, it checks to see if it should stamp a copy of itself as the winner on the game-over screen before shutting down all scripts. See Figure 7-32.

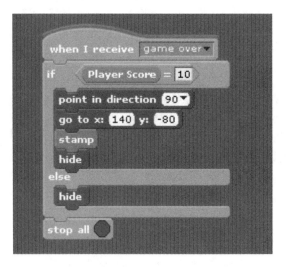

Figure 7-32.
Elephant game-over script

Once you have all the sprites and costumes ready, run Kinect2Scratch and ensure that the Kinect is launched and Scratch is receiving data. Run the game in full-screen mode (the easel icon in the top right of Scratch) and click the green flag to start. Raise your right hand for the instructions screen, and again to play. Move left and right to guide the elephant: remember to throw both hands over your head to spray him. Time your sprays well—you have only one at a time, and they are slow! The first player to accrue 10 points wins the game! Have fun playing, and make some of your own changes to the game. Maybe two-player mode?

Build a Kinect Space Shooter Game in Processing

Here's a great little shooter game developed by Jordi Llobet Torrens and Anna Fusté Lleixà. This Kinect Processing game is a throwback to classic gaming, but with a modern-day twist. The goal is to stay alive by shifting your body position from left to right while throwing your arms up in the air to shoot approaching enemies.

To download the full version with all files associated with the Processing sketch, go to *http://developkinect.com/resource/game/kinect-space-shooter*.

The sketch comprises four additional classes to accompany the *Main.pde* file. They consist of components such as a **Heart** class, which controls the speed of the falling hearts that provide additional "lives"; a **Bullet** class, which generates shots when the user raises his hands; and a **Particle** class, which is responsible for enemy movements and actions.

Begin by importing the library for Open Natural Interaction:

```
import SimpleOpenNI.*;
```

Next we'll issue the variable declarations, starting with the background image:

```
//Background Image
PImage backg, backg2, piSpaceCraft, piLife, piCalibrate, piCapture;
PFont pfFontCalibrate, pfFontGameOver, pfBig, pfSmall;
```

Set the amount of initial "lives" that the player receives when starting the game. Set the value to 5:

```
int iLifes = 5;
```

The walls are defined as follows: Wall 1: bottom; Wall 2: right; Wall 3: top; and Wall 4: left.

```
Wall w_Wall, w_Wall2, w_Wall3, w_Wall4;
PVector pNormal, pNormal2, pNormal3, pNormal4,
   pVect, pVect2, pVect3, pVect4, pPoint, pPoint2, pPoint3, pPoint4;
```

Here we specify the number of monsters in the game and initialization:

```
int iNumEnemies = 5;
Particle[] sParticles = new Particle[iNumEnemies];
boolean bParticlesExist = false;
```

Next up is the bullets and initialization. To begin the game, the user is allocated one shot at a time.

```
int iNumBullet = 0;
int iMaxBullets = 1;
Bullet[] b_Bullets = new Bullet[5];
```

Count lives (descending):

```
int iHearts = 0;
Heart h_heart;
boolean bHeartExist=false;
```

Set the screen size dimensions:

```
int iWidth = 1024, iHeight = 768;
```

Specify the user position:

```
PVector jointPos = new PVector();
```

Set the **SimpleOpenNI context** variable:

```
SimpleOpenNI  context;

//Screen variable:

0 - Menu
1 - Calibrate
2 - Game
3 - How to play
4 - Game over
5 - CountDown
6 - Credits

int iScreen = 0;
boolean bTrackingSkel = false, bInitPart = false,
  bInitWall = false, bPlayed = false;
// boolean to know if the photo has been taken
boolean bCapture = false;
```

Now we'll include the functions:

```
void setup()  {
```

Load fonts:

```
pfFontCalibrate = loadFont("data/Consolas-30.vlw");
pfFontGameOver = loadFont("data/Consolas-48.vlw");
pfBig = loadFont("data/Consolas20.vlw");
pfSmall = loadFont("data/Consolas14.vlw");
```

Load images:

```
backg = loadImage("imatges/fons-1024.jpg");
backg2 = loadImage("imatges/fonsInvertit-1024.jpg");
piSpaceCraft = loadImage("imatges/prota.png");
piLife = loadImage("imatges/vida.png");
piCalibrate = loadImage("imatges/calibrar.png");
```

Set up NITE and initialize context:

```
context = new SimpleOpenNI(this);
```

Mirror is enabled by default:

```
context.setMirror(true);
```

Enable depth map generation:

```
context.enableDepth();
```

Enable camera image generation:

```
context.enableRGB();
```

Initialize user segmentation:

```
context.enableUser(SimpleOpenNI.SKEL_PROFILE_ALL);
stroke(0,0,255);
strokeWeight(3);
size(iWidth, iHeight);

frameRate(30);
}

void draw()  {

switch(iScreen){
```

Calibrate:

```
case 0:
    background(backg2);
    iLifes = 5;
```

Update the context:

```
context.update();
```

The following text prepares the player for the Psi calibration pose:

```
fill(0);
  textFont(pfFontGameOver);
  text("Stay like this for a while!", 170, 80 );
```

Next we set the **image** along with the **depthImage**:

```
image(piCalibrate, (iWidth/2)-114, 250);
image(context.depthImage(),iWidth-100,iHeight-100, 100, 100);
break;
```

Case 1 is represented by the game:

```
case 1:
```

Increase the counting variable to throw hearts:

```
iHearts++;
```

Initialize particles just the first time:

```
if (!bInitPart){
  initParticles();
  bInitPart = true;
}
```

Initialize walls just the first time:

```
if (!bInitWall){
  InitWalls();
  bInitWall = true;
}
```

```
background(backg);
```

Update the context:

```
context.update();
```

Draw the depth image map at the right corner of the screen:

```
image(context.depthImage(),iWidth-100,iHeight-100, 100, 100);
```

The user moves out of the camera and back in. If it's a different user, we detect it like ID 1.

```
int userCount = context.getNumberOfUsers();
  if(userCount>0) {
    IntVector userList = new IntVector();
    context.getUsers(userList);
    int trackingListIndex = userCount-1;
    int trackingId = (int)userList.get(trackingListIndex);
```

Draw the craft if the skeleton is available:

```
if(context.isTrackingSkeleton(trackingId)) {
  drawSkeleton(trackingId);
```

```
        }
    }

        for (int iAux = 0; iAux < iNumEnemies; iAux++) {
```

Draw the particle and move it forward:

```
        sParticles[iAux].goAhead();
        sParticles[iAux].drawParticle();
```

Detect collisions with walls:

```
        sParticles[iAux].collision(w_Wall, pNormal, 1, pPoint);
        sParticles[iAux].collision(w_Wall2, pNormal2, 2, pPoint2);
        sParticles[iAux].collision(w_Wall3, pNormal3, 3, pPoint3);
        sParticles[iAux].collision(w_Wall4, pNormal4, 4, pPoint4);
```

Detect collisions with craft:

```
        if (sParticles[iAux].craftCollision(jointPos.x*iWidth/640)){
```

If a collision occurs, subtract one unit of life from the player:

```
        lifeDown();
    }
```

Detect collisions with a bullet:

```
        for (int i = 0; i < iNumBullet ; i++){
          sParticles[iAux].bulletCollision(b_Bullets[i]);
        }
```

Detect if there's still any monster in the game:

```
        if (sParticles[iAux].particleExists()) {
          bParticlesExist = true;
        }
    }
```

Every regular period of time, a heart falls.

```
    if(iHearts%500 == 0){
```

Initialize one heart:

```
        h_heart = new Heart(random(100, 400));
        bHeartExist = true;

    }
```

If there's a heart, move it forward.

```
if (bHeartExist){
    h_heart.goAhead();
```

Detect if the user catches the heart with the user position (scaled to our screen size):

```
if (h_heart.craftCollision(jointPos.x*iWidth/640)){
```

If there's a collision, destroy the heart and move one life up:

```
        bHeartExist = false;
        h_heart.destroy();
        iLifes++;


    }
}
```

If there are no lives left or all the monsters have been killed:

```
if ((iLifes == 0)||(!bParticlesExist)) {
```

Go to the final screen:

```
    iScreen = 2;

} else {
```

Reset to **false** variable **bParticlesExist**:

```
    bParticlesExist = false;
}

drawLifes();

if (!bCapture) {
```

Take a real photo of the player:

```
        piCapture = context.rgbImage();
        bCapture = true;

}

break;
```

Specify the game-over case:

```
case 2:
```

Update the camera:

```
context.update();
image(context.depthImage(),iWidth-100,iHeight-100, 100, 100);
fill(255);

if(iLifes == 0) {
  text("GAME OVER!", (iWidth/2) - 100, 200);
} else {
  text("YOU WIN!", (iWidth/2) - 100, 200);
}
```

Specify the **Init** variables:

```
bInitPart = false;
bInitWall = false;
image(context.depthImage(),iWidth-100,iHeight-100, 100, 100);
pushMatrix();
rotate(0.1);
image(piCapture, 270, 270, (iWidth/2) - 50, (iHeight/2)-100);
popMatrix();
break;


  }
}
```

Set up functions:

```
void initParticles(){
```

Initialize all particles with random values:

```
for (int iAux = 0; iAux < iNumEnemies; iAux++) {
  sParticles[iAux] = new Particle(random(300, 500),
    random(150, 250),
  random(-100, 100), random(-100, 100),int(random(3)));
  }


  }
```

Every regular period of time, a heart falls:

```
void InitWalls() {
```

Initialize wall 1 (the bottom wall):

```
w_Wall = new Wall(0.0, iHeight-35.0, iWidth, iHeight-35.0, 1);
pNormal = new PVector();
pVect = new PVector();
pPoint = new PVector();
```

```
        w_Wall.calculateNormal();
        pNormal = w_Wall.getNormal();
        pVect = w_Wall.getVector();
        pPoint = w_Wall.getPoint();
```

Initialize wall 2 (the right wall):

```
        w_Wall2 = new Wall(iWidth-25.0, iHeight, iWidth-25.0, 0.0, -1);
        pNormal2 = new PVector();
        pVect2 = new PVector();
        pPoint2 = new PVector();
        w_Wall2.calculateNormal();
        pNormal2 = w_Wall2.getNormal();
        pVect2 = w_Wall2.getVector();
        pPoint2 = w_Wall2.getPoint();
```

Initialize wall 3 (the top wall):

```
        w_Wall3 = new Wall(0.0, 0.0, iWidth, 0.0, -1);
        pNormal3 = new PVector();
        pVect3 = new PVector();
        pPoint3 = new PVector();
        w_Wall3.calculateNormal();
        pNormal3 = w_Wall3.getNormal();
        pVect3 = w_Wall3.getVector();
        pPoint3 = w_Wall3.getPoint();
```

Initialize wall 4 (the left wall):

```
        w_Wall4 = new Wall(0.0, 0.0, 0.0, iHeight, 1);
        pNormal4 = new PVector();
        pVect4 = new PVector();
        pPoint4 = new PVector();
        w_Wall4.calculateNormal();
        pNormal4 = w_Wall4.getNormal();
        pVect4 = w_Wall4.getVector();
        pPoint4 = w_Wall4.getPoint();


    }
```

Get the 3D joint data:

```
    void drawSkeleton(int userId)
    {
      PVector pvLeftHand = new PVector();
      PVector pvRightHand = new PVector();
      PVector pvNeck = new PVector();
```

Get the torso articulation position of the player:

```
context.getJointPositionSkeleton
  (userId,SimpleOpenNI.SKEL_TORSO,jointPos);
//convert 3d world coord to 2d coord
context.convertRealWorldToProjective(jointPos, jointPos);
```

Draw the craft at the player body's x position (we scale the position to our screen size):

```
image(piSpaceCraft, (jointPos.x)*iWidth/640 , 703);
```

Detect the three points needed to shoot. The user shoots when both hands are above the neck.

```
context.getJointPositionSkeleton
  (userId,SimpleOpenNI.SKEL_LEFT_HAND,pvLeftHand);
context.getJointPositionSkeleton
  (userId,SimpleOpenNI.SKEL_RIGHT_HAND,pvRightHand);
context.getJointPositionSkeleton
  (userId,SimpleOpenNI.SKEL_NECK,pvNeck);
```

Here's the function to convert the 3D world coordinates to 2D coordinates:

```
context.convertRealWorldToProjective(pvLeftHand, pvLeftHand);
context.convertRealWorldToProjective(pvRightHand, pvRightHand);
context.convertRealWorldToProjective(pvNeck, pvNeck);
```

Shoot:

```
if ((pvLeftHand.y < pvNeck.y) && (pvRightHand.y < pvNeck.y)&&
  (iNumBullet<iMaxBullets)){
    b_Bullets[iNumBullet] = new Bullet
      ((jointPos.x*iWidth/640)+50, 703);
    iNumBullet++;
}
```

Move bullets on the screen forward:

```
for (int i=0; i < iNumBullet; i++) {
  b_Bullets[i].goAhead();
  if(b_Bullets[i].getY() < 0){
    iNumBullet--;
  }
 }
}
```

This is the function to take one life away:

```
void lifeDown(){
  if (iLifes>0) {
    iLifes--;
  }
}
```

And here's the function to draw the actual lives of the player:

```
void drawLifes(){
  for (int i =0; i<iLifes; i++){
    image(piLife, 59.0*i, 10.0);
  }
}
```

When a new user is detected by the Kinect sensors:

```
void onNewUser(int userId)
{
  if (userId == 1) {
```

Start the detection of the pose to do the skeleton tracking:

```
    context.startPoseDetection("Psi",userId);
    println("New user Id: " + userId);
    println("Start pose detection");

  } else {
```

Don't calibrate if **userId** is different than 1:

```
    println("User "+userId+", We are not interested in.");

  }
}
```

Specify when a user is lost by the Kinect sensors:

```
void onLostUser(int userId)
{
  println("Lost User - userId: " + userId);
}
```

Specify when the user calibration starts:

```
void onStartCalibration(int userId)
{
  println("onStartCalibration - userId: " + userId);
}
```

Specify when the calibration is finished:

```
void onEndCalibration(int userId, boolean successful)
{
  println("onEndCalibration - userId: " + userId + ",
    successful: " + successful);

  if (successful)
  {
    println("  UserId = "+userId+" calibrated !");
```

Start tracking the user:

```
    context.startTrackingSkeleton(userId);
```

When the user is calibrated, we go to the next stage (the game):

```
    iScreen  = 1;


  }
  else
  {
```

If the calibration is not successful, we try to recalibrate the user:

```
    println("  Failed to calibrate user !!!");
    println("  Start pose detection");
    context.startPoseDetection("Psi",userId);


  }
}
```

Specify when the calibration pose is detected:

```
void onStartPose(String pose,int userId)
{
```

The following detects the user calibration pose. Once the user is detected, start to calibrate the skeleton:

```
    println(" onStartPose - userId: " + userId + ", pose: " + pose);
    println(" stop pose detection ");

    context.stopPoseDetection(userId);
    context.requestCalibrationSkeleton(userId, true);


}
```

Specify when the user stops doing the pose:

```
void onEndPose(String pose,int userId) {
    println("onEndPose - userId: " + userId + ", pose: " + pose);
}
```

HACK 50 Build a Processing Fridge Magnet Game

This gesture control Processing sketch was created by Jeramy Archer. It uses the SimpleOpenNI library to capture gestures, allowing the user to control her video window and combine letters to construct words or sentences. Think fridge magnets for the ultimate techno-geek (see Figure 7-33). It's not exactly a game, really, but definitely has the potential to be a pretty slick, fun-to-use learning tool. Perhaps you could add wrapping as a means of keeping score when matching the letters to some words? I'll leave that up to you to decide.

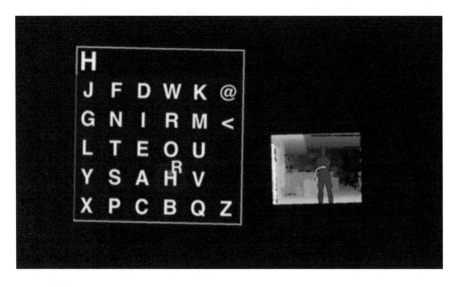

Figure 7-33.
Fridge Magnets UI

We'll begin by importing the SimpleOpenNI library and setting the screen size values:

```
import SimpleOpenNI.SimpleOpenNI;

int screenWidth = 1280, screenHeight = 800;

SimpleOpenNI openni;
ArrayList<Person> people;
ArrayList<Target> targets, targetsToAddNextCycle;
PFont monaco, helvetica;
Target fullScreenTarget;
```

This represents a single cursor and hand belonging to a figure on the screen:

```
class Hand {
    int x, y, z, deltaX, deltaY, deltaZ;
    int grabX, grabY;
    boolean grabbing, visible, isLeftHand;
    Person person;
    Target grabTarget;
    PVector start, direction;
```

Initialize this hand given its sidedness and parent:

```
Hand(Person p, boolean isLeft) {
    person = p;
    grabbing = visible = false;
    isLeftHand = isLeft;

    x = y = z = grabX = grabY = -1;
    deltaX = deltaY = deltaZ = 0;

    start = direction = null;
}
```

Move this hand to a new position. Internally, this method handles smoothing:

```
void moveHand(int newX, int newY, int newZ) {
    x += deltaX = (newX - x + 1) / 4;
    y += deltaY = (newY - y + 1) / 4;
    z += deltaZ = (newZ - z + 1);
```

Check for NaN: for complicated reasons, (1/0) != (1/0).

```
    if (x != x) x = 0;
    if (y != y) y = 0;
    if (z != z) z = 0;
```

Hide the hand if it is off-screen.

```
    visible = (x >= 0 && y >= 0 && x < width && y < height);
}
```

Render this hand on the current Processing canvas. It will look like a circle with a letter (L or R) attached.

```
void draw() {
    if (!visible) return;

    noStroke();
    if (grabTarget != null)
```

```
        fill(200, 0, 0);
    else
        fill(200, 200, 0);
    ellipse(x - 10, y - 10, 20, 20);

    fill(255);
    textFont(helvetica, 60f);
    text(isLeftHand ? "L" : "R", x - 10, y - 10);
}
```

Pull the latest data from the SimpleOpenNI instance.

```
void updateFromNI() {
    PVector projYourHand = new PVector(),
      yourHand = new PVector();
    PVector projYourTorso = new PVector(),
      yourTorso = new PVector();
```

Get the position of the hand, as a PVector. (c1 represents the certainty of that position.)

```
float c1 = openni.getJointPositionSkeleton(
    /* user ID */      person.getID(),
    /* joint */        isLeftHand ? SimpleOpenNI.SKEL_LEFT_HAND :
                            SimpleOpenNI.SKEL_RIGHT_HAND,
    /* destination */ yourHand
);
```

Get the position of the torso, as a PVector. (c2, as with the preceding case, represents the certainty.)

```
float c2 = openni.getJointPositionSkeleton(
    /* user ID */      person.getID(),
    /* joint */        SimpleOpenNI.SKEL_TORSO,
    /* destination */ projYourTorso
);
```

If we're fairly uncertain about either vector, hide this hand. Since the NI documentation is rather sparse on this topic, this factor is pretty arbitrary.

```
if (c1 <= 0.001f || c2 <= 0.001f) {
    visible = false;
    return;
}
```

Convert the perspective vectors (angle and distance) to real-world (x, y, z) vectors.

```
// openni.convertProjectiveToRealWorld(projYourTorso, yourTorso);
// openni.convertProjectiveToRealWorld(projYourHand, yourHand);
```

Scale the vectors arbitrarily to the screen size. They are currently in millimeters, so we need to convert them to screen (pixel) coordinates. Here, we're using a grab box of two meters wide, one meter tall, and about half a meter deep.

```
int newX = (int)(((yourHand.x - yourTorso.x) /
    1500.0 + 0.5f) * width);
int newY = (int)(((yourTorso.y - yourHand.y) /
    800.0 + 0.5f) * height);
int newZ = (int)(((yourTorso.z - yourHand.z) /
    450.0) * 100.0);
```

Move the hand to this new position.

```
moveHand(newX, newY, newZ);
    }
```

Detect if this hand is intersecting something on the hit image in the blue channel. The "hit image," in this case, is an image with all the objects rendered in a flat, per-object color, so that we can simply see the color at a certain (x, y) location to see what object lies there.

```
public int intersect(PImage hitTestImage) {
```

Disable if we're invisible (off screen). That's why we don't need a conditional here.

```
if (!visible) return -1;
```

There are a few things going on here. First, the image is scaled down to 10%, meaning that we need to scale both x and y by 10. We also need to linearize them (in row-major order). The result, which is a color, may have some alpha components, so we get rid of them and extract the blue component.

```
int value = hitTestImage.pixels
    [(x / 10) + (y / 10) * (width / 10)] & 0xff;
```

The blue component value of zero is black (#000), so we need to shift this guy down by one so that #000001 maps to 0 and #000000 maps to –1 (no intersection).

```
return value - 1;
    }
```

Detect if this hand is intersecting something on the hit image in the green channel. The "hit image," in this case, is an image with all the objects rendered in a flat, per-object color, so that we can simply see the color at a certain (x, y) location to see what object lies there.

```
public int intersectGreen(PImage hitTestImage) {
```

Disable if we're invisible (off screen). That's why we don't need a conditional here.

```
if (!visible) return -1;
```

There are a few things going on here. First, the image is scaled down to 10%, meaning that we need to scale both *x* and *y* by 10. We also need to linearize them (in row-major order). The result, which is a color, may have some alpha components, so we get rid of them and extract the green component.

```
int value = (hitTestImage.pixels
    [(x / 10) + (y / 10) * (width / 10)] >> 8) & 0xff;
```

The blue component value of zero is black (#000), so we need to shift this guy down by one so that #000001 maps to 0 and #000000 maps to −1 (no intersection).

```
    return value - 1;
}
```

Mark this hand as having hovered over another object, given the target's ID and secondary (green component) color index. If **t** is null, mark this object as not grabbing anything.

```
public void grab(Target t, int secondaryIndex) {
```

Record this object:

```
grabTarget = t;
```

If given a new target, tell that object to begin showing hover feedback.

```
    if (t != null)
        t.takeHoverDataFrom(this, secondaryIndex);
}
```

Set the target given the rendered hit image and numbered targets. The index of each object will be encoded in the blue channel of the **PImage**, so that, for example, object 0 (the first object in the list) will be encoded as #000001, object 1 as #000002, and so on.

```
public void setTargetFrom
    (PImage hitTestImage, ArrayList<Target> targets) {
```

If we're already hovering over something, unregister us from the object. If it turns out that we are still hovering over it with both hands, the **Person** class will register us as having grabbed it.

```
    if (grabTarget != null)
        grabTarget.setGrabbedBy(null);
```

Extract the blue and green indices from the hit image.

```
    int index = intersect(hitTestImage);
    int secondaryIndex = intersectGreen(hitTestImage);
```

If we're hovering over something, mark it as having been hovered over.

```
            if (index == -1) grab(null, 0);
            else grab(targets.get(index), secondaryIndex);
        }
```

Get the target we're currently hovering over.

```
        public Target getGrabTarget() {
            return grabTarget;
        }
```

Return whether this hand is on screen.

```
        public boolean getIsVisible() {
          return visible;
        }
```

Return the x coordinate (in screen pixels) of this hand.

```
        public int getX() {
            return x;
        }
```

Return the y coordinate (in screen pixels) of this hand.

```
        public int getY() {
            return y;
        }
```

Return the z coordinate of this hand. In practice, this will usually be in the range [−150.0, +150.0], but there isn't a defined rectangle as there is for x and y.

```
        public int getZ() {
            return z;
        }
    }
```

This is the controlling class for a person with two hands.

```
    class Person {
        Hand left, right;
        int userID;
        Target grabTarget;
```

Initialize this person given her ID in OpenNI.

```
        public Person(int id) {
            left = new Hand(this, true);
            right = new Hand(this, false);
            userID = id;
        }
```

Return the internal OpenNI identifier.

```
public int getID() {
    return userID;
}
```

Return the left hand.

```
public Hand getLeftHand() { return left; }
```

Return the right hand.

```
public Hand getRightHand() { return right; }
```

Update the current grabbing/hovering status, given the hit image and list of targets. The hit image is a rendered image with the various targets rendered as a silhouette in a flat color. The first object in the array is in color #000001, the second is #000002, and so on.

```
public void updateGrabbing(PImage hitTestImage,
    ArrayList<Target> targets) {
```

Update the hovering status for both hands.

```
        left.setTargetFrom(hitTestImage, targets);
        right.setTargetFrom(hitTestImage, targets);
```

If we're hovering over the same object with both hands, then mark the target as having been grabbed by us.

```
        if (left.getGrabTarget() == right.getGrabTarget() &&
            (left.getGrabTarget() != null))
            left.getGrabTarget().setGrabbedBy(this);
}
```

Get the average x position of the two hands.

```
public int getAverageX() {
    return (getLeftHand().getX() + getRightHand().getX()) / 2;
}
```

Get the average y position of the two hands.

```
public int getAverageY() {
    return (getLeftHand().getY() + getRightHand().getY()) / 2;
}
```

Get the angle [−pi, +pi] between the two hands.

```
    public float getHandAngle() {
        return atan2(getRightHand().getY() - getLeftHand().getY(),
                     getRightHand().getX() - getLeftHand().getX());
    }
```

Get the distance between both hands.

```
    public float getGrabRadius() {
        float dx = getRightHand().getY() - getLeftHand().getY(),
              dy = getRightHand().getX() - getLeftHand().getX();

        return (float)Math.sqrt(dx*dx + dy*dy);
    }
}
```

This represents a grabbable object on the screen.

```
    interface Target {
```

Render this object as a silhouette onto the **PGraphics** object given the value of the blue component.

```
        void drawHitRegion(PGraphics g, int blueComponent);
```

Render this object in full color.

```
        void draw();
```

Set this object as having been grabbed by the specified person. This method will be called a lot (every frame), so it should do little more than set a variable.

```
        void setGrabbedBy(Person p);
```

Move this object to the new location.

```
        void moveTo(int x, int y);
```

Rotate this object to the specified angle.

```
        void rotateTo(float angleInRadians);
```

Update the position and rotation of the object given the person grabbing it.

```
        void updateGrabbing();
```

Update the UI to respond (show feedback) to being hovered over by the specified hand. This method is also passed the green component of the color the hand is hovering over.

```
        void takeHoverDataFrom(Hand h, int secondaryIndex);
    }
```

This represents a target that is nested inside another.

```
interface SubTarget {
```

Render this object as a silhouette. The **PGraphics** will already be initialized with the proper color.

```
    void drawHitRegion(PGraphics g);
```

Render this object in full color.

```
    void draw();
```

Mark this object as currently being hovered over.

```
    void hoverOver();
```

Update this object given the current visibility of this **SubTarget**.

```
    void updateHovering(boolean enabled);
}
```

This represents an abstract rectangular target. By default, this class only draws a gray rectangle on the screen, but supports **SubTarget**s, rotation, and movement. Most other **Target**s are subclasses of this one.

```
class Rectangle implements Target {
    int x, y, w, h;
    float rotationAngle;
    Person grabbedBy;
    ArrayList<SubTarget> subTargets;
```

Initialize this rectangle with the default size, 500×300, and place it in the center of the screen.

```
    public Rectangle() {
        w = 500;
        h = 300;
        x = (width - w) / 2;
        y = (height - h) / 2;
        rotationAngle = 0.0f;
        grabbedBy = null;
        subTargets = new ArrayList<SubTarget>();
    }
```

Return **true** if this object can be bumped into full screen.

```
    boolean canBeMadeFullScreen() {  // meant to be overwriten.
        return false;
    }
```

Render this object in color. The coordinate system will already have been shifted and rotated so that the object should be placed to the right and below (0, 0).

Subclasses note: this method renders **SubTarget**s. If you intend to replace or override this method, you must manually render all **SubTarget** instances in this class, like so:

```
...

void drawTarget() {

...

  for (SubTarget target : subTargets) {
    target.draw();
  }
}

...

    void drawTarget() { // meant to be overridden.
        if (grabbedBy != null)
            stroke(200, 0, 0);
        else
            stroke(200, 200, 0);

        strokeWeight(5);
        fill(50);

        rect(0, 0, w, h);

        for (SubTarget target : subTargets) {
            target.draw();
        }
    }
```

Render this target as a silhouette onto the image buffer instance. The coordinate system will already have been shifted and rotated so that the object should be placed to the right and below (0, 0).

Subclasses note: this method renders **SubTargets**. If you intend to replace or override this method, you must manually render all **SubTarget** instances in this class. Likewise, before rendering, you must ensure that all objects are drawn in the proper color:

```
...
void drawTargetHitRegions(PGraphics g, int blueComponent) {
  g.fill(0, 0, blueComponent);

...

  for (int i = 0; i < subTargets.size(); i++) {
    g.fill(0, (i + 1), blueComponent);
```

```
            subTargets.get(i).drawHitRegion(g);
        }
    }
    ...

        void drawTargetHitRegions(PGraphics g, int blueComponent) {
            g.fill(0, 0, blueComponent);
            g.rect(0, 0, w, h);

            for (int i = 0; i < subTargets.size(); i++) {
                g.fill(0, (i + 1), blueComponent);
                subTargets.get(i).drawHitRegion(g);
            }
        }
```

Add a **SubTarget** to this list.

```
        void addSubTarget(SubTarget tar) {
            subTargets.add(tar);
        }
```

Draw this object in silhouette form in a color with the specified blue component, as defined in the interface.

```
        void drawHitRegion(PGraphics g, int blueComponent) {
```

Determine if the entire screen has a single component.

```
        if (fullScreenTarget != null) {
```

If we're in full screen mode, render the entire screen as the same color. It's wasteful, but cycles are plentiful nowadays.

```
            if (fullScreenTarget == this) {
```

Transform our coordinate system and render.

```
                g.pushMatrix();
                g.fill(0, 0, blueComponent);
                g.rect(0, 0, width, height);
                g.translate(width / 2, height / 2);
                g.scale(Math.min(((float)width) / w, ((float)height) / h));
                g.translate(-w / 2, -h / 2);

                drawTargetHitRegions(g, blueComponent);
                g.popMatrix();
            }
        } else {
```

Transform our coordinate system and render.

```
g.pushMatrix();
g.translate(x, y);
g.translate(w / 2, h / 2);

g.rotate(rotationAngle);
```

If we're grabbing, increase the size of the object to make it easier to grip.

```
if (grabbedBy != null) g.scale(1.5);

g.translate(-w / 2, -h / 2);
drawTargetHitRegions(g, blueComponent);

g.popMatrix();
    }
  }
```

Render this object in full color.

```
void draw() {
```

Determine whether one component is blocking the entire screen.

```
if (fullScreenTarget == this) {
```

If we're in full screen mode, simply transform and render.

```
pushMatrix();
translate(width / 2, height / 2);
scale(Math.min(((float)width) / w, ((float)height) / h));
translate(-w / 2, -h / 2);
drawTarget();
popMatrix();
```

Retransform and put an axis through both hands to indicate that distance is how a full screen view is maintained.

```
pushMatrix();
strokeWeight(1);
stroke(255, 255, 255, 50);
noFill();

translate(grabbedBy.getAverageX(), grabbedBy.getAverageY());
rotate(grabbedBy.getHandAngle());

ellipse(0, 0, 0.6 * width, 0.6 * width);
line(-width * 10, 0, width * 10, 0);
```

```
      line(0, -height * 10, 0, height * 10);

    popMatrix();
  } else if (fullScreenTarget == null) {
```

If no target is in full screen mode, then transform and render in the normal place.

```
        pushMatrix();
        translate(x + w / 2, y + h / 2);
        rotate(rotationAngle);
        translate(-w / 2, -h / 2);
        drawTarget();
```

If we've been grabbed, render an overlay of crosshairs and an outer radius.

```
        if (grabbedBy != null) {
          translate(w / 2, h / 2);

          strokeWeight(1);
          stroke(255, 255, 255, 50);
          noFill();
          line(-width * 10, 0, width * 20, 0);
          line(0, -height * 10, 0, height * 20);
          ellipse(0, 0, 100, 100);
          ellipse(0, 0, 40, 40);
        }

        popMatrix();
  }
```

Update the status of all **SubTarget**s. Pass true if this **SubTarget** is visible.

```
        for (SubTarget tar : subTargets) {
          tar.updateHovering((grabbedBy == null &&
            fullScreenTarget == null) ||
            fullScreenTarget == this);
        }
  }
```

Mark this target as having been grabbed.

```
    void setGrabbedBy(Person p) {
      grabbedBy = p;
    }
```

Update hovering data from the given hand and highlight the target.

```
    void takeHoverDataFrom(Hand p, int greenComponent) {
      if (greenComponent != -1) {
```

```
                SubTarget tar = subTargets.get(greenComponent);
                tar.hoverOver();
            }
        }
```

Move the rectangle to the specified *x* and *y* positions.

```
        void moveTo(int newX, int newY) {
            x = newX - w / 2;
            y = newY - h / 2;
        }
```

Rotate this rectangle to the specified angle from the horizontal.

```
        void rotateTo(float angleInRadians) {
            rotationAngle = angleInRadians;
        }
```

Update the position and rotation of this object given the position of the grabbing hand.

```
        void updateGrabbing() {
            if (grabbedBy != null && fullScreenTarget == null) {
```

If no one is in full screen mode, then move and rotate this block.

```
                moveTo(grabbedBy.getAverageX(), grabbedBy.getAverageY());
                rotateTo(grabbedBy.getHandAngle());
```

If the hands are close enough together, pop into full screen mode.

```
                if (grabbedBy.getGrabRadius() < 100) {
                    fullScreenTarget = this;
                }

            } else if (fullScreenTarget == this) {
```

If we're out of full screen mode and the hands are too far apart, pop out of full screen mode.

```
                if (grabbedBy == null || grabbedBy.getGrabRadius()
                    > 0.6 * width) {
                    fullScreenTarget = null;
                }
            }
        }
    }
```

Here is a movable view of NI's depth image, colored for calibration.

```
    class SceneViewTarget extends Rectangle {
```

By default, this view is half the pixel width of NI's scene image.

```
SceneViewTarget() {
    w = openni.sceneWidth() / 2;
    h = openni.sceneHeight() / 2;
    x = width - w;
    y = height - h;
}
```

This can be made full screen. When in full screen mode, it displays a four-up view of IR, the scene, depth, and RGB information.

```
boolean canBeMadeFullScreen() {
    return true;
}
```

Render the NI scene image, with overlays for the arms and torso.

```
void drawSceneView() {
    rect(0, 0, w, h);

    image(openni.sceneImage(), 0, 0, w, h);

}
```

Render this control.

```
void drawTarget() {
```

Draw the scene view.

```
    if (fullScreenTarget == this) {
```

Draw the scene view in the top-left.

```
        pushMatrix();
        scale(0.5, 0.5);
        drawSceneView();
        popMatrix();
```

Render the IR, depth, and RGB images. IR and RGB cannot be viewed at the same time for technical reasons.

```
        if (openni.irImage() != null)
            image(openni.irImage(), w / 2, 0, w / 2, h / 2);
        image(openni.depthImage(), 0, h / 2, w / w, h / 2);

        if (openni.rgbImage() != null)
            image(openni.rgbImage(), w / 2, h / 2, w / 2, h / 2);
    } else {
```

In regular mode, just render the scene.

```
                pushMatrix();
                drawSceneView();
                popMatrix();
            }
        }
    }
```

This represents a textual label that can be placed and moved.

```
    class RefrigeratorMagnet extends Rectangle {
        String label;
```

Initialize this widget given the string to display. It will be placed randomly on the screen (with caveats—can you see why?) and with enough width to display the message.

```
        RefrigeratorMagnet(String s) {
            textFont(helvetica,90);

            w = (int)textWidth(s) + 20;
            h = 100;
            x = (int)random(width - w);
            y = (int)random(height - h);

            label = s;
        }
```

Render the magnet. It will be drawn in Helvetica with a colored border, depending on its status.

```
        void drawTarget() {
            if (grabbedBy != null)
                stroke(200, 0, 0);
            else
                stroke(200, 200, 0);

            strokeWeight(5);
            fill(10);

            rect(0, 0, w, h);

            fill(255);
            textFont(helvetica, 90);
            text(label, 10, 80);

            for (SubTarget target : subTargets) {
```

```
                target.draw();
            }
        }
    }
```

A collection of key widgets allows the user to type letters and make textual "refrigerator magnets," as shown previously.

```
    class KeyboardTarget extends Rectangle {
```

The keys were chosen this way based on relative word frequency in English: the most common words are in the center, which (theoretically) makes them more accessible.

There are some special characters: the at sign (@) represents enter, or newline; the back-chevron (<) represents backspace or delete; and the space represents "no button."

```
    String topRow = "JFDWK@",
        secondRow = "GNIRM<",
         thirdRow = "LTEOU ",
         forthRow = "YSAHV ",
         fifthRow = "XPCBQZ";

    String letters;
```

Initialize this keyboard at a size of 600×600, so that each key gets 100×100.

```
    KeyboardTarget() {
        x = y = 0;
        w = width / 3;
        h = width / 3;
        letters = "";

        String[] rows = { topRow, secondRow, thirdRow, forthRow,
            fifthRow };
        int sz = w / 6;
```

Loop through and create buttons for each key.

```
        for (int i = 0; i < 6; i += 1) {
            for (int j = 0; j < 5; j += 1) {
                if (rows[j].charAt(i) != ' ') {
                    addSubTarget(new ExplodingButton (
                        /* location and size */
                        i * sz, j * sz + sz, sz * 9 / 10, sz * 9 / 10,
                        /* label */       rows[j].substring(i, i + 1),
                        /* parent */      this
                    ));
```

```
                    }
                }
            }
        }
```

Draw the containing rectangle and render the keys for this keyboard.

```
        void drawTarget() {
```

Render a border around the keys that is colored based on text-entry status.

```
            if (grabbedBy != null)
                stroke(200, 0, 0);
            else
                stroke(200, 200, 0);

            strokeWeight(5);
            fill(10, 0, 0);

            rect(0, 0, w, h);
```

Render the keys.

```
            for (SubTarget target : subTargets) {
                target.draw();
            }
```

Display the current text entered.

```
            fill(255);
            textFont(helvetica, w / 6 * 9 / 10 * 0.8f);
            text(letters, w / 6 / 10, w / 6 * 9 / 10 * 0.8f);
        }
```

Handle the entry of a single character.

```
        void typeLetter(String letter) {
            if (letter.equals("@")) {
```

As mentioned previously, an at sign represents enter, and creates a "refrigerator magnet" containing the current text entered.

```
                targetsToAddNextCycle.add(new RefrigeratorMagnet(letters));

                letters = "";
            } else if (letter.equals("<")) {
```

Likewise, a back-chevron deletes the previous character entered, if there is one.

```
              if (!letters.equals("")) {
                  letters = letters.substring(0, letters.length() - 1);
              }
          } else {
```

Anything else is simply appended to the buffer.

```
              letters += letter;
          }
      }
  }
```

This flamboyantly named `ExplodingButton` class represents a single key on the keyboard. The way this works, in practice, is that hovering over a single key gradually causes it to "heat up" until it "pops" and enters the letter into the keypad.

```
class ExplodingButton implements SubTarget {
    int x, y, w, h;
    float powerLevel;
    boolean hoveredOver;
    String letter;
    KeyboardTarget parent;
```

Create a new key given its position relative to its container and letter to display.

```
    ExplodingButton(int newX, int newY, int newW, int newH,
      String newLetter, KeyboardTarget t) {
        x = newX;
        y = newY;
        w = newW;
        h = newH;
        powerLevel = 0.0;
        hoveredOver = false;
        letter = newLetter;
        parent = t;
    }
```

Draw a silhouette—in this case, a rectangle.

```
    void drawHitRegion(PGraphics g) {
        g.noStroke();
        g.rect(x, y, w, h);
    }
```

Render this key for visual presentation. Importantly, there is visual feedback of the "power level" (really more like "heat") so that the user "feels" the button becoming hotter up to the point of creating the letter. Why programmers are stereotypically immature, I have no idea.

```
void draw() {
    fill(((powerLevel   / 100.0 * 0.9 + 0.1) * 255.0, 0, 0, 100);
    stroke(((powerLevel / 100.0 * 0.9 + 0.1) * 255.0, 0, 0, 150);
    strokeWeight(10);
    rect(x, y, w, h);

    fill(255);
    textFont(helvetica, h * 0.8);
    text(letter, x + (w - textWidth(letter)) / 2, y + h * 0.8);
}
```

Mark this key as having been hovered over within the last frame.

```
void hoverOver() {
    hoveredOver = true;
}
```

Update the heat of the button. The button heats up much faster than it cools down, because that somehow feels more natural.

```
void updateHovering(boolean enabled) {
    if (enabled && hoveredOver) {
        powerLevel += 5.0;
    } else {
        powerLevel -= 2.0;
    }

    if (powerLevel > 100.0) {
        parent.typeLetter(letter);
        powerLevel = 0;
    }

    powerLevel = (float)(max(0, powerLevel));

    hoveredOver = false;
}
```

Return the current power level to indicate how close this key is to producing a keypress.

```
    float getPowerLevel() {
        return powerLevel;
    }
}

void setup() {
    size(screenWidth, screenHeight);
```

```
        openni = new SimpleOpenNI(this);
        openni.setMirror(true);
        openni.enableScene();
        openni.enableDepth();
        openni.enableUser(SimpleOpenNI.SKEL_PROFILE_ALL);
        openni.enableHands();
        openni.enableIR();

        people = new ArrayList<Person>();
        targets = new ArrayList<Target>();
        targetsToAddNextCycle = new ArrayList<Target>();

        targets.add(new SceneViewTarget());
        targets.add(new KeyboardTarget());

        monaco = loadFont("Monaco.vlw");
        helvetica = loadFont("Helvetica-Bold-48.vlw");
    }
```

Specify an OpenNI callback for whenever a person enters the view of the camera.

```
    void onNewUser(int userID) {
        System.out.println("New User: " + userID + ";
          start autocalibration!");

        openni.requestCalibrationSkeleton(userID, true);

        people.add(new Person(userID));
    }
```

Specify an OpenNI callback for whenever a person leaves the view of the camera.

```
    void onLostUser(int userID) {
        System.out.println("Lost User: " + userID);
```

Remove the person from the list of people.

```
        int foundIndex = -1;

        for (int i = 0; i < people.size(); i++) {
            if (people.get(i).getID() == userID) {
                foundIndex = i;
                break;
            }
```

```
        }

        people.remove(foundIndex);
    }
```

This is called whenever a user has successfully been calibrated.

```
    void onEndCalibration(int userID, boolean successful) {
        System.out.println("Calibrated User ID : " + userID + "
            successful : " + successful);

        if (successful) {

            openni.startTrackingSkeleton(userID);
        } else {
```

If the first attempt at calibration was unsuccessful, retry the pose detection, and hopefully things will work out better this time.

```
            openni.startPoseDetection("Psi", userID);
        }
    }
```

This is called whenever the person makes the Psi pose successfully.

```
    void onStartPose(String pose, int userID) {
        println("onStartPose - userID: " + userID + "; pose = " + pose);
```

Begin calibrating the sensor from the skeleton.

```
        openni.stopPoseDetection(userID);
        openni.requestCalibrationSkeleton(userID, true);
    }

    void draw() {
```

Render the hit region.

```
        PGraphics miniRender = createGraphics
            (width / 10, height / 10, JAVA2D);
        miniRender.beginDraw();
        miniRender.scale(0.1);
        miniRender.noSmooth();
        miniRender.fill(0);
        miniRender.rect(0, 0, miniRender.width, miniRender.height);

        for (int i = 0; i < targets.size(); i++) {
            miniRender.fill(color(250, 0, i + 1));
            miniRender.noStroke();
```

```
            targets.get(i).drawHitRegion(miniRender, (i + 1));
    }

    miniRender.endDraw();
    miniRender.loadPixels();
```

Pull data from OpenNI.

```
    openni.update();

    for (Person p : people) {
        p.left.updateFromNI();
        p.right.updateFromNI();
        p.updateGrabbing(miniRender, targets);
    }
```

Handle grabbing.

```
    for (Target t : targets) {
        t.updateGrabbing();
    }
```

Move new targets into the list.

```
    for (Target t : targetsToAddNextCycle) {
        targets.add(t);
    }
    targetsToAddNextCycle.clear();
```

Begin drawing code.

```
    background(0);
```

Render normal drawing.

```
    for (Target t : targets) {
        t.draw();
    }
```

Render hands.

```
    for (Person p : people) {
        p.left.draw();
        p.right.draw();
    }
  }
```

If you'd like to obtain this Processing sketch in its entirety, go to Jeremy Archers GitHub page at *https://github.com/fatlotus/common-report*.

8

Robotics and Natural User Interfaces

This chapter is all about interacting with machines. Whether it's your own PC or an autonomous robot, the Kinect is perfect for interpreting your gestures and applying them to a particular interface. We'll touch on controlling a Mac by dragging and exposing windows, using a wide variety of gestures to control everything from browsing to picture viewing on your Windows PC, and controlling your mouse with the Kinect using Ubuntu.

One of the most compelling and futuristic Kinect applications is using it to control autonomous robots. Practical uses for this include being able to control the movement of the robot's arms and legs from a remote location. Imagine being able to send a robot into a small area and control it remotely by walking on a treadmill and moving your arms.

This is all possible thanks to Taylor Veltrop's amazing work with the Kinect along with his NAO Robot avatar. In this chapter, you'll be introduced to some coding examples applied to robotics using OpenNI and NITE along with the Kinematics Dynamic Library (KDL) and the Robot Operating System (ROS).

HACK 51 Control a Robotic Arm

This hack explains how to control a robotic arm with four degrees of freedom through the Kinect. It requires the usage of OpenNI and NITE. NITE provides skeleton tracking of the Kinect user. It's really just a simple matter of plugging NITE's skeleton API into the joint control API of your robot, with a little bit of math in the middle. To do the necessary matrix multiplications and trigonometry, we will use the KDL library. Many other mathematical libraries are usable here, but KDL was chosen because it is used within ROS.

We won't get into depth about how to set up the entire skeleton tracking program with OpenNI. I recommend that you take a look at the Sample-NiUserTracker program that is supplied with OpenNI/NITE. You can use this code as a starting point. If you would like to see what a complete solution looks like, check out the veltrop-ros-pkg repository on SourceForge at *http://veltrop-ros-pkg.svn.sourceforge.net/* and look inside the veltrobot_teleop stack.

First, we need to aquire joint positions and angles from the human Kinect user. We need information about the torso, both shoulders, left elbow, and left hand.

```cpp
// To understand the meaning of "user" and "UserGenerator" refer to
// the OpenNI UserTracker Sample

#include <kdl/frames.hpp> // For KDL::Vector, KDL:Rotation, etc

XnFloat* m; // Temporary variable for accessing matrix elements

// Get torso xyz position
XnSkeletonJointPosition xn_pos_torso;
UserGenerator.GetSkeletonCap().GetSkeletonJointPosition(user,
        XN_SKEL_TORSO,
        xn_pos_torso);
KDL::Vector torso(joint_pos_torso.position.X,
                  joint_pos_torso.position.Y,
                  joint_pos_torso.position.Z);

// Get torso rpy rotation
XnSkeletonJointOrientation xn_orient_torso;
UserGenerator.GetSkeletonCap().GetSkeletonJointOrientation(user,
          XN_SKEL_TORSO,
          xn_orient_torso);
m = xn_orient_torso.orientation.elements;
KDL::Rotation torso_rotation(m[0], m[1], m[2],
                             m[3], m[4], m[5],
                             m[6], m[7], m[8]);

// Get right shoulder xyz position
XnSkeletonJointPosition xn_pos_r_shoulder;
UserGenerator.GetSkeletonCap().GetSkeletonJointPosition(user,
        XN_SKEL_RIGHT_SHOULDER,
        xn_pos_r_shoulder);
KDL::Vector right_shoulder(xn_pos_r_shoulder.position.X,
                           xn_pos_r_shoulder.position.Y,
                           xn_pos_r_shoulder.position.Z);

// Get left shoulder xyz position
XnSkeletonJointPosition xn_pos_l_shoulder;
```

```
UserGenerator.GetSkeletonCap().GetSkeletonJointPosition(user,
        XN_SKEL_LEFT_SHOULDER,
        xn_pos_l_shoulder);
KDL::Vector left_shoulder(xn_pos_l_shoulder.position.X,
                          xn_pos_l_shoulder.position.Y,
                          xn_pos_l_shoulder.position.Z);

// Get left shoulder rpy rotation
XnSkeletonJointOrientation xn_orient_l_shoulder;
UserGenerator.GetSkeletonCap().GetSkeletonJointOrientation(user,
        XN_SKEL_LEFT_SHOULDER,
        xn_orient_l_shoulder);
m = xn_orient_l_shoulder.orientation.elements;
KDL::Rotation left_shoulder_rotation(m[0], m[1], m[2],
                                     m[3], m[4], m[5],
                                     m[6], m[7], m[8]);

// Get left elbow xyz position
XnSkeletonJointPosition xn_pos_l_elbow;
UserGenerator.GetSkeletonCap().GetSkeletonJointPosition(user,
        XN_SKEL_LEFT_ELBOW,
        xn_pos_l_elbow);
KDL::Vector left_elbow(xn_pos_l_elbow.position.X,
                       xn_pos_l_elbow.position.Y,
                       xn_pos_l_elbow.position.Z;

// Get left hand xyz position
XnSkeletonJointPosition xn_pos_l_hand;
UserGenerator.GetSkeletonCap().GetSkeletonJointPosition(user,
        XN_SKEL_LEFT_HAND,
        xn_pos_l_hand);
KDL::Vector left_hand(xn_pos_l_hand.position.X,
                      xn_pos_l_hand.position.Y,
                      xn_pos_l_hand.position.Z);
```

These joint positions and angles must be corrected based on the user's torso position
and angle. We can't use the data directly. If we use it directly, then when the user's
body rotates, the skeleton data we get about the shoulder will have been both trans-
lated and rotated. This is because all of the data we get is relative to the Kinect camera
position. We need it to be relative to the user.

```
// We need this inverse rotation to correct all of the other
// joints' XYZ and RPY into a torso-relative space.
KDL::Rotation torso_rotation_inverse = torso_rotation.Inverse();
```

```
// Right shoulder position - Remove torso rotation and translation
right_shoulder = right_shoulder - torso;
right_shoulder = torso_rotation_inverse * right_shoulder;

// Left shoulder rotation - Remove torso rotation and extract angles
left_shoulder_rotation =
  left_shoulder_rotation * torso_rotation_inverse;
double left_shoulder_roll, left_shoulder_pitch, left_shoulder_yaw;
left_shoulder_rotation.GetRPY(left_shoulder_roll,
        left_shoulder_pitch,
        left_shoulder_yaw);

// Left shoulder position - Remove torso rotation and translation
left_shoulder = left_shoulder - torso;
left_shoulder = torso_rotation_inverse * left_shoulder;

// Left elbow position - Remove torso rotation and translation
left_elbow = left_elbow - torso;
left_elbow = torso_rotation_inverse * left_elbow;

// Left hand position - Remove torso rotation and translation
left_hand = left_hand - torso;
left_hand = torso_rotation_inverse * left_hand;

// Now all of our data considers their (X,Y,Z) and (R,P,Y) to have
// their (0,0,0) at the torso rather than at the Kinect camera.
// These coordinates are now ready to process to create useful joint
// angles to send to a robot.
```

The joint positions that we calculate here may not be immediately usable for your robot. The "zero" position of your robot may be different. Or if it does not obey a righthanded coordinate system, the sign of the final joint angle may need to be flipped. For example, your robot may consider the "zero" position of the shoulder pitch joint to be when an arm is straight out, but my examples are based on the arms being straight down along the sides of a humanoid. So, in this case, you would have to either add or subtract $\pi/2$.

Robots usually use a righthanded coordinate system, where positive x is pointing forward out of a humanoid robot's chest. Positive y points out of the robot's left side, and positive z points up. Unfortunately, the Kinect has a different interpretation about the coordinate system of the user's skeleton it tracks. In this case, positive x comes out of the user's right side, positive y is pointing up, and positive z comes out of the user's back. So the robot's (x, y, z) equals the Kinect's (−z, −x, +y).

Figure 8-1 shows how the coordinate system of the Kinect and robot avatar differ, and how coordinate frames are initially relative to the Kinect camera, but become relative to the torso after we correct them.

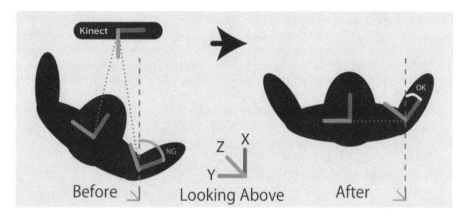

Figure 8-1.
Coordinates relative to the Kinect camera become relative to the torso

We use the words roll, pitch, and yaw. These are rotations around the x-, y-, and z-axis, respectively.

We will need the following vectors for the trigonometry used to generate the final joint angles for your robot.

```
// The following vectors are normalized so that when we create
// triangles out of them we can treat them as being within the unit
// circle, and the trigonometry is simplified.

// These first two vectors have the shoulder as the origin. Useful
// for calculating left shoulder pitch and roll.

KDL::Vector left_shoulder_right_shoulder
  (right_shoulder - left_shoulder);
left_shoulder_right_shoulder.Normalize();

KDL::Vector left_shoulder_elbow(left_elbow - left_shoulder);
left_shoulder_elbow.Normalize();

// These last two vectors have the elbow as the origin. Useful for
// calculating the elbow angle.

KDL::Vector left_elbow_shoulder(left_shoulder - left_elbow);
```

```
left_elbow_shoulder.Normalize();

KDL::Vector left_elbow_hand(left_hand - left_elbow);
left_elbow_hand.Normalize();
```

If you don't understand the trigonometry that follows, I suggest reviewing sine and cosine and drawing out the triangles of the vectors that we declared.

The following code is responsible for calculating the robot's left shoulder roll.

```
static double robot_left_shoulder_angle_roll = 0;
if (xn_pos_r_shoulder.fConfidence >= 0.9 &&
    xn_pos_l_elbow.fConfidence >= 0.9 &&
    xn_pos_l_shoulder.fConfidence >= 0.9)
{
  // Calculate the angle between two vectors. By comparing the
  // left elbow, left shoulder, and right shoulder positions, we
  // can get the inner angle.

    robot_left_shoulder_angle_roll = acos(KDL::dot
        (left_shoulder_elbow, left_shoulder_right_shoulder));

  // Shift the angle to consider arms down as zero position

    robot_left_shoulder_angle_roll =
      robot_left_shoulder_angle_roll - HALFPI;
}
```

Now we'll calculate the robot's left shoulder pitch.

```
static double robot_left_shoulder_angle_pitch = 0;
// static: if a confidence check fails, previous iteration's value
// is used.

if (xn_pos_l_shoulder.fConfidence >= 0.9 &&
    xn_pos_l_elbow.fConfidence >= 0.9)
{
  // Remember, Y from the Kinect coordinate system is actually Z
  // on the robot. This considers a triangle where the hypotenuse
  // is your arm. We want to take the inverse sign of the forward
  // component of your arm to calculate the angle that we should
  // send to the robot's pitch joint.

    robot_left_shoulder_angle_pitch = asin(left_shoulder_elbow.y());

  // Shift the angle to consider arms down as zero position
```

```
    robot_left_shoulder_angle_pitch =
        robot_left_shoulder_angle_pitch + HALFPI;
}
```

Next up is the robot's left shoulder yaw.

```
// left shoulder yaw
static double left_shoulder_angle_yaw = 0;
if (xn_pos_l_shoulder.fConfidence >= 0.9)
{
    // In this case, we can take the rotation directly from the Kinect
    // data. However, this method isn't very reliable. The rotational
    // information for joints from NITE is very unreliable. In
    // certain positions of the user's arms, this method will fail.
    // I suggest that you try to make a better trigonometric solution.
    // Remember, robot yaw = kinect roll because robot Z = kinect Y

    left_shoulder_angle_yaw = left_shoulder_roll;
}
```

Now calculate the robot's left elbow angle.

```
static double robot_left_elbow_angle = 0;
if (xn_pos_l_hand.fConfidence >= 0.9 &&
    xn_pos_l_elbow.fConfidence >= 0.9 &&
    xn_pos_l_shoulder.fConfidence >= 0.9)
{
    // Calculate the angle between two vectors. By comparing the left
    // shoulder, left elbow, and left hand positions, we can get the
    // inner angle.

    robot_left_elbow_angle = acos(KDL::dot(left_elbow_hand,
                                        left_elbow_shoulder));

    // Shift the angle to consider arms down as zero position

    robot_left_elbow_angle = left_elbow_angle - PI;
}
```

The skeleton data we get from the Kinect with NITE does not give us rotational information about the hands. It is possible to add some Nintendo Wii remotes to the mix to get hand orientation data. Or perhaps you can think of an entirely new approach that uses the NITE hand tracker instead of the skeleton tracker!

If your robot is capable of receiving torso-relative *xyz* goal coordinates for hands, and can do the inverse kinematics on its own (such as the Aldebaran NAO), then you have it easy. Simply subtract the Kinect user's torso position from the right hand position, scale it down a bit, and send it into the inverse kinematics engine. This approach can be very accurate and intuitive if a user is trying to manipulate tools with the robot; however, it is much slower. The direct method that this hack explored works in real time.

HACK 52 Control a Robot's Navigation

This hack is much simpler than controlling a robotic arm. Here, we will explore the possibility of moving a robot around by using the Kinect. Once again, we need OpenNI/NITE and the user's skeleton data. But this time, we care only about the user's torso position and orientation. What you need on your robot is a system that can receive commands like "go forward," "stop," "rotate clockwise," etc.

As in the previous hack, acquire the torso position and orientation. We can use this information quite directly to drive the robot. The logic is simple: if the user's z position is less than the initial position, make the robot go forward. If the user steps farther forward, the robot could go forward faster. When the user steps back to the initial position, tell the robot to stop. Likewise, if the user's rotation is counterclockwise or clockwise, tell the robot to rotate accordingly. When the user returns to his initial body orientation, tell the robot to stop.

> To make this easier to operate, you may want to put some tape or a diagram on the ground that tells you how far you need to step or rotate to achieve the desired operation from your robot.

HACK 53 Use Candescent NUI

We'll start off the PC side of the NUI by demonstrating a few components of Candescent NUI. Developed by Stefan Stegmueller, Candescent NUI is an application that lets you detect where the fingers are and even in what direction they are pointing (see Figure 8-2). This feature is still missing in all the official development kits. It has many applications like image and video manipulation.

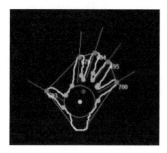

Figure 8-2.
Candescent NUI finger tracking

The requirements are:

- Windows 7 64-bit
- NET Framework 4 (*http://www.microsoft.com/download/en/details.aspx?id=17851*)
- OpenNI (*http://www.openni.org*) (1.5.2.23 or newer)

Download the newest binary version from CodePlex. You can also download the source code, if you have Visual Studio 2010, from *http://candescentnui.codeplex.com*.

The following sample is the minimum code to initialize Candescent NUI. You'll find this and more samples in the project *CCT.NUI.Samples*. The referenced file, *Config.xml*, is included in the release. It contains configuration options for OpenNI.

First you create the data source factory; here, it is an OpenNIDataSourceFactory. This class is used to initialize OpenNI and to prepare everything. Next you create a hand data source. The event **NewDataAvailable** is invoked every time a new frame is available. The last thing we have to do is to start the data source.

```
private IDataSourceFactory dataSourceFactory;

private void Initialize()
{
    this.dataSourceFactory = new
        OpenNIDataSourceFactory("Config.xml");
    var handDataSource = new HandDataSource(
        this.dataSourceFactory.CreateShapeDataSource());
    handDataSource.NewDataAvailable += new
    NewDataHandler<HandCollection>(handDataSource_NewDataAvailable);
    handDataSource.Start();
}

void handDataSource_NewDataAvailable(HandCollection data)
```

```
    {
        foreach (var hand in data.Hands)
        {
            foreach (var finger in hand.Fingers)
            {
                //Do something with the location
                //finger.Location.X
                //finger.Location.Y
            }
        }
    }
```

For more on the many features that Candescent NUI has to offer, be sure to check out the CodePlex page at *http://candescentnui.codeplex.com* and follow Stefan's blog at *http://blog.candescent.ch*.

HACK 54 Use Kinect Jesture for Mac

Kinect Jesture was written by Takashi Nishibayashi (@hagino3000 on Twitter). The program allows you to control your Mac by using gesture-based commands. With this great openFrameworks application, you can control your Mac's mouse and perform a few of those handy trackpad-swipe actions as well. The multiwindow display feature has been added as well; you access it by holding both hands up simultaneously. This application runs only on Mac OS X and requires a few dependencies before you can get started.

You'll need to download the 0062 FAT (10.6) version of openFrameworks, located at *http://www.openframeworks.cc/download/older.html*.

Download the ofxKinect add-on from *https://github.com/ofTheo/ofxKinect* and place it in your *addons* folder within the extracted *of_preRelease_v0062* directory. Download the latest build of Kinect Jesture from *https://github.com/hagino3000/KinectJesture* and place it in the *apps/examples* directory.

Alternatively, you can use git clone *to download the most up-to-date build if you have Git installed.*

Navigate to the *jestureCap.xcodeproj* file inside of *of_preRelease_v0062_osxSL_FAT/ apps/examples/KinectJesture* directory and launch the file.

Xcode will open, and you should have two projects indexed.

Before you run the project, change the Base SDK for the project and target to 10.6. If you are using the OS X Mountain Lion version of Xcode (v4.4), see this openFra-meworks forum post: http://bit.ly/VpnTfk. *See Figure 8-3.*

Figure 8-3.
Change the Base SDK to run Kinect Jesture

Ensure that your Kinect is plugged into a power source and also connected via USB.

If all goes well, you will be presented with the settings interface for Kinect Jesture. Here you are able to adjust settings such as the tilt angle, mirror mode, the detect range, and mouse controls. Press the space bar once you are ready to begin. See Figure 8-4.

You will now be able to control your mouse by motioning with your hand. Make a fist and open it to trigger a left-click action. Hold your fist closed to grab and move windows. Hold both hands up at once to bring up the MacBook Pro trackpad Expose multiwindow display.

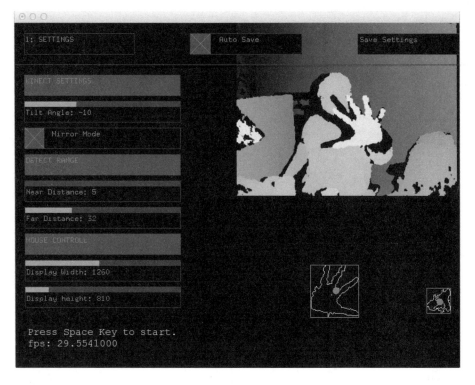

Figure 8-4.
Kinect Jesture settings interface

You may find it a little difficult to use the mouse right away, but that's what the settings are there for. Play around with the distance and mouse configurations to get it just right. Also, if you lose all mouse control, try turning the Kinect around, or hold down Command, tab over to the Xcode build, and press the space bar to go back to the settings interface.

HACK 55 Use Linux Gesture-Based Mouse Control

This easy-to-set-up hack allows a user to control the mouse for Ubuntu. The current version doesn't allow for any click commands but is still a great start. It may prove to be a good jumping-off point if you are interested in developing a *Minority Report\-* type interface for Ubuntu.

First up, you'll need to install a few dependencies. Start off by adding the personal package archives (PPA) for Freenect. Open a terminal and enter the following:

```
sudo add-apt-repository ppa:arne-alamut/freenect
```

Resynchronize the package list:

```
sudo apt-get update
```

Now for the rest, input:

```
sudo apt-get install freenect libncurses5-dev freeglut3-dev
  libX11-dev
sudo apt-get install libxtst-dev libxmu-dev cmake git
```

Next up, we'll need to build the Kinect-Mouse project. Create a *Kinect* directory somewhere that you can access easily and use Git to download the latest version of Kinect-Mouse.

```
mkdir ~/Kinect
cd ~/Kinect
sudo git clone https://github.com/Ooblik/Kinect-Mouse.git
```

Create a *build* directory within Kinect-Mouse and run **make** to install it.

```
mkdir build
cd build
cmake ..
make
```

Plug your Kinect into a USB port, and also make sure the Kinect is plugged into a power outlet. Then run **kmouse**.

```
sudo ./kmouse
```

Make sure you're situated at a distance where your body appears in white but your hand is red. This is the Kinect-Mouse "sweet spot," if you will. You'll notice that as soon as you're calibrated properly, your mouse cursor will begin to move with your hand. See Figure 8-5.

Figure 8-5.
Kinect-Mouse control for Ubuntu

Use Winect for Windows

Daniel Ho has developed this great Windows gesture-based–control software that uses OpenNI. It also incorporates a sign recognition algorithm to allow the user to control a Windows OS interface. The user makes simple hand-based gestures to evoke left mouse clicks, middle mouse clicks, and right mouse clicks. Other features, such as back and forward gestures for browser navigation and zoom controls, have been included as well. See Figure 8-6.

Figure 8-6.
Winect hand recognition window

Here are the prerequisites:

- SensorKinect-Win-OpenSource32-5.0.3.4
- OpenNI-Win32-1.3.2.3
- NITE-Win32-1.4.1.2
- Microsoft NET 4.0

The best way to install all three Kinect-related prerequisites is to use the Windows Zigfu bundle installer from *http://bit.ly/TAqCac*.

Once you have those prerequisites installed, download Winect from *http://bit.ly/ RWINm7*.

Before you launch the application, ensure your Kinect is plugged into a USB port as well as into a power source. Launch Winect, and you should be presented with a small window that shows you a real-time display of your hand being tracked by the Kinect. Once a proper hand gesture has been detected, you will be able to control your Windows interface by simply using the gesture commands that Winect supports.

For a detailed list of all the included hand gestures and commands, go to http:// ixorastudios.com/products/winect/.

Index

We'd like to hear your suggestions for improving our indexes. Send email to index@oreilly.com.

About the Author

Jared St. Jean lives in Toronto, Ontario, and is the application services manager at web.net, one of the leaders in delivering open source websites and web-enabled applications to social enterprises. Jared is the founder, writer, and web administrator for developkinect.com, a community-driven site aimed at promoting and assisting all areas of programming and development for the Microsoft Kinect sensor. He is also a video game enthusiast who has been covering all aspects of the gaming industry for the Dashhacks Network.

Colophon

The text and header fonts are Benton Sans, and the code font is Ubuntu Mono.

Have it your way.

Get even more for your money.

Join the O'Reilly Community, and register the O'Reilly books you own. It's free, and you'll get:

- $4.99 ebook upgrade offer
- 40% upgrade offer on O'Reilly print books
- Membership discounts on books and events
- Free lifetime updates to ebooks and videos
- Multiple ebook formats, DRM FREE
- Participation in the O'Reilly community
- Newsletters
- Account management
- 100% Satisfaction Guarantee

Signing up is easy:

1. **Go to: oreilly.com/go/register**
2. **Create an O'Reilly login.**
3. **Provide your address.**
4. **Register your books.**

Note: English-language books only

To order books online:

oreilly.com/store

For questions about products or an order:

orders@oreilly.com

To sign up to get topic-specific email announcements and/or news about upcoming books, conferences, special offers, and new technologies:

elists@oreilly.com

For technical questions about book content:

booktech@oreilly.com

To submit new book proposals to our editors:

proposals@oreilly.com

O'Reilly books are available in multiple DRM-free ebook formats. For more information:

oreilly.com/ebooks

Spreading the knowledge of innovators   oreilly.com